COUNSELING AND PSYCHOTHERAPY

A
TRANSPERSONAL
APPROACH

Second Edition

BARRY WEINHOLD
GAY HENDRICKS
University of Colorado – Colorado Springs

LOVE PUBLISHING COMPANY
Denver, Colorado 80222

Library of Congress Catalog Card Number 91-077046

Copyright © 1993 Love Publishing Company
Printed in the U.S.A.
ISBN 0-89108-224-7

1995

Contents

4   Being and Personality   75
Gay Hendricks

5   Transpersonal Uses of Human Energy Patterns   87
Barry Weinhold

6   Developmental Process Work in Marriage and Family Therapy   107
Barry Weinhold and Janae Weinhold

1

An Overview

Gay Hendricks

In the past three decades we have seen the emergence of a robust new force in psychology—the transpersonal approach. Transpersonal psychology, with striking implications for all fields of human endeavor, most directly impacts education and the helping professions. Counseling and psychotherapy are often the natural proving ground for any new approach, and transpersonal psychology—sometimes called the *fourth force* because it followed the Freudian, behavioral, and humanistic movements—must be carefully examined to determine if it can contribute something of new and lasting value to our understanding of personality and its transformation.

DEFINING THE INDEFINABLE

Anthony Sutich, one of the founders (with Abraham Maslow) of both the Association for Humanistic Psychology and later the Association for Transpersonal Psychology, once said that *transpersonal* was indefinable and should remain so. Concerned with the tendency of definitions to limit a phenomenon, he believed that transpersonal psychology, of all things, must not be limited. Nevertheless, it may be possible to suggest several broad definitions that, when considered in their essences, communicate the scope of the field without placing limiting boundaries upon it.

The Latin prefix *trans* has several meanings. It can mean *connecting,* in the sense of a transatlantic telephone cable. It can also mean *through,* in the sense of a transparent pane of glass. A third meaning is *beyond,* as in the word transcendental. Adding these three meanings of *trans* to the word *personal,* we have a term that refers to bridging and connecting the personal, through the personal, and beyond the personal.

What can this be? What is it that connects all people, is at the essence of all of us, and is beyond the purely personal? To answer these questions, let us explore the latin root of *personal.* In Latin, the term *persona* means mask. A *persona* is a mask that one dons for a certain purpose. An example of the use of this term in English is our word denoting person-ality, which is based upon *persona.* Personality can be understood as a set of masks we don to gain recognition and approval, or to protect ourselves from pain. Assemble a variety of *personas*, or masks, and you have a personality. Transpersonal can therefore refer to that which is through the *persona*, beyond the *persona,* connecting all *personas.*

Much of Western psychology can be regarded as ego psychology because it deals with processes of the *personality* by which we seek recognition and protect ourselves from pain. The term *ego* comes from a word that means *I.* Thus, the *I* of most Western psychology refers to ego. In his important book, *Realms of the Human Unconscious,* Grof defined transpersonal experiences as those that go beyond the normal boundaries of the ego.[1] The ego, then—the central focus of study for much of the psychology of the West—is but the jumping-off place for transpersonal psychology.

What remains after the masks of *persona* have been removed? What is beyond the strivings of the ego? What aspects of human experience go beyond and through the personal while connecting all persons? Abraham Maslow, known for a positing a hierarchy of human needs, was one of the founders of transpersonal psychology. Frequently depicted in the form of a pyramid, the hierarchy arrayed human needs as follows:

The middle three sets of needs, including safety/security, love/be-longing, and self-esteem, can be regarded as ego needs because they involve acquiring and maintaining a set of successful personas with which to get one's needs met. Maslow's "highest need" was self-actu-alization, the emergence of one's true self in some form of creative expression. By "higher" he did not mean better. Just as the higher rungs

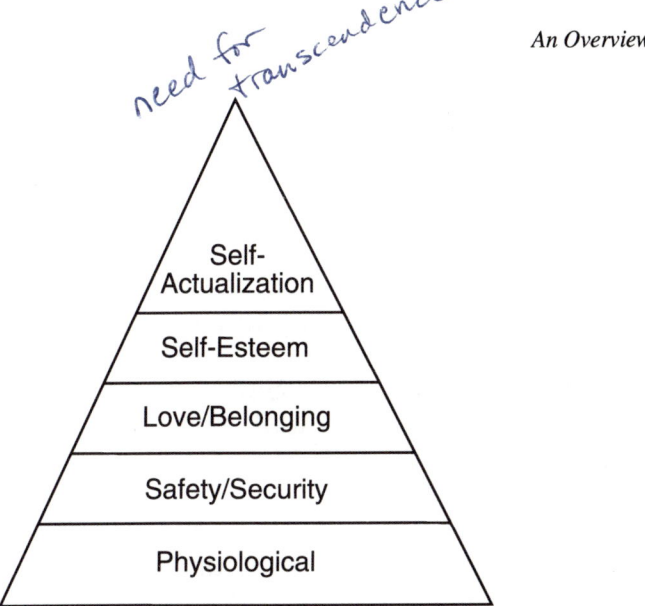

need for transcendence

Figure 1.1
MASLOW'S HIERARCHY OF HUMAN NEEDS

of a ladder are no better than the lower, the higher human needs were so placed because they depend upon successfully meeting the lower, more basic needs.

In the final version of the hierarchy, published toward the end of Maslow's life, he made a revealing addition. At the top of the pyramid, beyond self-actualization, Maslow placed a need for transcendence. A modified version of the pyramid might look like this:

Transcendence, or surrender into an expanded sense of self, is the need that grows out of self-actualization. The higher needs are likely present in a subtle form throughout our development but must await the successful meeting of more basic needs before they can be acknowledged. Before the ego needs can be met, breakfast must be served. Before self-actualization can get under way, we must have a workable sense of self. Then, with a full stomach, an effective ego, and an emerging relationship with our true and creative self, we can set about the task of dissolving our personal conception of ourselves and begin to surrender to the transpersonal.

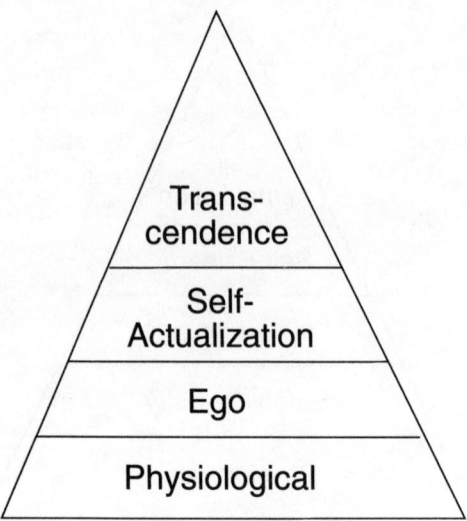

Figure 1.2
MODIFIED HIERARCHY OF NEEDS

A TRANSPERSONAL CONTEXT

As part of the transpersonal approach, counselors incorporate a set of activities and processes designed to change thoughts, feelings, and behaviors. A counselor may meditate with a client, for example, or may use intuition to tune in to some aspect of a client's life. But basic to determining whether counselors are working from a transpersonal approach are their attitudes and views. Some attitudes that many transpersonal therapists would agree are part of a transpersonal context are: oneness, an expansionist view, acceptance and use of full human potential, spiritual dimensions, observation and love, among others.

Oneness

The ego, by its very nature, is a seeker. It restlessly scans the environment in search of recognition. It tirelessly protects against threats to itself. It is on the make, on the run. It sees separateness; that is its job. But a transpersonal therapist knows the ego is only part of the picture. The ego has been compared to being the mayor of New York City—important, yes, but to be kept in perspective.

Mystics throughout the millennia have emerged from their meditations with a simple, profound truth that has life-changing implications:

We are one. They mean that we are one both within ourselves and without. Most psychological problems can be viewed as stemming from forgetting that we are all one. For example, our emotions per se are not what causes so much difficulty; rather, it is our attempts to disown our emotions. We may have a feeling like anger that would soon dissolve if we were to acknowledge, accept, and express it. If, however, we do not accept it or express it, we tie up energy in suppressing it. If this tendency to hold emotions at arm's length, instead of embracing them, becomes a lifestyle, we have a problem that is likely to affect our relationship with ourselves and with others. Conversely, knowing that we are all one can help us befriend the disowned parts of ourselves and allow us to develop a sense of unity.

Problems in relationships between people have the same root as do psychological or emotional problems. When we forget that we are one with all other humans, when we regard each other as separate ego entities, we tend to misunderstand others and feel alienated.

A transpersonal world view, which transcends ego boundaries, sees all parts as being equal in the whole, all humans as having similar needs, feelings, and potentials.

An Expansionist View

Transpersonal approaches tend to be expansionist rather than reductionist in their view of the human personality and potential. As the fourth force in psychology, the transpersonal has built upon contributions of the first three forces: Freudian, behavioral, and humanistic. Whereas an approach such as classic behaviorism tends to be reductionistic, in reducing large sets of phenomena to fit smaller sets of processes (reinforcement, stimulus, response), transpersonal approaches tend to be open-ended and inclusive. So, although a behaviorist (for example) might not acknowledge transpersonal phenomena, a transpersonalist would almost certainly acknowledge behavioral phenomena such as reinforcement and conditioning.

Transpersonal approaches draw upon the first three forces while going beyond to see humans as intuitive, mystical, psychic, and spiritual.

5

Above all, humans are viewed as unifiable, having the potential for harmonious and holistic development of all their potentials.

Acceptance and Use of the Full Human Potential

One of the hallmarks of the transpersonal approach is the acceptance and use of the farther reaches of human potential. Among the extraordinary phenomena the transpersonal therapist acknowledges and puts to use are altered states of consciousness, mystical insight, paranormal powers, and the human quest for unity and contact with the divine.

The use of altered states of consciousness in counseling might take several forms. Transpersonal counselors may use relaxation training, guided fantasy, or meditation to accomplish various goals in counseling. Relaxation training, for example, has proven helpful in dealing with common problems including test anxiety, in addition to more serious problems such as agoraphobia and anorexia nervosa. Furthermore, relaxation, centering, and similar skills can be taught to students in school as a preventive mental hygiene tool, regardless of whether a problem does or does not exist.

The concept of altered states of consciousness has another fundamental application in counseling. It communicates to the client that valid alternatives to ordinary, linear, waking consciousness are available. In Western Culture the linear, logical approach to solving problems is highly valued. This is the state of consciousness that builds bridges, conducts experiments, smashes atoms. But life presents other problems, emotional difficulties, communication blocks, crises not easily handled through the rational approach. Actually, many problems may be *caused* by an overly rational approach to life. I recall a session with an engineer and his wife in which he was being confronted because he was unable to hear and respond to his wife's feelings. "Feelings?" he asked in puzzlement. "I've worked my whole career at getting the human error out of situations, and now you want me to listen to somebody's *feelings?*"

Nonrational processes such as dreaming and meditation can truly yield material relevant to therapy, material that may have been elusive in ordinary working consciousness. To give an example, I once worked with a person who was trying to make a decision about taking a new job. The change had many implications, and this client had worried over it for several months without being able to come to a decision. I suggested to him that his logical processes probably had considered the issue from every angle, and perhaps it was time to find out what the innermost part of him had to say about it. I asked him to pay attention to his dreams for a couple of nights to see if they would yield any useful information. That night he dreamed of crossing a large body of water. The journey was fraught with difficulty, but as he reached the shore on the other side, he saw a traffic light. It was green. On awakening, he felt he had received the go-ahead from the deeper part of himself, and he took the new job. Now, after several successful years, he feels it was the right move for him at the time.

Along with altered states of consciousness, the transpersonal approach takes into account the insights received from mystical and psychic experiences. Though other approaches might see these processes as irrelevant or even pathological, the transpersonal approach makes room for and even celebrates explorations into the farther reaches of human potential.

For anyone who reads the literature in the field, there is no question that events such as telepathy and precognition do happen. How they work is not known, because psychic processes do not readily lend themselves to scientific investigation. One of the aims of the transpersonal approach is to regard psychic processes as normal rather than paranormal. Not enough is known about these to determine just how they may be used best in therapy. Nevertheless, we can make space for psychic events in our conceptual framework so that we can be open to their occurrence. We can take on a willing attitude of inquiry toward them. Then they may surprise us by how they work.

In recent years I have been experiencing more and more seemingly telepathic contact when working with clients. In the first session of working with one couple, I had an impulse to tell the wife to give the husband more latitude and leeway regarding a specific issue. The thought entering my mind was, "Get off his back." I kept silent, as I was not sure I had good enough rapport with the wife to confront her this directly. The next week she came in and excitedly told me the problem had cleared up in a particularly unusual way. When I asked her how this had happened, she replied that several hours after our first session, she had suddenly realized, "I need to get off Carl's back." Coincidence could be a useful explanation in one or two events like this, but after accumulating a sizable number of them, I now find telepathy to be a sounder explanation.

Spiritual Dimensions

The transpersonal view also acknowledges the human spiritual quest. Transpersonal therapists accept the human need for growth along spiritual dimensions such as unity, ultimate truth, and direct perception of the divine. Humans are seen as ultimately spiritual in addition to physical, emotional, and mental.

Namaste

A traditional Indian greeting, *namaste*, can be translated as, "I salute the light within you." This term captures an important attitude that transpersonal therapists can transmit to clients. We each have a light within us. Counselors often see people who have lost perspective; they have become identified with their problems. It can be a true revelation for them to learn that even though they may *have* problems, they are more than their problems. We can perceive a part within us that is essence, free of all the conditioned elements of the personality. Whether this is termed a soul, a spirit, or a self, it is the timeless part of all of us that is beyond conditioning.

We might think of ourselves as a lantern with a light shining brightly within. Life experiences, parental conditioning, societal pressure, and other factors put smudges on the chimney of the lantern, making the light less perceptible to ourselves and others. Working on ourselves through counseling, meditation, or other practices can polish the chimney so the light can shine through.

Transpersonal therapists have trained themselves to see the light in themselves and others, even when it is buried beneath a lifetime of smudge.

Wisdom is Beyond Belief

Psychological growth depends upon the transcendence or erasing of a person's history of conditioned thoughts, feelings, and behavior. Georges Gurdjieff proffered that humans were asleep, mechanically responding in a conditioned manner. Awakening could come only through self-observation and "work on oneself" through mental and physical discipline. The Indian teacher Krisnamurti once remarked that the word *guru* was widely misunderstood to connote a person who dispensed some sort of knowledge, whereas the true and original meaning of the term meant a person who *dispelled* knowledge. The guru's task is to help seekers cut through the knowledge they have about the world and themselves and, by doing so, to tap into the creative source of knowledge beyond their conditioned purview.

What we know about our world is often what someone else has trained us to think and believe about it. The task of growth is not to learn something else but instead to erase the distorted knowledge we already have so we can see the world inside and outside afresh.

Karma

The concept of *karma* figures largely in Asian spiritual systems. Although the term, particularly in the Hindu system, is used to imply the transfer of destiny from one lifetime to another, a more personal, here-and-now understanding can be useful with clients. In our understanding, karma refers to the unconscious patterns of behavior we have learned from adults who taught us. Unless one becomes conscious of these patterns and changes them, they can go on unabated from one generation to another and seem to be predetermined.

Another way of understanding karma is to see it as an opportunity to embrace what we have in the past repelled. We may have within us the fear of being alone, for example. But by withdrawing from this fear, we propel ourselves into situations that call forth the fear. Thus, in trying to withdraw from an experience, we create a destiny in which we are forced to confront that experience.

As an application of this concept, say we have an aversion to someone. We may turn away to avoid confronting the person or our own feelings about the person, but we curiously find that the person pops up everywhere in our lives, either in person or in our minds. Until we act to *embrace* our own reactions and the actual person, we reinforce our reactions rather than changing them. If we view the experience through an understanding of karma, we will create a destiny full of opportunities for embracing it. We must, in truth, forgive that person and what he or she represents in ourselves before we can embrace the perfection of the universe as it operates through us.

Understanding the concept of karma gives us an entirely different way to look at our lives. Viewing life as a series of opportunities rather than obstacles is in itself a radical change in consciousness.

Observation and Love

Observation—seeing things the way they are—is a key part of many systems of psychological and spiritual growth. Observation means the ability to see thoughts, feelings, and behavior as they are with no evaluation. It is original meeting original without anything in between. When we observe things as they are, without judgment, they begin to change. This is because we have added awareness to the equation, and awareness is not just one of the powers that make us fully human; it is an agent of change. Then, when we can learn to *love* things as they are, they are no longer that way! When we learn to love our fear or our anger, we replace the feeling with acceptance. When we learn to love a previously hated body, we transform the energy that was trapped in hatred. Thus liberated, the energy can be used for change.

This is why it works: Most of us waste energy in resisting, in setting up a duality between what is and what we want it to be. Here we refer primarily to what is within us—our fear, anger, sexual feelings, all the things we usually dislike ourselves for having. To accept and love others is difficult until we do the same for ourselves. We continue to resist *what is*, though—often in the name of self-improvement. Tremendous energy is required to maintain a stance of resistance, particularly because the feelings, thoughts, and behaviors we most resist seem to be those that recycle most frequently. Paradoxically, then, the only ultimately successful way to change is by lovingly accepting all parts of us, just as we are.

The Sufi poet Rumi once wrote, "The astrolabe of God's mysteries is love." The astrolabe was a navigational device for finding one's way around the stars. So Rumi was saying that love is the tool for navigating through the mysteries of ourselves.

Love may be the only part of us that needs awakening; once we know how to love ourselves and all our reactions to things, we have the tools needed to explore our psychodynamic and spiritual potentials.

Here are some questions about love that clients have asked, along with the answers to them:

Q: Is loving ourselves the same as egotism?

A: No, egotism is an attempt to convince the world and ourselves that we are lovable after we have come to hate ourselves.

Q: What can we do if we can't love ourselves?

A: We can love ourselves for not being able to love ourselves.

Q: If we love ourselves for all our anger, sexuality, and violence, won't we go around being angry, violent, and incontinent?

A: No, we act out anger and other feelings inappropriately because we resist them until they explode. If we lovingly accept all our feelings, they can be channeled into appropriate expression.

Other Transpersonal Attitudes

A commonly held transpersonal attitude is that the way out is *through*. The only way to stop feeling scared, or angry, or sad is to go ahead and give ourselves total permission to feel that way, if only for a moment. For example, a young girl had experienced some problems in relating to boys, and her counselor suspected she was still angry at her father for some things he did and didn't do when she was younger. The counselor encouraged her to express the anger, and when she had, the counselor asked her to love herself for feeling angry. Afterward, she realized that she did not have to be attached to that anger any more, that she could let it go. A smile spread over her face, and she looked transformed. She had opened up, accepted her anger, expressed it, and let it go. In the process her consciousness expanded to embrace something that before was resisted and contained.

In summary, we may say that transpersonal approaches take a broader view of humans than do most approaches to therapy. Transpersonal counseling, like other therapies, sees people as hindered by psychodynamic conflicts, but the transpersonal orientation takes into account the human impulse toward higher states of consciousness. Transpersonal therapists may draw from spiritual systems in addition to psychological systems for explaining phenomena in the therapeutic quest. And they may use techniques (e.g., meditation, energy awareness, imagery, relation, love) that tend to go beyond those traditional therapists use.

THE CORE NATURE OF HUMANS

According to the transpersonal view, the core of the human personality is not ego. Transpersonal definitions of ego place it among the components of human personality. The core is really where all life energy resides and where our connection with universal energy begins. This core, along with those dynamic processes that tend to obscure the core, can be illustrated by an open circle and five expanding circles around it, as in Figure 1.3.

The Core

We have within us something that is essence, free from the residue accumulated by conditioning and the unfinished business of living. A metaphor for this open space could be a window through which others can see the inner light of ourselves, and through which we can receive the world the way it is, without distortion. When all the screens have been removed from the window and it has been lovingly polished, a new set of possibilities opens for us.

This human core might be regarded as the most basic of the transpersonal common denominators. Most of us have come to think of a common denominator as the lowest level at which two or more entities come together, but here is a paradox: The core at once unifies all humans on the *highest level*—the level at which, free from the conditioned differences in feeling, thought, perception, and behavior, we are all the same, and one.

Feeling

Early in life a second circle is placed over the open space. Although quite translucent, it is the beginning of a process of distortion. This circle is emotion, feeling. Feeling does not severely distort the essence. The basic feelings are only a few: fear, anger, sadness, happiness, excitement, as depicted in Figure 1.4. When we do not resist them, when we experience them fully, we have access to the core. Thus, our feelings are one of the most direct avenues to the spiritual essence within. Were we to be in contact with our most basic feelings daily, we would be living close to the core. But a more serious distortion occurs as parental and societal conditioning begins. We call this layer of distortion pseudo-feelings.

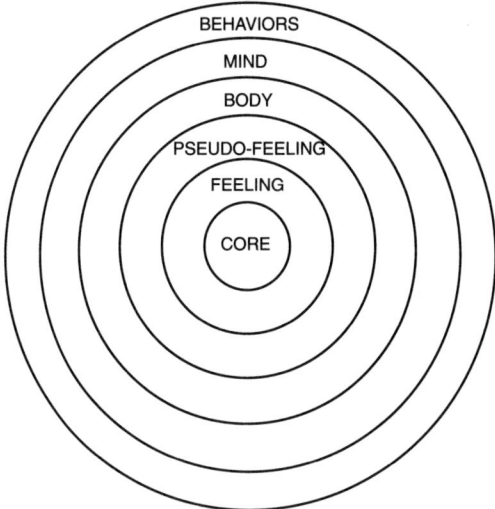

Figure 1.3
COMPONENTS OF HUMAN PERSONALITY

Pseudo-Feelings

We use pseudo-feelings to defend ourselves against the basic feelings beneath. An example of this is the learned use of anger when the real feeling beneath is fear. Those who have not been given permission to feel or express fear often turn it into anger, which may get the attention of the people around them. Other people cover deep anger with fear; they are, in essence, scared of their anger. The pseudo-feelings are a troubling distortion because they seem like real feelings but instead are among the most difficult to penetrate of all the layers of defense against the basic feelings. Pseudo-feelings include blame, guilt, shame, depression, frustration, nervousness, irritation, and boredom, as Figure 1.5 illustrates.

The Body

This body circle is denser and more material. It is the physical layer of defense, depicted in Figure 1.6. Some examples are:

—muscular tension (unnecessary contraction of skeletal muscles).
—postural attitude (examples: head forward, shoulders hunched, locked knees, stomach sucked in, tensed brow).
—postural imbalance (weight carried unevenly front to back or side to side).

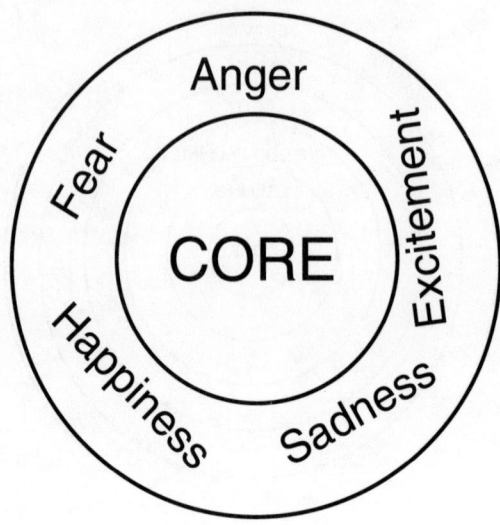

Figure 1.4
THE FEELINGS OF COMPONENT

—automatic hyperarousal (fast heartbeat, excessive sweat production, rapid respiration).
—psychosomatic illness (asthmas, rashes, ulcers, colitis).

Excess muscle tension, a common example, causes a number of problems. First, muscle tension warps the body and pulls it out of alignment with gravity. Second, tension is associated with many psychosomatic symptoms, from headaches, many of which are caused by tension in the muscles on the back of the head and neck, to high blood pressure, in which tense musculature restricts the flow of blood. Third, tense muscles constitute a barrier to feeling. The rigid muscles act as a wall of defense against the feelings trapped inside and against the feelings of others.

The Mind

In proceeding from the inner layers of defense to the outer, the distortions become more complex, and now we come to a defense system so infinitely complex that few ever get beneath it. This is the mental layer of distortion, containing all our beliefs, biases, prejudices, perceptions, and conditioned ways of thinking, shown in Figure 1.7. Of course, not

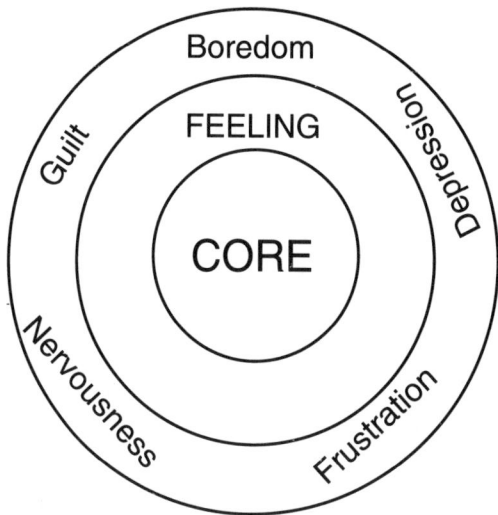

Figure 1.5
PSEUDO-FEELINGS

all mental activity is problematic. We can use mental mechanisms to handle information and solve problems. But if we observe ourselves closely, we can see that much of our mental activity is unproductive and uninvited, and it distorts our ability to see things clearly.

Behaviors

The outermost layer of distortion and defense, shown in Figure 1.8, consists of all our observable verbal and nonverbal behaviors. These include the way we talk, the roles we occupy, our gestures, and all the "games people play." Not all of these behaviors are problematic either. People can solve problems, communicate effectively, enjoy intimacy, and take on meaningful roles. Nevertheless, few of us feel satisfied with our ability to do these things with satisfactory frequency or consistency. Most of us present to the world a limited repertoire of conditioned verbal and nonverbal behaviors. And the conditioned patterns of acting and speaking perpetuate our problems rather than solve them.

An Illustrative Example

To illustrate the various levels of reality represented by the circles, let us use an example of a set of twins. At the core, Joe and Jill simply *are*.

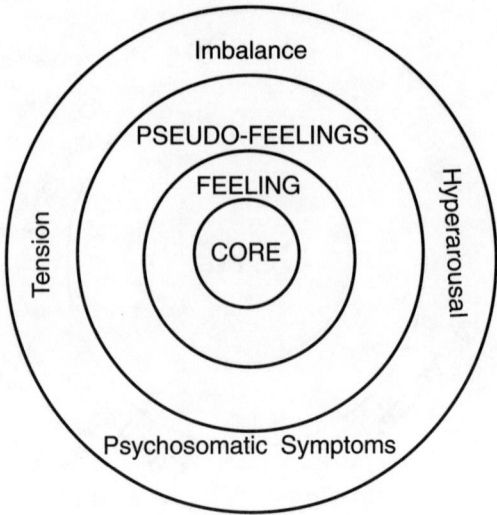

Figure 1.6
THE BODILY LAYER OF DEFENSE

They are essence, pure being, uncolored and unsullied by any concept, notion, or conditioning that can be applied to them. At this deepest level, they are simply representatives of life energy.

At the feeling level, some differences between the two begin to emerge. Although both Joe and Jill have all the feelings common to humans, Joe gets angry more often than Jill. She, on the other hand, becomes afraid more often. At the level of pseudo-feelings, their differences emerge more clearly. Joe deals with his anger by pouting, sulking, and getting depressed. Jill deals with her fear by being nervous. Joe's shoulders are tense and held back, and a shoulder massage hurts him. Jill has relaxed shoulder muscles, but she has a tight stomach, accompanied by frequent stomach upsets.

Jill is highly critical of herself in her mind. If criticized, she automatically thinks she is in the wrong. Joe, in contrast, thinks he is right and others are wrong. If criticized, he is likely to be defiant and start an argument.

As you can see, the farther we get from the core, the more complex the phenomena become. At the core, there is oneness. At the levels of mind and behavior, there is infinite difference. With all the conditioned layers of feeling, thinking, and acting serving as screens, we can see why the core is obscured, why so few are in touch with the essence within.

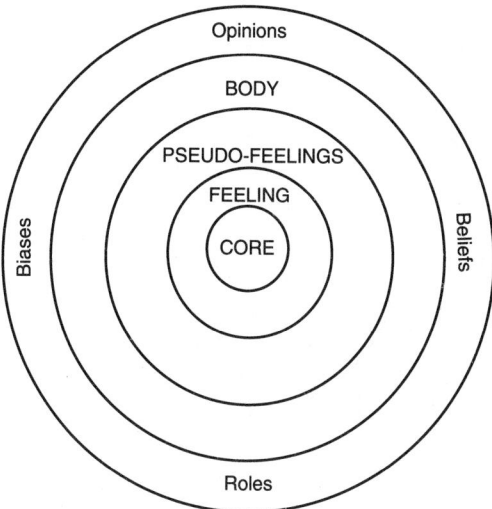

Figure 1.7
THE MENTAL LAYER

We also can see why some people who have experienced the reality of their core continue to be troubled by problems on the most external levels of themselves. People who experience the core during meditation practice still have to dissolve the emotional, physical, mental, and behavioral barriers before they can live totally free of distortion. Dissolving these barriers takes time, awareness, and immersion in the experience of one's feeling, body, mind, and actions.

The rewards are worth it because, as we begin cutting through the layers of conditioning, we begin living transpersonally; we begin dying to the old and experiencing rebirth on a moment-to-moment basis. We are propelled in this process by a powerful energy, for as we approach the core—our common connection with all life energy—we get just the amount of energy needed to dissolve the very next layer of conditioning that must be removed to keep growing. The choice is always ours. We may choose at any moment to withdraw our awareness or to expand it to what is here and real.

IN SUMMARY

Every approach to human behavior seeks to explain what motivates us. By finding out who or what is driving us, we may learn how better to

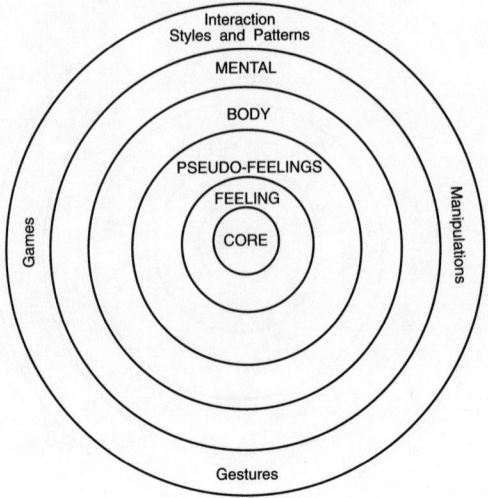

Figure 1.8
VERBAL AND NONVERBAL BEHAVIORS

change directions. To the orthodox Freudian, sex is the driver. To the behaviorist, the search for reinforcement and the avoidance of punishment drive us. To the humanist, self-actualization is a motivating force. To all of these, the transpersonal therapist says yes. But there's more. In the *expansive* transpersonal view, something in us seeks freedom, wholeness, connection with all. We have an urge to play, to create, to go where no one has gone before. There is something beyond the strivings of the ego and the masks of the personality. It is this nameless thing that is the home ground of the transpersonal approach.

NOTES

1. Stansilav Grof, *Realms of the Human Unconscious* (New York: Viking Press, 1974).

2

The Transpersonal Therapist

Barry Weinhold

A transpersonal approach to counseling and psychotherapy includes many goals and techniques of the traditional therapies, but places them in a larger, more expanded context for understanding human behavior. As part of this transpersonal context, the therapist teaches clients how to expand their view of themselves, how to ground their behavior and experiences within this context, and how to assume complete responsibility for their behavior and experiences. Also, the concept of "the therapeutic experience" is enlarged to encompass all of life's experiences. The therapist teaches clients how to utilize this expanded context in their daily lives. In addition to the more conventional therapeutic techniques, the transpersonal therapist may use a variety of alternative methods, such as meditation, prayer, and affirmations to help clients expand their awareness and reduce their attachments to more limited forms of awareness.

I want to begin by sharing one of my most unusual experiences with transpersonal therapy.

One of my most significant transpersonal therapists was an 800-year-old physician who "rented out" the body of a middle-aged woman. The woman's name was Trina, and she was a trance medium who channeled the words of Dr. Duran, an English physician who presumably lived in London in the twelfth century.

My first encounter with Dr. Duran was when I attended a trance circle in Denver one summer evening in 1979. I arrived at the house where the circle was held, and at about dusk the trance circle began. After a group song, Trina lowered her head and dropped into a trance. When she raised her head, a man's voice started to "come through" her.

He asked who was there for the first time, and I spoke up. He began to speak to me as if I were an old friend of his from past lifetimes. He began to tell me things about myself and my life that no other living person knew. He told the people I had lived many different lifetimes and was now a master, adding, "The trouble with you is that you don't recognize you are a master."

Then he began asking me questions: "Barry, do you know that you cannot make any mistakes?"

I replied, "No, I don't know this."

He repeated the question, speaking louder this time. When my reply was the same, he continued, now shouting at me. If you have never been shouted at by an 800-year-old spirit, I doubt that you can fully appreciate my situation.

Finally I began to understand what he was saying. I reasoned that in the perfect harmony of the universe, there are no mistakes, so, as part of the universe, I have to accept this perfection. As a parting shot to me, he said, "Barry, I also want to tell you that you are about to have the relationship you have always wanted."

As I drove back to Colorado Springs, I pondered all these things. When I arrived home, my wife was waiting eagerly to find out about the trance circle. We had been experiencing much conflict, and we both knew our relationship was in need of change. I thought perhaps Dr. Duran's statement about the relationship I always wanted might mean that things would improve between us.

As I began to share the events of the evening, I talked about what Dr. Duran had told me about my relationship, which led us into a four-and-one-half-hour discussion about what each of us wanted from the relationship. By the end of the discussion, we came to a mutual decision to get a divorce. We both realized clearly that night that we each wanted a different kind of relationship and that neither of us was wrong or bad for wanting something different than the other. I had come close to this point before but always backed away, afraid I was making a mistake. Dr. Duran's words echoed in my brain that night: "You cannot make a mistake."

I had an internal feeling of rightness about this decision, but I was still scared about the risks involved and afraid of an unknown future. I now see that this was an important step for me. It sent me on a journey of growth and transformation that could not have happened otherwise.

In a transpersonal context the therapeutic process also is expanded to include the possibility of a high degree of mutuality between therapist and client, in which both are working on themselves and teaching one another. Because they share a common growth-oriented intention for therapy, there is usually less distance between therapist and client than in conventional approaches. Therapy traditionally has been a process whereby one person, presumably with more experience and knowledge, tries to share his or her interpretations of that experience and knowledge with those who presumably have needs in those areas. This process inadvertently can teach clients how to invalidate their own knowledge and experience in favor of someone else's. Many clients now have gained sufficient understanding of their own behavior so that this process seems insulting to them.

We have to expand our concept of therapy to include the validation of personal experience. Inherent in this expanded view of therapy is the recognition that this form of therapy is possible every moment of the day. All the people, situations, and events of our day have potential for teaching us everything we want to know about ourselves, other people, and the world around us. The following illustrates this principle:

> I was about to say something when John closed his eyes and took in a slow, deep breath. The air became still, and I was aware of sounds I had not heard before. I heard bees working in the flowers bordering the veranda, the birds calling in the valley, the wind rustling the leaves, a dog barking in the distance, and the faint sound of some children playing—but it seemed that I could hear them *all at once*. It was an extraordinary experience, for I realized, at that moment, that normally it only seems that we hear, or see, more than one thing at a time. Perhaps for a brief moment I knew the meaning of consciousness as a form of energy, for it was possible to realize that all the sounds were taking different lengths of time to reach my ears, and thus to hear them all at once, I had to transcend space and time as we normally perceive it.[1]

Therapists are only the easels for displaying the experiences of life. These experiences, not the easels, are what we wish to examine in detail. Your experience of life can teach you everything you need to know if you are but awake enough to receive the message.

Many people—mothers, fathers, professional teachers, friends, marital partners, even our own children—have served as potential therapists for all of us. Everyone you encounter is a potential therapist for you, and you are a potential therapist for them. Finding these therapists at first seems to be a random process, but one senses that certainly some unconscious purpose could be behind these encounters. There is an awareness that you are dealing with more than the specifics of the moment. For example, you likely have patterns of learning that go beyond what we refer to as a lifetime. When you meet another person who seems familiar, but someone you never could have met, you possibly are remembering a relationship from generations gone by or from generations yet to come. Time seems to have little to do with this kind of therapy.

I often tell my clients that a mythical place called "central casting," decides what people to send into your life to help you learn your important lessons. You will know these actors and actresses from central casting by the way they affect you. They may disturb you, enrage you, seduce you, or attract you, but they all bring something to help you become more aware and conscious. If you choose to open yourself to the "gifts" these people bring, you are involving yourself in a form of transpersonal therapy.

Who, then, is a transpersonal therapist? A transpersonal therapist is anyone who chooses to be one. The main qualification is that you have made a deliberate choice to see your core self as being the same as other people's. You see that, through choosing to learn from others or to teach others, you can best learn everything in life you need to know. Transpersonal therapy takes place when you can see that everything you are focusing on in others is some aspect of yourself. In this context, other people bring gifts to you that may remind you of things you may or may not have accepted or understood in yourself.

DEVELOPING A TRANSPERSONAL PERSPECTIVE

Essentially, three steps are involved in developing a transpersonal perspective:

1. Become aware that all life experiences usually seen as external to yourself are actually projections of the inner self onto the screen of outer reality.
2. Learn how to reclaim these projections. This may involve learning specific tools for checking your perceptions of reality to determine if projections are present and learning to read your own "early warning signals" that tell you when you may be projecting unwanted aspects of yourself onto others.
3. Finally realize that what you experience as inside and what you experience as outside are not different. This is called "Unus Mundus," or one Reality that connects the inner and outer realities. They are now seen as the same thing.

SOME BELIEFS OF TRANSPERSONAL THERAPISTS

Transpersonal therapists are those who have begun to integrate this expanded way of understanding the therapy experience. Some of their key beliefs are:

1. To do therapy is to receive therapy; the therapist and client are the same, and are both involved in teaching and learning.
2. You cannot help anyone else, only yourself. Doing therapy with others is an excellent way of teaching yourself.
3. Anyone you meet is a potential therapist and client for you.
4. Therapy is a constant process that goes on every moment of your day and continues even into your sleep.
5. To do therapy is to demonstrate. What you demonstrate is who you are (or think you are) and what you believe your relationship with others to be.
6. The formal content of your therapy approach may be irrelevant to the way it is being given and being received.
7. Ultimately you are your own therapist. This means people must be given the tools to work with themselves.
8. Everything you see outside yourself is a projection of what is going on inside yourself. It seems easier to see it first in others or outside yourself before seeing it in yourself.
9. Thoughts are a form of energy that manifest and create your experience.

10. The therapy path you take doesn't matter. There are thousands of paths, and they all lead to the same place. All the answers are available to you if you are aware enough to recognize them.
11. The validity of your internal experience can be trusted. Therefore, an internal therapist has to be a part of you that you trust will give you information to guide and direct you in understanding your life experiences.

Let's take a closer look at each of these beliefs.

To do therapy is to receive therapy. This understanding is difficult to grasp at first because it seems to run counter to most of what we are taught about therapy. Yet it is the cornerstone of a transpersonal approach. At first you may have to behave as if this were true, until you can experience the truth of the statement at a personal level. Therapy is a way of validating what you believe to be true about yourself.

Therapy with others is self-therapy. This grows naturally out of the first belief and is stated separately for emphasis. If you have this focus, you certainly open up the possibility of learning more about yourself. It requires only a change in attitude but, once changed, adds a richness to all your therapy situations, whether formal or informal.

Everyone is your therapist and client. All people we encounter have the potential to be our therapist, our client, or both. You will attract people you need to help solve your problems. Everyone you meet brings you a gift, even though you may not be ready to receive that gift. Your job is to determine the true nature of the gift and then learn how to utilize the gift to solve your problems. Likewise, you have gifts to offer others, who will be attracted to you and you to them for what you can bring to them and them to you.

Therapy is a twenty-four hour a day process. This, too, expands the focus of therapy to include all of life's experiences. It really means that no matter what you are doing, the opportunities for self-improvement are always there. In all of life's experiences, you are confronted either with lessons to be learned or with bliss. Once you have learned the lessons, you have more time to experience the bliss.

To do therapy is to demonstrate. In his fine book *Illusions*, Richard Bach has defined *learning* as finding out what you already know, and *teaching* as reminding others what they already know. *Doing*, according to Bach, is demonstrating what you already know. *Therapy* is a form of witnessing for yourself and others. It enables you to show yourself and others what you believe to be true.[2]

Embedded therapy transcends formal content. What a therapist is saying is usually only a small part of the therapeutic effort. All the words do is get other people's attention long enough for the real therapy to occur. Your level of awareness is the true therapist. It is often transmitted nonverbally or can be conveyed by the sound of your voice. These sound vibrations are actually doing the therapy no matter what you are saying at the moment.

People have to receive self-therapy tools. If your focus has been on external rather than on internal sources of information, you may need help in refocusing. Meditation, prayer, yoga, journal keeping, affirmations, and energy awareness itself are all tools that help you refocus this energy. Many of the tools mentioned in this book are readily available to all of us without much added training.

Projection is an inner reflection. This is the major way people invalidate themselves. It is how we keep from dealing with issues pressing into our awareness. Therefore, refocusing on self-energy requires a clear awareness that what you see outside yourself is *all* a projection of what is going on inside yourself. Without this awareness, you will remain hopelessly stuck in limiting forms of awareness.

Thought is creative. This belief is basic to understanding the transpersonal therapist. You have to understand that you are the source of all your thoughts and that the manifested results of your thoughts serve as therapist for you. Your results tell you clearly what your thoughts have been. If you don't like your results, you have to change your thoughts.

The single path is a myth. Many different approaches are presented as the only way to salvation. Transpersonal therapists know this isn't true, that the path they choose is one of thousands of valid paths. In choosing a way or developing a path of your own, though, you must have some idea about how fast you usually are expected to move along that path (you could get trampled by going too slowly). Measure this against how fast you would like to move, and then decide on a path that you can move along comfortably.

The internal therapist evolves from trust. You probably were taught not to listen to your internal "voices," so developing a reliable internal therapist may be difficult at first. One suggestion is to listen to your heart energy. The voice of your heart generally is a good source, although it may have to be balanced by some thinking. Trust that you will know by your results, if nothing else, which inner voices to listen to and which to ignore. Meditation can be useful in opening yourself to hear more clearly your internal therapist. It can cut down the "noise" or chatter that your surface mind is engaging in.

SPECIAL TECHNIQUES

The transpersonal therapist has no special techniques. The only focus is on learning the lessons embedded in all life experiences. Therapy happens everywhere without any formal structure. There is no person or situation from whom or which transpersonal therapists cannot learn. Likewise, there is no one they cannot reach. All those you meet, therefore, form a therapeutic relationship, and there is really no accident in this. If you didn't have anything to teach each other or learn from each other, you would not have met.

Some of these therapeutic situations are quite casual. Perhaps a stranger sits down next to you on an airplane. Do you talk to the person or ignore him or her? Perhaps two students in a formal class are assigned to do a project together. Do they agree or protest?

At a more sustained level (two or more people, say), a professional therapist and a group of clients may meet for a prescribed time and then disperse. A relationship with a friend may go on for some time, and then the friend might move away. Some therapeutic situations are more intense. One such situation is described here, showing how a transpersonal therapist used a temporary relationship to learn some important lessons.

We formed a committee to help all the school staff better serve the needs of minority youngsters in our student body. We hired an expert in the field, a black fellow named Dr. Robinson. As our work with this man progressed, I realized I just didn't like the fellow. To handle these feelings of dislike, I did the usual things such as trying to see what things in him that I disliked might really be things in myself I wasn't happy with. Then I looked into what he might be doing that I wished I could get away with. I still couldn't come up with the reason I disliked him.

Then one day it came to me. Dr. Robinson, being black, had experienced many occasions of hostility and prejudice from the white community. As could be expected, I summarized that he held a lot of anger and resentment within him. In fact, it seemed to me that anger seemed to fill the air with a negative energy. Although he was absolutely brilliant at disguising it with anything verbal he expressed, I could feel that anger energy, and I would get uncomfortable in his presence.

I came to the next meeting with a better understanding of what I felt about him. The meeting started out much as usual. I was sitting across the circle from Dr. Robinson and looking at him intently. Slowly the other people in the room began to fade from my consciousness, and I realized all my thoughts were centered on him. It was almost as if something that had been blurred was coming into focus, and as the focus sharpened, I saw Dr. Robinson as unbelievably lonely, isolated from people of all races, even though he was at the top of his field, respected, admired. I saw him so lonely that it was hard to imagine the intensity of his loneliness, my loneliness. Then, suddenly, the loneliness broke something within me and I loved him. It was as if the total love of the universe was flowing through me to him, surrounding him with a loving energy so intense that my whole being was vibrating with it as it flowed through me. It wasn't that I was doing anything but, rather, that I was being used as a channel for this loving energy.

I noticed a gradual change in Dr. Robinson. He had laughed before —I remembered that—but it had been in a sarcastic way. I'd never seen him smile, and suddenly he was smiling in a relaxed, peaceful way. He had refused to speak about his own children. Now he was using them as examples in a warm, human way. I noticed the other people in the room were becoming more relaxed and talking more openly than they had in any of the previous meetings. I myself was amazed by what had happened, but I attributed it to my own solving of my reaction to Dr. Robinson. I didn't dare believe this sudden flow of loving energy through me had wrought the changes I was feeling and seeing.

Not until two days later did I have reason to speak with anyone about what had happened. Then I saw one member of our committee, who remarked, "Wasn't that some change in our meeting the other day? Dr. Robinson seemed like a *person*, a *real person*, for the first time. I felt that we really got somewhere with the meeting." I started to shake inside. Maybe the love that had been flowing through me had made a difference after all. The committee member went on to talk about the change in Dr. Robinson. He had become someone to whom she could easily relate.

I could hardly wait to talk with other members of the committee and when I did, I found that all had noticed a difference, ranging from how changed Dr. Robinson had seemed to how much more on target the whole meeting had been. All I could do was throw out my hands in a gesture of wonder and amazement, and to feel thankful that I had been a vehicle through which the universe poured this love energy.[3]

Finally, therapeutic situations can be embedded in relationships that are lifelong. Marital partners, for example, are those who choose to make permanent their therapeutic relationship because they see unlimited opportunities for self-improvement. The closer the two become, the closer they are to their true selves and the richer the therapeutic opportunities become.

Frequently, couples who come for counseling tell me about how wonderful the early years of their relationship were, and then unforeseen problems and conflicts began to arise. I usually say to them, "Congratulations. Your relationship has now gotten close enough and safe enough for the unfinished business you each brought to this relationship to surface and now is available for you to resolve." At first, couples are shocked by the idea, but when they begin examining their conflicts from this context, they can see it is true. A relationship can be a rich source of intimacy when two people agree to cooperate with each other to understand the unmet needs they brought to the relationship.

THERAPEUTIC TOOLS OR METHODS

Many therapeutic tools or methods are available to the transpersonal therapist. These are discussed in other chapters. The main tool or method of therapy available, however, is the awareness of and control over your own energy patterns. The ability to change your vibrational level and respond with an energy pattern necessary to deal with any given situation is a precise art. Many masters have studied a lifetime to learn to develop even a small amount of control over their own vibrational energy patterns. A few individuals apparently have gained enough control over this process to be able to dematerialize and rematerialize themselves. Jesus Christ appeared to have achieved that level of mastery. Most of us, however, would settle for pulling ourselves out of a low energy period or making an illness, such as a cold, disappear.

ACTIVITIES

Following is a set of writing activities designed to help you develop a context for your life and work. I hope it is broad enough to include everything in your life. These three activities are followed by a self-inventory checklist.

Activity 1: Clarifying Your Purpose

Rationale. Your first task as a transpersonal therapist is to have a clear purpose that is broad enough to include all major areas of your life. Your purpose is defined as the overall context against which you can measure all experiences. In this way, you can always check how "on purpose" you are in what you are doing. A major criterion of success for you is the progressive realization of your purpose in life.

Step 1. Take a blank paper and write the following open-ended sentence on it: "My purpose in life is…." Complete that sentence, using as few words as you can that pull together all aspects of your life. An example of a purpose statement is: "My purpose in life is to experience myself as perfect, divine, and complete, and to encourage others to experience themselves in this way."

Step 2. Take your complete purpose statement and ask yourself the following questions:

- ❏ Is this broad enough to include everything I do?
- ❏ Will I ever complete my purpose? (Purpose goes on infinitely.)
- ❏ Is it clear enough so I could explain it to others and they would understand?
- ❏ Is it written in simple enough terms?
- ❏ Is the statement reduced to its basic level?

If your answer to any of these questions is no, continue playing with your statement of purpose until you feel complete with it.

Step 3. Write another purpose statement: "My purpose in being a transpersonal therapist is…." Complete that sentence, using as few words as possible to create a context for your work. Then compare your purpose statement to the overall purpose statement you wrote in *Step 1.*

Activity 2: Clearing Up Your Intentions

Rationale. Your intentions or wants are the motivating forces or energies that take you from your overall purpose to specific goals. The trick is to bring these energies in harmony with your purpose so your wants support your overall purpose.

Step 1. Under each of the five categories of Money, Work, Recreation, Relationships, and Self-Esteem, write specific wants. (For example, under Money, you might write, "I want to make $50,000 this year," or

"I want enough money to pay my bills.") List as many "I wants" as you can under each category.

Step 2. Go back over each want and place a checkmark beside those that seem to support your purpose, a questionmark next to those you aren't sure about.

Step 3. Examine the wants that may not support your purpose and those that clearly do not support your purpose. Attempt to change them so they do support your purpose, or cross them out.

Activity 3: Goal Setting for the Transpersonal Therapist

Rationale. Goals are ways of measuring how "on purpose" you are in an area of your life at a given time. By setting a goal, you are agreeing to give yourself a certain amount of time to find out how successful or on purpose you can be during that time frame. Many people avoid verbalizing goals because they are afraid they will be trapped by them. All goals are really made with yourself, so you can always change them if you want.

Step 1. Keeping in mind the five categories (Money, Work, Recreation, Relationships, Self-Esteem) used in Activity 2, write a letter to a friend and date it one year from today's date. Tell this friend all the things you accomplished in the year that just passed (which is actually the year to come). Be as specific as possible, and fantasize all the things you think might be possible for you to do during the coming year. State them in the letter as if they already had been completed.

Step 2. Extract specific goal statements from the letter, and write them under each of the five categories (e.g., "I have made $50,000 this year").

Step 3. Take these specific yearly goal statements and "back them up" to six months from now. Write specific statements about where you expect to be with your yearly goal six months from today's date (e.g., "I have made $25,000 by this time").

Step 4. Reduce each goal statement to three-month and one-month goal statements. These breakdowns give you an opportunity to examine each goal again and decide whether you are or are not willing to put forth the effort to reach the goals. Based upon that feedback, you may wish to eliminate or change some of your goals.

Self-Inventory on Attitudes of Transpersonal Counselors and Therapists

Directions

Place a checkmark in the column that best represents how you think, feel, and act relative to each statement. (Generally, your first impression is the best one.)

	Never	Sometimes	Usually	Always
a. I enjoy planning the learning of other people.				
b. I would rather learn from others than from myself.				
c. I am a good judge of what is best for me.				
d. Other people seem to ignore what I tell them.				
e. I feel dissatisfied with myself.				
f. I see other people as being generally happy.				
g. I recognize that my thoughts create my experiences.				
h. I learn best in a formal teaching/ learning situation.				
i. I don't understand why things happen to me.				

	Never	Sometimes	Usually	Always
j. I see the world as generally a scary place for me and others.				
k. I have trouble seeing the unpleasant behaviors of others as a self-projection.				
l. I like myself.				
m. I worry about whether I am on the right track for me.				
n. I have trouble motivating myself to do things.				
o. I feel lonely even when I am with others.				
p. I think about all the mistakes I have made.				
q. I find that I have a lot in common with others.				
r. I have trouble spending time by myself.				
s. I find it easy to forgive myself and others when something goes wrong.				

	Never	Sometimes	Usually	Always
t. I see other people as generally able to learn from their experiences.				

Scoring Procedures:

Each item carries a weight of 1, 2, 3, or 4. In some cases, items are keyed with the "Always" column weighted at 4, and others are keyed with "Never" weighted at 4. Items scored 1, 2, 3, 4 (Never = 1; Sometimes = 2; Usually = 3; Always = 4) are c, f, g, l, q, s, and t. Items scored 4, 3, 2, 1 (Never = 4; Sometimes = 3; Usually = 2; Always = 1) are a, b, d, e, h, i, j, k, m, n, o, p, r.

After completing the inventory, go over each item and write the corresponding number in the column where you placed a checkmark. Add all the numbers to get a personal score. Place this score on the continuum below and look at the suggested interpretation of your score.

20	30	40	50	60	70	80

Suggested Interpretation of Your Score

20-29 Little in common with transpersonal therapy concepts.

30-39 Some awareness of transpersonal therapy concepts.

40-49 Some identification with transpersonal therapist; move slowly.

50-59 Ready to proceed with learning to be a transpersonal therapist.

60-69 Go for it.

70+ You are truly a transpersonal therapist!

A Dialogue Between the Authors

Gay: Barry, I would like to ask you a question. Do your remember a particular person or a significant event in your life that moved you in a transpersonal direction or assisted you in entering that transpersonal level in your life?

Barry: One event that I described in the chapter on developmental perspectives (Chapter 3) probably did the most to open up my ideas in the transpersonal domain. It happened over twenty years ago when I had a death/life experience. I experienced something that I couldn't explain psychologically. It transcended everything I knew at that time.   I had no frame of reference to understand it. That experience, probably more than others (and there were lots of others), stands out in my mind as the one that kept coming back to me over the last twelve or thirteen years. I found myself asking, "What did that really mean, and what was that experience telling me about myself?"

Gay: It seems to me the one thing that makes a transpersonal therapist is that he or she is willing to take experience to the limit, is willing to go all the way with a particular experience or experience in general.

Barry: I agree. I think that would be a good description of what I've done with that experience and many others I've had since then. Each time I've had an experience like that, I've always had a choice. I either put it aside and say, "I don't understand it; I don't want to look at it and deal with it," or I can go ahead and take that experience as far as I can.

Gay: ...to be willing to experience it intensely, to the limit.

Barry: Yes.

Gay: That's one thing I think of frequently in terms of training transpersonal therapists. I come back time after time to the awareness that it is what the therapist is willing to experience that defines the quality and depth of the therapy that is going to take place. In other words, your client is only going to be able to go up to the place at which your willingness to experience has come.

Barry: I find that to be true, too. A lot of clients and others who have come to me have told me that. The other day a client said she had experienced many transpersonal events in her life—precognitions and things. When she had tried to talk to another therapist about them, the therapist told her they were worthless. She was admonished not to pay any attention to them.

Gay: The implication was that they were pathological.

Barry: Yes. The therapist put some kind of label on them that indicated there was something wrong with her. So when she brought them up again, I helped her put them in a context that would enable her to use these experiences to understand them and to broaden her concept of herself. What she needed to do was not wall all that off but accept those types of experiences as reflecting valid parts of herself.

Gay: That's a good point. Any aspect of life that one walls off will eventually cause a problem, because any aspect of life that you disown—feelings, the past, your potential, telepathy, your body or spirit—is going to come back eventually and seek recognition.

Barry: To help people go through whatever their resistances are is exciting. In my own life, there are things I have disowned, such as my rage and my own fear. When I understood how they are part of me, I could accept them.

Gay: When I think of those kinds of experiences in my own life, I remember one in particular when I became willing to feel fear. I kept going down into it, shaking with it, being with it, vibrating with it; and I kept choosing over and over again to feel this. I was thirty years old when I realized that I had never allowed myself to experience fear because I come from a background where you weren't supposed to admit you were scared. You were supposed to tough it out. So I had gone through my whole life defending against fear. When I got down to the bottom of the fear, I found that after a while I spontaneously started dancing. I happened to be by myself at the time, and I turned on some music and began to dance. Fear turned out to be something that I could actually dance with!

This experience taught me a lot about transpersonal therapy and a transpersonal view of life. It is those very disowned experiences that can be a tremendous source of energy once I allow them to participate in me.

Barry: Yes, I've seen it happen frequently. People who allow themselves to fully experience their fears may suddenly transform all their fears into joy and ecstasy. What are some other experiences you've had that have moved you toward a transpersonal perspective?

Gay: I can think of a couple—one from a teacher—which really moved me. I was listening in 1971 to a talk given by Krishnamurti. In a way it was the most disquieting experience of my life, but in a way it was the most healing experience up until then, because Krishnamurti simply described the way it is in life. He described the problem carefully and came right up to the end. Everybody in the audience was saying, "Now tell us how it's going to be," "Tell us it's going to end all right." At that moment he stopped the speech and said, "Now you must ask yourself how it is from now on." I've described the way it is right up until this moment, and now only you can be your own guru from this moment on."

It was the most electrifying thing. I partially leaped up off my seat and ran out of the auditorium. I was rattled and also healed, because he in a sense gave me permission to ask the questions myself that I wanted to know. All my life I had been looking for the answers out there somewhere.

I see that same process with my clients. My goal is to get them to experience things the way they are, not to hold out a hope that it's going to get better, or guarantee them that if they make a certain change, everything will end all right. All I can do is say: Experience it the way it is now. The emphasis must be on developing the willingness in myself and my clients to experience life the way it is right now. I want to teach them that if they are willing to take it the way it is rather than live an illusion, they get to experience the truth that lies just under the pain. The first thing that has to be gone through is that pain we've been holding onto, but underneath is a tremendous sense of joy and truth—a clear relationship with life.

Barry: It's deceptively easy for people to look outside themselves for the sources of their problems and also for the solutions to them. Not only are the problems inside themselves, and of their own making, but also the solutions are there. When people realize this, they are profoundly moved.

For example, about ten years ago I began to be aware that sometimes I felt fragmented while I went about my daily routine and other times everything seemed to flow and it was almost effortless. I tended to blame those fragmented days on other people or external conditions. The days when everything flowed I credited to luck.

One day it occurred to me that maybe I could influence these external events by my thoughts and perceptions. I began to experiment with myself. I decided to focus on how everything I was doing was connected, to see if I could actually create the flow I spoke of. Much to my surprise, when I did focus on how everything I was doing was connected, the flow would be there, and when I would forget and not focus on this aspect of my daily routine, I would tend to lose the connected feeling.

The more I practiced this, the better I got at producing this flow until I could sustain the flow for weeks, sometimes months. I also found, much to my surprise, that I could now do almost three times as many things without expending any more energy. My whole life unfolded more rapidly.

Gay:　That reminds me of the other event I wanted to mention. I realize I need to see things and experience things myself now, in order to prove they are so for me. I'm no longer willing to take anybody else's word for things, unless I can personally experience them. My first occasion of seeing a transpersonal experience in action was six or seven years ago. A client I was working with was feeling scared, so I asked her to just allow herself to experience it. I had known that if I allowed myself to experience my fears fully, I would eventually come to a place of clarity that was underneath the fear, and I could get to that place only by allowing myself to experience my fears fully. I had not seen that process unfold in anybody else, so the first time it happened, I looked on in total awe as this client went down through layer after layer of fear and allowed herself just to be with it until it subsided.

Then a very amazing thing happened. Not only did she feel quiet and serene and at peace with herself but also bubbled a number of solutions to the problem she was dealing with, solutions she hadn't seen fifteen minutes before. I was profoundly moved by that, because it told me once and for all that people actually do have direct access to the truth and to all solutions they need, in themselves. It's like the statement you quoted by Richard Bach about how learning is discovering what you already know. That's such a paradox I would not have believed it until I saw it with my own eyes.

Barry: One of the things I'm interested in is how you got trained as a transpersonal psychologist. How did that happen? Was it a planned thing, or did it happen accidentally? What is your perception on that, and what do you say to people when they ask you that question?

Gay: I had a lot of training, in my formal graduate studies, in the three main forces in psychology. When I was at the University of New Hampshire, I had quite a bit of training in client-centered counseling. Then, when I was at Stanford, I had considerable training in behavioral counseling. During this time I also learned about psychodynamic concepts. All those approaches had value for me. In a sense, they built one on the other, and I now see that I learned many things from each of these approaches.

I eventually got to the place—I believe it was along about the time when I heard Krishnamurti talk—where I suddenly realized I had to take my education into my own hands. So, somewhere in the early seventies, while I was still working on my Ph.D., I began seriously asking myself, "What do I really want to know?" I found that what I really wanted to know was not only psychology but also the whole spiritual element of life. I found myself asking, "Is there a bridge between psychotherapy and spirituality?" "Is there some sort of meeting ground between those two things?" I knew that all the religious and spiritual and psychic experiences I'd had must follow some kind of laws and obey certain types of principles, and I knew that all the psychological experiences I'd had obey some kind of principle, and I wanted to know where those two met. I had never heard the term "transpersonal" before that time, and I began looking around for people who also were asking these questions and whom I could discuss these things with.

At that time I met Jim Fadiman. He asked me what I was interested in, and when I told him, he said, "Oh, you're interested in transpersonal psychology." I said, "Great. Tell me about it.

What is it?" He described it, and I decided I was definitely a transpersonal psychologist. He said that it was the fourth force in psychology that was being built on top of the humanistic tradition. It seemed for me the only unlimited psychology I could find. It was the only boundless one. It was the only one that seemed to reach for the sky beyond.

After that meeting I began taking responsibility for my own education and, as a transpersonal psychologist, spent hours reading esoteric books. I spent the rest of my graduate education sitting on the floor in bookshops, reading things I didn't have enough money to buy but wanted to read. I began reading about various Indian philosophies, Chinese philosophies, trying to find out what they were really saying about how transformation takes place. I guess the question I kept returning to again and again was: "What is the one thing that allows transformation to take place?" Zen is talking about it. Sufism is talking about it. Freud sometimes alluded to it. I wanted to know what that one thing is that allows transformation to unfold in a person.

Barry: It sounds like a real exciting discovery process that led you to find transpersonal psychology.

Gay: Yes. It made life a lot easier to have a limitless container to hold it all in.

Barry: Yes.

Gay: How does that mesh with some of your training and background?

Barry: As you know, we come out of similar traditions, in one sense. All of my graduate training was at the University of Minnesota, and some of your major professors were people who either taught there or were trained there also.

Gay: Yes.

Barry: The "Minnesota point of view" seems to describe how I put myself together therapeutically and theoretically. I was exposed to all the major therapies in my graduate training. In my master's level training, like yours, I had client-centered training, and in my doctoral work I learned behavioral counseling approaches in therapy, but I didn't learn to apply psychoanalytic theory until later. I deliberately went out of my way while at the university to pick up the psychoanalytic theory of development and then later learned how to put all that together. Like you, my process was one of constantly wanting to know more.

Even this broad framework didn't quite give me answers to the questions I would encounter with clients and the questions within myself I couldn't answer. I was seemingly led to something more complete. I felt a desire, a quest to know more. I wanted to expand the context with which I did therapy with myself and other people. Like you, I just decided to find out more and began reading articles and books in the transpersonal literature. I started to be pulled toward the transpersonal literature, and I started to understand more about aspects of my own behavior and experiences. I found that these people were opening up areas of human endeavor that I wanted to look at. I think, more than anything else, it was the journey I was on.

Also, the one transpersonal concept that has always appealed to me, which grounds me with my own training, is that you don't want to leave any of your troops at home when working with people. It helps me to create the broadest possible context for working with people. All the other approaches would always say, "We have the answers now. You have to cast the rest aside and do what we say." I was so glad I'd found an approach to therapy that was saying to me, "Don't cast anything aside. Include it all. Learn to use it. Learn how to integrate it."

Gay: That's what I like about transpersonal psychology. It says "yes" and gives me permission to explore and understand things that other theories just don't look at. Other approaches ignore inconsistencies or reduce them to some level of understanding that leaves out a lot of the complexities. I think it's sometimes helpful to look at behavior in that way, but it tends to be a little bit too reductionistic to handle some of the spiritual aspects of human behavior.

Barry: As I look back, a big part of becoming a transpersonal psychologist relates to my graduate training. It gave me a transpersonal perspective, because I wasn't trained in one specific approach. It encouraged me to find what worked for me, to learn how to use it, and then learn how to integrate what I have learned with other things. I learned to approach a systematic, but expansive, point of view. I really credit my teachers at the University of Minnesota for having the wisdom to teach me that way.

Gay: I think good teachers are those who give their students total freedom and permission to go farther than they themselves have gone.

Barry: I agree. The other principle they taught me indirectly was not to create a special guru for myself and not to create a mentor whose ideas I had to overcome. They all gave me permission to do the type of things that made sense to me and not to do what they were doing exactly. It wasn't that they ever came right out and said that, but it was clear by their behavior that's what they were saying. I think that's a really valuable thing.

I remember seeing a film of Warren Bennis interviewing Carl Rogers. He asked Rogers what contributed most to his ability to develop his theory—this expansive theory of understanding human behavior. Rogers said he didn't have to overcome the teachings of a mentor, and he had permission to explore in ways that none of his teachers had taught. When I heard that, I really picked up on it and said to myself, "Yeah, that's true." I see how people can limit themselves by following a certain mentor or a certain approach.

Something is to be said for mentors, because they are good at what they do and they can achieve excellent results with a given approach. I don't want to discredit that kind of focus, but I needed something broader and more expansive—and permission to explore more complex issues in human behavior that my mentors and teachers chose not to explore.

Gay: Barry, I've mentioned a couple of people who've been instrumental at different points in my life, either by delivering a certain message to me that I really needed to hear or by giving me a certain permission that I needed. Who were some of the significant people in your development as a transpersonal psychologist?

Barry: Really, I have to credit some of my graduate instructors—particularly Donald Blocher, who impressed me with his tremendous insight into human behavior. He's articulate and so clear about his understanding of human behavior. I loved to sit and listen to him for hours just articulate different aspects of how to work with people. Also, he gave me permission to find my own niche, not to follow his. That was an important permission for me.

Carl Rogers certainly influenced my thinking. I was profoundly interested not only in what he did but also in the way he did it. He certainly was a man who was willing to explore and to break down established barriers. He advanced our field in ways that probably we're just beginning to understand. He took some risks and did some things that nobody else in his time was willing to do. We wouldn't be here today calling ourselves transpersonal therapists had it not been for Carl Rogers.

Maslow—although I never knew him or worked with him directly—had that same kind of feeling for psychology. Here was a man who was willing to risk asking questions that no one else would ask. Indirectly, he gave me a lot of permission to explore my hunches.

I think of other people who briefly touched my life, like George Leonard, who happened to be my partner in an aikido class taught by Bob Nadeau. I learned so much in just a brief encounter with that man. He was such a powerful person, who knew how to channel his energy so effectively. Also, I remember going to an AHP convention in Berkeley and hearing a speech by Jean Houston. I'd never heard anyone speak as eloquently about psychology and human behavior. It profoundly moved me. I've since read some of her books and heard some of her other speeches, and I've always had the same kind of sense of here's a person who is asking the kinds of questions I'm asking. She's a fellow traveler in the transpersonal realms, and I felt a lot of kinship and support. This led me to study intensively with her for several years.

At the same AHP Convention I remember listening to another speech by Leonard Orr, the founder of rebirthing. It was confusing to me. He had a very informal way of delivering a speech—not the usual formal lecture—and while he talked, he did a lot of breathing and sighing. Part of what interested me was the audience reaction. Some people became highly incensed and walked out; some people became hysterical and started laughing at everything he said and couldn't stop laughing. I got so caught up watching the reactions of the people around me that I didn't hear the speech. Fortunately, I had it on tape, and I had to listen to the tape many times before I heard his message. Again I followed my internal guidance and sought training in rebirthing and have now integrated breath work into my daily spiritual practices.

You know, I basically don't need any special teachers. My own kids are my teachers. All my clients are my teachers. All my students are my teachers. All my experiences are my teachers. I'm open to learn from whoever is there teaching something.

Gay: That's one thing about transpersonal psychology. I think it opens up space for everything to be a teaching-learning situation. You can learn as much from these pine trees we are sitting among right now as you can from a particular mode of teaching or a gifted teacher.

Barry: It does seem incomplete to say these are the people who helped me get where I am. When I refer to them, they are people who stand out in my mind, and I know there were many others. I could go on naming people. I remember some of them. Others ... I don't even know their names, but they were there. They had something—a gift to bring—not always one I wanted to receive at the time. My willingness is much less limited now.

What seems most important to me now, when it comes to teachers, is their ability to teach out of their own wounds. I have found only a few teachers who meet that qualification. Robert Bly is one of them. I remember when I first encountered him back about 1982, he was not able to teach from his wounds. But in recent years he learned how to do that. Now I find what he has to say quite valuable. Since I'm interested in male psychology and the development of my own deep masculine aspects, I regard him as a mentor for me. I recently thanked him in person for being my mentor. He asked, "What did I do?" I said, "You taught me how to use my own wounds in my teaching and are a role model for me." He understood immediately.

John Bradshaw has been another mentor for me for the same reasons. John goes on national television and teaches from his wounds. What a powerful way to teach the masses. I believe transpersonal therapists can best reach people if they are willing to tell their own story and expose their woundedness. This takes courage and maturity.

Barry: What is the essence of being a transpersonal therapist?

Gay: I think the essence is having an unblinking focus on what actually *is* while at the same time having an infinitely expanded view of the possibilities. At its worst, the transpersonal approach is used as a vehicle for the therapist's speculative belief systems—from aromatherapy to Zoroastrianism—and can be a retrograde influence in the client's life. When transpersonal ideas are ill-used, they keep clients from embracing reality by introducing them to an immature and premature form of transcendence based on fear. At their best, transpersonal concepts engender a relationship with reality grounded in oneness and love.

Transpersonal therapists dance along the edge of the central paradoxes of reality. To what extent does the mind affect the body? Where does one mind leave off and another begin? To what extent do we perceive ourselves as embedded in or separate from the universe? Do we use our concepts as an embrace of or an escape from reality? To transpersonal therapists, these issues are not idle intellectual curiosities. They are the living reality of what goes on in the consulting room. These questions are what the transpersonal therapist does for a living.

NOTES

1. Reshad Feild, *The Invisible Way: A Love Story for the New Age* (New York: Harper and Row, 1979), pp. 93–94.
2. Richard Bach, *Illusions: The Adventures of a Reluctant Messiah* (New York: Delacorte, 1977).
3. Personal account given to the author by a friend; names changed by request.

3

Human Development: A Transpersonal Perspective

Barry Weinhold

From a transpersonal perspective, the process of human development represents the broadest conceptualization of human development that I can utilize in a practical sense in my work with people. My thinking about the subject is always in a state of change, so what you are about to read represents the point to which my thinking had evolved at the time I wrote this chapter (January 1991).

CONTRIBUTIONS FROM OTHER THEORIES

A number of attempts have been made to extend the work of traditional developmental psychologists such as Freud, Erikson, Piaget, and others to include the more spiritual, mythic, psychic aspects of human development. Maslow's hierarchy of needs was one of the approaches that postulated a higher level of development, which he termed *self-actuali-*

zation. Jung's work also added the concept of the *Self*, which represented wholeness and divine connections, but he looked at it as emerging only during the second half of life.[1] Later, some of his followers described the Self as the original totality of the person before the ego develops.[2]

Loevinger developed a theory involving ego development, which seems to include some of the same characteristics found in Maslow's self-actualized person but which did not reach beyond that level.[3] Wilber's book, *The Atman Project: A Transpersonal View of Human Development,*[4] attempts to go beyond the highest level of the ego psychologists and includes a reinterpretation of their work as well as an extension of human development to include transpersonal stages.

The research of Margaret Mahler[5] has added much to our understanding of early childhood development. She was able to chart the course of early childhood development, particularly how the important bonding and separation needs of infants are met. She helped us better understand the importance of the psychological birth and why so few people actually complete this process at the appropriate age of two or three.

My attempt to make some sense and order out of human development, from a transpersonal perspective, includes much of this previous work on human development done by the major psychoanalytic and ego development theorists, along with a number of humanistic and transpersonal theorists. My description of this complex, much-studied subject has to be limited here, so the following account is naturally somewhat sketchy and brief. Nevertheless, I hope to capture the essential ingredients of the process and highlight some of the key concepts.

THE KEY ASSUMPTION OF A TRANSPERSONAL VIEW OF HUMAN DEVELOPMENT

The key assumptions of a transpersonal perspective of human development include the following:

1. Emphasis is placed on the importance of the *prenatal period* and the *birth process.* Few developmental theories have accounted for the importance of the prenatal period of development and the birth process itself as they both set the tone for all future development. Therefore, these may be the most important periods of development in people's lives.

2. Special attention is given to the actual *bonding process*, and to the long-term effects of improper bonding. Few developmental theories account for these effects in their theoretical paradigms. Tremendous breakthroughs in our understanding of maternal-infant bonding have occurred in the past twenty years.

3. The *psychological birth process* is another focal point. Few theorists have looked at the psychological or second birth process, which also has tremendous implications for future development. This process should be completed as early as age two but, for most of us, is never completed during our lifetime.

4. Emphasis is given to *continuous development*, with no break between ego development and so-called higher states of being. In this framework, transcendence is a process that occurs at each stage of development rather than a grand and glorious event that signifies "death of the ego." Actual transcendence beyond the stage of full ego development is not seen as a quantum leap or a major break with the ego. Instead, it is seen as movement to the next higher and more integrated stage of development while incorporating everything learned from the previous stages.

5. *Development is seen as sequential* and presumes that any developmental task not learned at the age-appropriate time is simply carried along to the next stage, to be added to the tasks to be completed at that stage. It is always there and will remain a part of our unfinished business until it is completed—which, for many, is later in life or never at all.

6. *Age-specific stages are deemphasized.* Rather, the emphasis is on completing the ego functions at each stage to better equip the person to handle the next emerging stage. Each stage leads to an eventual re-membering (uniting) who we really are and then expanding even more as a conscious unified being.

7. Special attention is directed to the *tendency to inflate the ego* rather than to complete the stages leading to full ego development. This refers to the propensity to look "enlightened" or Godlike in place of the real thing (being enlightened and being God).

8. The *newborn child is seen as highly aware and connected* to the infinite, transpersonal realms of existence. This is similar to Jung's central unifying archetype, which he termed the Self. If this core self or transpersonal core receives nurturing and support, it will grow and remain a vital force. If it is not supported and

nurtured, the infant will become cut off from the core self. The person then is left with the difficult task of re-membering (uniting) this core self.

Hubert Benoit stated the case this way:

> Man is born the son of God…but he is forgetful of his origin…Amnesic, he suffers from illusorily feeling himself abandoned by God, and he fusses about …in search of affirmations to support his divinity which he cannot find.[6]

PRENATAL DEVELOPMENT

In the past twenty years we have developed much of the technology necessary to study the life of the unborn child. We always have been fascinated by "old wives' tales" about how we can influence later development of the child by the books the mother reads or the music she listens to or the messages she sends to her unborn child, but medical science usually has dismissed any reported effects as nonsense. Now, with the new development of tiny ultrasensitive sensors and sound equipment, medical science can study more thoroughly the world of the unborn child.

Medical research has confirmed many of the old wives' tales and discovered that the unborn child is far more developed than we ever imagined. For example, studies have shown that by the fifth week of fetal development, the child has already acquired a complex set of reflex actions. By the eighth week, the child is moving its head, arms, and trunk with ease and has developed a primitive body language, usually expressed in deliberate jerks or kicks. Thomas Verny, a physician, states that medical research has confirmed that the fetus can see, hear, experience, taste and on a primitive level, even learn in utero…[7]

Fetal Development of Boys and Girls

We have known for some time that from conception until the twelfth week, the gender of the fetus is always female. If a male child is going to develop, drastic changes start about the twelfth week and continue until the time of birth. These changes disrupt the flow of development of the male fetus, whereas the female fetus does not experience these disruptions. Because of this developmental disruption, girl babies are developmentally advanced over boy babies at birth, and this developmental gap increases and continues until about age sixteen. During this time, the gap between boys and girls can be as much as one or two years.

This may account for the fact that almost ninety percent of all birth defects and genetic abnormalities occur in males, and eighty percent of all infant crib deaths are male children. Young male children often suffer untold damage to their self-esteem because of their inability to match the performance levels of female children, who usually crawl, walk, talk, and respond earlier than male babies.

Early Signs of Fetal Development

By the fourth month, the unborn child can frown, squint and grimace. If the eyelids are touched, the fetus will squint. If the lips are touched, the fetus will start sucking. By the sixth month, the unborn child is as sensitive to touch as a one-year-old. If cold water is injected into the amniotic fluid, the child will kick violently. Also, by this time the child has developed a good sense of taste. If saccharin is added to the amniotic fluid, the child's rate of swallowing responses doubles. The addition of a foul-tasting, iodine-like substance will cause the swallowing rate to drop, accompanied by facial grimaces.

From the sixth month on, the child listens all the time—and a pregnant woman's abdomen and uterus are indeed noisy places. The loudest sounds the unborn hears are the mother's stomach rumblings. Voices of the mother and people around her are also audible to the unborn. The mother's regular heartbeat is the constant sound that lets the unborn child know all is well. Perhaps this is why later a young child can be lulled to sleep by the ticking of a clock. Researchers found that when adults were asked to set a metronome at the rate that pleased them most, they chose fifty to ninety beats per minute—the range of the human heartbeat. Some people believe that musical talents also are awakened in the womb by the rhythms of the mother's heartbeat. Unborn children prefer largo music (sixty beats per minute) to rock music, which causes them to kick violently.[8]

Vision develops more slowly in the darkness of the womb. Even so, from the sixteenth week on, the unborn child can be easily startled by shining a light directly on the mother's abdomen. At birth the child is dreadfully myopic but has excellent vision at six to twelve inches, the distance from the mother's breast to the mother's face.

Early Signs of Consciousness and Memory

Early sensory development is necessary for learning to occur. Consciousness exists from the twenty-eighth week on.[9] By that time, the cerebral cortex is as advanced as that of a newborn, so thinking, feeling, and remembering are possible from then on. Brain waves are apparent from the thirty-second week on, and even REM (rapid eye movement) sleep patterns can be detected, which suggests that dreaming may be occurring.

Adult subjects in LSD research by Stan Grof[10] reported clear memories from the womb that were verified as accurate. Other researchers have looked at the emotional life of the unborn child through follow-up studies of children who, while in an unborn state, were exposed to marital strife between their mother and father.

In a study of more than 1,300 children, and their families, one researcher concluded that "a woman locked in a stormy marriage runs a 237 percent greater risk of bearing a psychologically or physically damaged child than a woman in a secure, nurturing relationship."[11] This risk actually was rated higher than other known recognized risks, such as physical illness, smoking, or performing back-breaking labor during pregnancy. This research showed that unhappy marriages produced babies who were five times more fearful and jumpy than children from happy marriages. At age four or five, these children were undersized, timid, and highly dependent on their mothers.

Another long-term, follow-up study showed similar results.[12] A group of researchers at the Fels Research Institute tested unborn babies for changes in heart rate when an external stimuli (a loud noise made near the mother) was introduced. They hoped to see if those who had few changes in heart rate as a result of the loud noise (low reactors) would maintain this personality trait long after birth. When these children were tested in the same way fifteen years later, they still exhibited the same few changes in heart rate when a loud noise was made. The group of high reactors showed equally persistent patterns of rapid increase in heart rate as a reaction to a loud noise. Another finding of this study was that the high reactors were more creative and better able to identify feelings in themselves and others than were those in the low reactor group, who tended to be much more concrete.

Several other studies have confirmed that mothers who consciously and subconsciously wanted to be pregnant produced much healthier babies, emotionally and physically, at birth and afterward than mothers who did not want to be pregnant. One group of mothers consciously said they wanted to be pregnant, but psychological tests showed they really did not want to be pregnant. The offspring of these mothers seemed to know this subconscious reality and, as a result, had an unusually large number of behavioral and gastrointestinal problems in early childhood.[13]

In the same study, another group of mothers was identified as having many doubts and fears about being pregnant, but the psychological tests showed that, despite the conscious doubts and fears, they really wanted to be pregnant. Children from these mothers seemed to pick up both messages and were confused. At birth, an unusually large number of these children were apathetic and lethargic.

These studies are just the beginning, and there is so much still to know about prenatal development and its effects on later development. Each of the studies answers some limited questions but leaves many more questions to answer.

During Grof's LSD research, hypnotherapy, and breath work clients could describe in great detail events from their unborn state. Some even reported a memory trace of their own conception.[14] We do know that much of what we previously had labeled as old wives' tales turned out to be accurate statements about mothers' ability to influence the subsequent development of their children while still in the womb. If I were pregnant (which I never will be), I think I would do everything I could to provide positive emotional, physical, and intellectual experiences for my unborn child. I would read, talk, sing, eat good food, play classical music, and do anything else I could think of to provide a positive climate for the development of my unborn infant.

Also, the research strongly suggests that the marriage or couple relationship should be strong and healthy and that both parents should want the child. Less than half of all children born are wanted by their parents, and fewer than that number are actually planned.[15]

BIRTH: THE BLUEPRINT FOR ALL FUTURE DEVELOPMENT

Until recently, most obstetrical practices were designed to rush people through the birth process as quickly as possible. The belief seemed to be that the quicker it was, the better it would be for everyone concerned. The work of the French obstetrician Frederick LeBoyer caused people to begin questioning these practices, and in the past fifteen to twenty years a virtual revolution has taken place in the way we give birth.[16]

New research findings also suggest a strong need to change many traditional practices and beliefs.[17] What has been affirmed is that the newborn is highly sensitive to all sensory stimulation, as opposed to the belief in a lack of sensory development.

Imagine for a few minutes what your birth must have been like. Pay attention to your reactions as you read these words describing the standard obstetrical practice still used in many hospitals: After hours of struggle made more difficult by the birthing position of your mother (feet in stirrups, lying on her back), you emerge (if not sucked or pulled by use of forceps) into a cold, noisy world of bright lights, being semi-drugged, over-stressed, and exhausted. Before you have the opportunity to take a breath on your own, you are hooked up to a respirator or held up by the heels and slapped on the back. Already out of breath from the journey, your next ordeal is to have suction devices stuck in your mouth, nose, and ears, your eyelids peeled back, letting painful light and even more painful chemicals enter your tender young eyes.

Next the umbilical cord is cut, whether you are breathing on your own or not, and then the blood from your mother's episiotomy is cleaned from your body and you are laid on cold, hard scales to be weighed like a piece of choice roast beef. If this isn't enough, you are then wrapped tightly in a blanket and whisked away to the nursery or incubator, either screaming in pain and terror or in a semi-conscious state from all the anesthetic administered during the birth process. If you were born in a hospital, this is probably what your first encounter with this world was like.

Consider what you might have learned about the world in this first encounter with it. Remember, you moved from a soft, warm, dark, quiet, totally nourishing place into a harsh, sensory bombardment. You were physically abused, violated in a number of ways, and subjected to physical pain and insult, all of which could possibly be overcome if it weren't for one additional act of cruelty: You were isolated from your mother. This final barbaric act is almost impossible to overstate. No court of justice could hand out a punishment severe enough to account for this crime against helpless humanity. The final isolation from your mother robbed you of the bonding necessary to overcome the effects of your ordeal.

In the last twenty years we have seen many changes in the way we birth babies, although the above-described practices still prevail in many hospitals. LeBoyer insisted that babies be birthed in soft light at a comfortable room temperature with soft music playing. He also placed the newborn on the mother's belly or near the breast even before the cord was cut, allowing the child to take the first breath spontaneously. Following this, the child is bathed in warm water and gently massaged to activate brain cells.

Other pioneering obstetricians added more to his research. A Russian doctor, Igor Charkofsky, started birthing children in water.[18] This environment allows the mothers to squat or lie in the water and stay more relaxed as the water environment supports and soothes them. In more than twenty-five years of using this procedure, he reported almost no complications and almost no need for drugs or pain killers. The baby is born under water and breathes through the umbilical cord, which is still attached. Charkofsky also suggests that during the first few months mother and child spend several hours each day in the water, which is the natural environment of the prenatal child. He reports rapid rates of physical, emotional, and mental development in these children. Charkofsky's "water babies" walk, talk, and develop much faster than "land babies" who don't receive water therapy.

The home-birth movement, led by many courageous midwives, has done more than anything to change the way hospitals now birth children. Facing the prospect of losing revenue, hospitals have created "birthing centers," where some of these new procedures can be used under the care of trained medical practitioners. Fathers are now allowed to be present and assist in the birth process, and mother, father, and child are allowed time to bond in the period immediately after birth. Siblings and other relatives can visit the newborn in the hospital. We know that anyone present during the birth of a child and in the first two days following the birth is bonded to that child.

BONDING: A VITAL PROCESS

We now know that mother-infant bonding, which takes place during the first twelve to twenty-four hours, is necessary to relax muscles tightened during the birth process, to fully activate the central nervous system, and to activate the reticular formation necessary for full mental-physical coordination and learning. If allowed to, a newborn bonds or attaches to his or her mother almost immediately after birth. The sound of her voice, the sight of her face during feeding, the feel of her skin, the smell of her body—all are clear signals of safety and security in this otherwise foreign and harshly demanding world. Naturally, this attachment requires a significant amount of private mother-infant contact during the first several days, including skin-to-skin contact between mother and child during the first hours after birth.

The original mother-infant bonding is the blueprint for all the infant's subsequent attachments and is the first step in the psychological birth process. Throughout your lifetime the quality of this first attachment influences the quality of all your other bonds with other individuals.

Klaus and Kennell have contributed much to our understanding of the bonding or attachment process. They summarized their research findings into seven crucial components of the bonding process.[19]

1. The optimal period for bonding is the time starting from the first minutes after birth on through the first twelve to twenty-four hours. Both mother and father should make maximum physical and sensory contact with the newborn during this time. It is crucial for healthy completion of the later stages of development.
2. Mothers and fathers make species-specific responses to the infant immediately after birth, and these are necessary to activate the infant's sensory attachments. For example, hearing mother's or father's voice has a critical orienting function for the infant.
3. Mother and father become attached to one child at a time. In multiple births this factor has to be taken into account so each infant receives time alone with the parents.
4. The infant has to respond to the parents to give them a signal that they are making contact. Otherwise they can get discouraged and withdraw, making the attachment more difficult.
5. Anyone who witnesses the birth process is likely to become strongly attached to the infant. This suggests that if more members of the immediate and extended family can be present, more attachment possibilities are created.
6. Mothers and fathers often have difficulty attaching to an infant if that infant has some life-threatening illness or problem during the

attachment period. They cannot attach freely and at the same time be worried about the possible loss of the infant. Also, a father whose wife has life-threatening complications during the birth process could have difficulty attaching to the infant.

7. The parents' emotional condition during the first few hours after birth has long-term effects on the child's development. For example, a mother's anxiety about the well-being of her baby, who has a temporary illness in the first day following the birth, may result in long-lasting concerns about her child's health and this could adversely shape the child's development.

According to Klaus and Kennell's work, considerable care must be taken to help prepare parents to deal psychologically with the attachment process. To not do so is to invite disaster. If something goes wrong during this early attachment process, according to their overwhelming research evidence, it will have long-term and perhaps lasting effects on the child's development.

THE PSYCHOLOGICAL BIRTH: A CRUCIAL JOURNEY

The term *psychological birth* was used by Louis Kaplan to describe the next important developmental process.[20] This "second birth" occurs when the infant has separated successfully from the symbiosis with mother. The human infant at birth is not ready to take its place in the world as a fully functioning human being. The infant must be taught carefully so it can develop into a fully functioning human being. Infants who have accidentally been placed with animals at this stage have grown up with more animal than human traits. We know that the kind of teaching one gets during these early years is extremely important to subsequent development; yet, much of the teaching is random, unconscious, and narrow in focus.

Successful completion of the psychological birth process from a bonded infant to separate individual takes one through at least four distinct stages of development, each involving a major transformation into the next stage. Figure 2.1 illustrates the psychological birth process starting with the physical birth. At, birth, the Self is present before any ego functions develop. Gradually the ego forms, first as a separate part of the person, and finally is integrated with the Self following completion of the psychological birth.

Unlike the case of the inflated ego (discussed later in this chapter), the integrated Self and ego allow a wholeness of the individual to emerge. When the lower self (ego) and higher self (Self) are in harmony and not separated from each other, one always has access to the aspects of the other necessary to function effectively in most situations. This is unlike the Jungian conceptualization, in which the ego and Self are seen as separate until later in life, when they begin to come together.

Now let's retrace those early stages of development briefly so you can begin to identify with this crucial journey. As a newborn infant you moved quickly from the confused state of a stranger in a strange land to a oneness with the mothering one. This bonding or attachment was necessary for your survival. It happened both gradually and all at once, as your mother and you explored your new relationship. From your perspective there were literally no boundaries between you and your mother. You two were one. In that oneness was your security and relief from the stress and anxiety of being in a world where no one knew what you were like. At first everything seemed perfect and comfortable, but gradually you came to experience displeasure, discomfort, a return of the anxiety. By about five months you begin to complete this initial symbiotic stage of development.

To balance the need for oneness, a strong urge to move out into the world stirred in your being. This was the beginning of your psychological birth as a separate person. By about eight months you were able to venture out a little more as you began to be able to hold constant an image of your mother even when she was not present. This object constancy would later become your major security as you ventured out farther. The onset of this object constancy enabled you to begin practicing the skills you needed to develop in order to become a separate human being.

By one year your moves away from your mother became more courageous. You could walk away on your own, and you began to feel like the conqueror of your world. You jumped, ran, climbed, labeled, and claimed your world. Still unable to understand that you and your mother were not separate persons, you believed your world to be an extension of your mother.

Around eighteen months you came to the wonderfully frightening realization that your mother was actually a separate person. This event more than any other heralded the crisis of your second birth. Your previously joyful mood turned into sadness and anger with the terrifying realization that you were actually alone. For the next year or two you

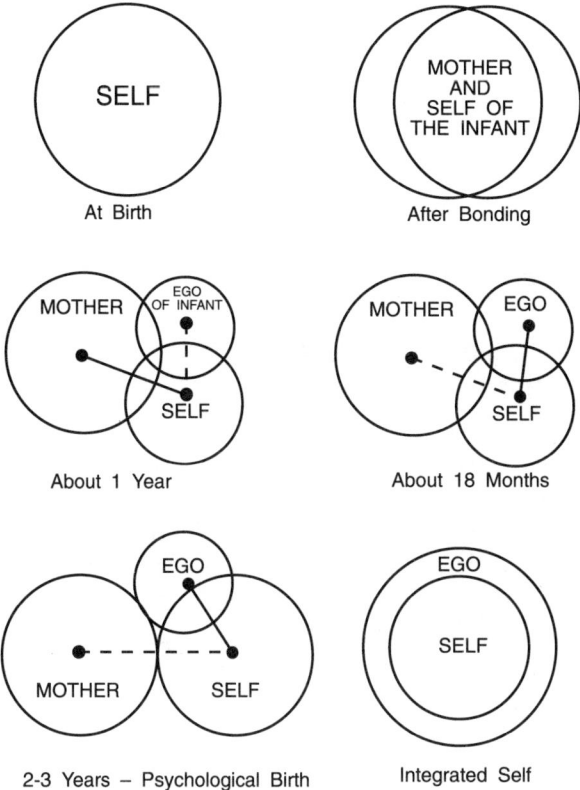

Figure 3.1
PSYCHOLOGICAL BIRTH PROCESS

were learning that it was possible to be a separate person without giving up your sense of wholeness. Above all, you learned that you could still get love from your parents and hold on to a sense of self-love, too.

By about age three you may have developed an initial sense of yourself separate from your mother. You had become an individual, but the struggles between oneness and separateness still persisted. If your image of yourself as a separate being was strong, you developed an emotional acceptance of yourself and others as whole persons. You were able to experience all your emotions, including both love and hate. You were able to reconcile your longings for perfection with the down-to-earth reality of an imperfect world. You were able to form a lasting primary relationship, a partnership of two whole multidimensional human beings loving and respecting each other's separateness. You had a clear sense of your boundaries as a person and knew how to function within those boundaries, as well as how to constantly expand the boundaries through increased awareness and growth. You knew how to get close to people without fearing you would lose your identity.

By completing your psychological birth, you gain the tools to function effectively in the world as a whole person.

The journey just described is the ideal, the way it should have been for all of us. Unfortunately, most adults are still struggling to complete aspects of their psychological birth because of some malfunction in this process during those first two or three years. So many things can influence this process that it is hard to document all of them. The most important factor seems to be the extent to which those around you during that time had completed their own psychological birth. They were your models and guides, so by looking at their level of functioning, we usually can tell what likely went wrong at various stages.

POSSIBLE ADULT PROBLEMS RELATED TO THESE EARLY EXPERIENCES

Effects of the Birth Trauma

When Frederick LeBoyer was asked on a TV interview what events besides birth are important to people's development, he replied that there were no other events—only the repeated experience of one's birth trauma until it is released.[21] What are some manifestations of the birth trauma experience?

I call this one the "watch out" problem. When people are feeling uninhibitedly happy, they often shut down their good feelings in anticipation of the bad things that will follow. People actually seem to place a personal quota on how long they can feel good at any one time.

From a transpersonal perspective another effect that seems related directly to the trauma associated with birth is the damage done to the core self, which does much to destroy the connection the child has with the universal or transpersonal. As adults, we must laboriously rebuild that connection. In his research on therapeutic uses of LSD, Grof found that many of his subjects relived their whole birth process, often releasing the traumatic effects of birth. He wrote that those who completed their LSD session with a reliving of the final stage of birth experienced "the often dramatic alleviation or even disappearance of previous psychopathological symptoms and a decrease of emotional problems of all kinds."[22] His patients reported having a strong recall of the odor of anesthetics used during their birth, the sounds of surgical instruments, and other clear images of their birth scene. His patients also reported "feelings of enormous decompression and expansion of space. The general atmosphere is that of liberation, redemption, salvation, love and forgiveness."[23]

Breathing as a Therapy Tool

I do not work with psychedelic drugs, but in my breathing work with people, I have seen results similar to Grof's. Before the term *psychotherapy* took on more medical meanings, it referred to the process of working with breathing. Through this process, some clients describe tremendous physical and psychological releases of old traumas, which resemble the descriptions of Grof's patients. Some have complete recall of the whole birth scene, including the ability to know the thoughts and feelings of those in attendance.

One client reported, following a breathing session, that she saw her father at her birth, which was filled with complications for both mother and child. She said she intuitively read his thoughts to be, "If someone has to die, let it be the child and not my wife." She reported excitedly that this might explain why her father always seemed to act so guilty around her. She was relieved at this insight and began to talk to her father about what had happened. The father had actually forgotten the source of his guilt, but when the client reported what she had experienced, her father acknowledged that he did have those exact thoughts.

The breathing process I use is simple and direct. It is similar to the process Leonard Orr and others use in what they call rebirthing.[24] I do recommend special training for those doing breath work. The study of the breath may seem simple, but it is highly complex and can require a lifetime of study to truly master.

I generally take a fairly detailed family and medical history on clients who are going to do breath work, with particular interest in illness and death patterns in the family. I ask them to go back at least three generations to look for patterns. Then I form hypotheses, which the breath itself will validate or deny. During the first session I also go over expectations to make sure clients' expectations are not too high or too low. In the first instance they could be disappointed, and in the second instance they could become shocked and scared by what typically happens. Without creating any definite expectations of my own, I attempt to ground clients' expectations within a range of possibilities. The grounding is necessary for some and not for others.

I ask the client to lie flat on his or her back with arms at the side, being as relaxed as possible. The breathing itself consists of connected breathing in and out, either through the nose or the mouth, without pauses in the process. I usually ask the client to visualize a circle with the inhale being one half and the exhale the other half, with the two halves connected. The client is to pull on the inhale and let go on the exhale, without pushing out.

My function during this process is to be supportive and instruct the person on minor changes to even out the breathing cycle. I also pay attention to the position of the breath and any difficulties encountered on inhale or exhale. For example, some people who don't inhale fully don't let in the world fully and suffer from being too closed or restricted in their lives. Some who don't exhale completely are likely to hold on to old hurts and get stuck in repeating many old patterns. People who can't breathe fully into the upper chest (fully expanding the upper lobes of the lungs) are likely to have difficulty with expressing love or sadness. Those who are "belly breathers" are more in touch with fear, anger, and sexual feeling. Many other such variations and subtleties present themselves during an observation.

Although breath work is a simple and direct way of working with people, the results are far from mundane. Like Grof's LSD patients, people who experience this process can go through many levels of awareness and change. Many physiological and biological changes occur along with vivid memories and psychological insights. Generally, clients experience a release from past burdens and anxieties and are often able to feel connected to their mind, body, and spirit in ways they never have before through other forms of psychotherapy or spiritual practices such as meditation or yoga. Many people actually experience re-membering themselves physically, psychically, and psychologically. Quite a few clients experience intense love feelings for themselves and for others as a direct result of the release they get from breath work. I typically work with people for a minimum of five to ten sessions, instructing them on how to practice the breathing between each session. This phase of the process is completed for me when clients can get approximately the same results on their own as they can get when I am there.

The process can be done in a group but should be done only after certain safeguards are in place. First, clients must have good boundaries so they don't take in the "psychic junk" being released by others in the room. Also, the therapist should provide enough trained assistants to help handle any complications. I suggest having one trained assistant for every three or four clients. This is powerful work and can be damaging if not enough support is provided.

One of the most important times during the process comes when clients realize they are doing this themselves through their breathing. They often try to attribute some magic to my instructions or just my presence. When they realize I am not doing it to them or for them, they have learned perhaps the most important lesson of life. I emphasize the importance of this learning and look for signs of their taking full responsibility for their own results.

Grounding the Awareness

Another important, but difficult, part of the process is helping clients ground the results and learn to integrate their new awarenesses with their everyday world. This takes time and patience, so I do a number of things to support the process. With some clients I use a combination of individual and group therapy. Without some form of follow-up and support, the effects can be short-lived or can lead to further confusion and, possibly, increased anxiety.

Effects of Partial Bonding

Most people are only partially bonded. This is seen often in their safety concerns. The partially bonded person is preoccupied with checking out, "Am I safe?" Whereas the more fully bonded person might be asking, "What is happening?" and then take appropriate action. The concern for survival, safety, and well-being often forces partially bonded persons to evaluate an experience before it can be incorporated, or even before it is experienced. Clients might say, for example, "I don't think I'll like to do that because it sounds too hard." They tend to restrict their lives to things that are safe, and then may feel unhappy and jealous of others who seem to be able to have more fun.

Most people are busy tiptoeing through life, hoping to make it safely to death. The definition of jealousy I use with these clients is "watching others have the fun you won't give yourself permission to experience."

In working with safety issues, I get to their bottom-line fear, which is usually a fear of death. I then help them understand where they learned their fear of death, which invariably leads them to their parents and family. When they begin to see that they blindly accepted their parents' fears, they often can begin to rid themselves of these inhibiting messages. The case example later in this chapter describes a process I use to help clients deal with their fear of death.

Another common problem related to poor bonding is the inability to express anger. The underlying fear is that expressing anger will destroy or weaken the bond even more. These people often interpret unexpressed anger in others close to them as potentially damaging to their bond, and they generally attempt to placate or remove the cause of the anger. They fear that if they were to express the anger, the bond couldn't stand its expression. The result is often repressed fear, rage, and anxiety.

From a transpersonal view anxiety in general can be seen as the result of incomplete bonding. Those who over-focus on personal safety, survival, and well-being are doing so to avoid the anxiety they feel from the lack of complete bonding. Comfort issues are apt to get redefined into safety and survival issues.

Unfortunately, partially bonded children often have to deal inordinately with safety and survival issues while they are growing up. Frequently they did not receive the safety information necessary to take good care of themselves. Also, studies have shown that parental neglect and abuse is twice as high in infants who were separated from their parents at birth during the optimal bonding period.[25]

Therapy Tools

The most important intervention I can make with clients with this type of problem is to get them to experience their feelings fully and completely. Without the knowledge that can come only from experiencing their feelings fully, they will likely remain stuck. Once they experience their fears and find out that many are fears of death, they can begin to deal with the issue of their mortality. Then they also can begin to examine the process by which they acquired these fears. In all cases, the fears are learned from our parents and other significant adults in our lives while we were growing up.

[margin handwriting: inability to express anger]

Not all clients are ready to take responsibility for this area of their life. I proceed cautiously and try to keep the discussion grounded in their reality. Ultimately, it means taking responsibility not only for one's illnesses but also for one's death. Some people may be able to see that they caused themselves to get a cold but won't see that they could cause themselves to get cancer or die. I call this process "unraveling your personal birth-death cycle." It involves some or all of the following steps:

1. Experience your fear of death and face it squarely.
2. Begin to understand where this fear came from. You were not born with it. During the birth process you may have been close to the feeling of death, but primarily you learned it. Sometimes I can teach people this by having them trace the major illnesses and causes of death in their family back at least three generations. The patterns often are so clear and striking that the client may begin to see the relationship between family beliefs and sickness or death.
3. Recognize that your mind controls your body. The causes of illness and death are your thoughts. The thought that death is inevitable is the largest single cause of death in all recorded history. If the thought is creative, you may be able to change your own death thoughts.
4. Develop a frame of mind that supports life rather than one that fears death. Positive affirmations to surface subconscious emotional responses can help you support life. The basic one I use is, "I am alive now; therefore, my life urges are stronger than any death urges. As long as I keep strengthening my life urges and weakening my death urges, I will continue living in increasing health and vitality." If you have any death fears, repeating this affirmation can bring these to your attention.
5. Master some so-called spiritual purification techniques such as prayer, meditation, martial arts, yoga, or breathing.
6. Experiment with a variety of body-mind mastery techniques such as the mastery of food and diet, physical laws (levitation through meditation), or other bodily functions such as breathing, sleeping, pulse and heart rate, temperature, and the like.
7. To get support and encouragement, visit or talk with others who are doing similar work.

Case Examples

I would like to begin with my own story. More than twenty years ago I attended a workshop in which the leader talked about how we all repress our fears of death and we hope that by avoiding any thoughts of death, we can magically avoid dying. He said that he was developing a process for helping people face their death fears and wanted to know how many were interested in volunteering to participate in a session to be held that evening. I volunteered, mostly because I was curious.

Along with four others who were equally curious, I received instructions that evening to imagine my own death. Each of us was asked to go through the whole process, including attending our own funeral. My only previous vivid experience with death had been that of my grandfather, who died of cancer in a hospital at the same time I was there for surgery. So I began imagining I was dying of cancer in a hospital. Almost immediately my breathing changed, and my body began to shake and vibrate much like convulsions. At first I thought I had consciously created these bodily reactions through my breathing changes, but I soon realized that I had no control over them, and that's when the fear hit me. I thought, "My God, I must be dying." The more afraid I got, the more the shaking and vibrating continued. I began to notice that when I relaxed and stopped trying to control all this, the shaking also subsided and what I experienced was very peaceful. I remember deciding that I liked the peacefulness so much that I was just going to relax my way through the shaking and enjoy the peaceful interludes.

Gradually the peaceful times became longer and the shaking lessened until finally I sank into the most peaceful feeling I had ever experienced. I thought, "This must be what death really is." Then I felt myself rising out of my body. I rose up to about four feet and I remember looking down and seeing my body still lying there. Finally I rose up through the roof of the building and began to fly through the dark space at an incredible rate of speed. I could see objects and bright flashes of light going past me. The colors were bright orange, blue, green, violet—all the basic colors, all vibrant and clear.

Slowly the deep blackness of space began to get lighter and lighter until my whole consciousness was filled with a brilliant light. I remember thinking that this must be the dawning of the universe. Shortly after that, everything faded and I opened my eyes to see several people crowded around me with concerned expressions. Later I found out the leader was quite worried about me and had considered trying to bring me out of the experience. He had closely observed my alternate shaking and peaceful patterns and at the final release saw my lower jaw unhinge and my closed eyes roll back into my head. I was totally unaware of any of this and was surprised at his and other people's concern.

For weeks after the experience, I didn't really know what to make of it. One day I told a friend about it and, following my description, he asked me if I had read the *Tibetan Book of the Dead*.[26] I hadn't, so he told me that what I had described was recorded in that book as the experience of people who had died and come back to relate what it was like. Since then, I have read other descriptions of people who were clinically dead and then came back. There is a strong resemblance to what I experienced.

The final piece of the puzzle came to me some nine years after that initial experience. In December 1978, I went through the process of rebirthing, and what I experienced during that first rebirthing session was almost exactly what I had experienced nine years before. These and other experiences have helped me begin to piece together some hypotheses about the connections between birth and death experiences. I have come to understand the expansion and contraction of life energy forces as they flow through me and how I can experience death and rebirth as a normal everyday experience, all part of a continuous life energy flow. Integrating these seeming opposite energy forces has enabled me to see everything I do and say as connected in some way.

I have worked with a number of clients who became interested in working out their birth-death cycle. One of them, Gloria, came to me after she had a breast removed following a diagnosis of cancer. She was interested in exploring why she would give herself cancer. She could not understand how she had done that.

In my work with her, which lasted more than two years, I focused on helping her see the personality patterns and beliefs she had that had led to her getting cancer. At first she resisted everything I suggested, but finally she began to make contact with a long-buried part of herself that was crying out to be recognized. Having grown up in a fairly traditional upper-middle class family, only a narrow band of ideas was tolerated. She recalled having a number of thoughts and experiences, while growing up, that were labeled silly or unacceptable. Gradually, through reframing and breathing techniques, she was able to accept that part of herself she had tried so hard to suppress. Finally she realized that the long-term suppression of her spiritual quest had led to her cancer.

Undoubtedly many quieter and more gentle reminders went unheeded over the years, but the life-threatening roar of cancer finally got her attention.

Since then, Gloria has worked hard to bring her spiritual side into the light of day and re-member herself. This has not been easy, and at times her spiritual courage has been put to severe tests. But each time, with support, she has been able to pick herself up and keep going. Her marriage almost crumbled several times, but she continued to broaden her context, and now she and her husband report having the best relationship they have ever had.

Effects of Incomplete Psychological Birth

If properly nurtured and supported, the psychological birth process can be completed by about age three or four. If that foundation is laid, there are usually no other insurmountable developmental hurdles. By completing this process early enough in their development, people are equipped to handle the vicissitudes of life and can learn to function at higher and higher levels of effectiveness. Unfortunately, most of our parents did not know how to facilitate the successful completion of that process, so most of us are still making our way through life trying to be born psychologically.

Co-Dependency

A number of problems face adults who are dealing with this issue. The most prevalent one I see is a tendency to create co-dependency-type relationships, or what I call *need-obligate relationships* between two persons, in which neither is a complete, separate individual and both attempt to manipulate the partner to get what they want. The way this kind of relationship operates is that I (one member) find something that you (the other member) are afraid you can't do for yourself and then I do it for you, which obligates you to me. The reason I want you obligated to me is that I can then get you to take care of me and now do something in exchange that I am afraid I can't do myself. In this way you can obligate me to stay with you as well. These relationships are filled with power plays and manipulation; they are unfulfilling but believed necessary, so they continue.

Object Constancy

Another persistent problem growing out of failure to complete the psychological birth is associated with *constancy*. Object constancy refers

object constancy

to our emotional acceptance of ourselves as we are capable of feeling all our feelings and still maintaining a sense of wholeness and integrity. When object constancy is weak, we tend to protect our highly valued feelings from our so-called bad or unwanted feelings by splitting them off and building compartments for each. When this happens, we are unable to experience ourselves as whole and, instead, feel fragmented and disjointed in our lives. Also, we are unable to appreciate or recognize the wholeness of others. Without constancy, the apparent contradictions between oneness and separateness cannot be reconciled. Things look all good or all bad. We can feel highly elated when our image of perfection is maintained or feel totally crushed when it isn't. The same is true for our perception of others. We can almost worship those who momentarily help us hold onto our self-perfection image and then see the same person as an arch enemy when that person frustrates or somehow tarnishes us by his or her behavior.

Some people with weak object constancy use up "perfect partners" one after another, first overvaluing them, then undervaluing them and replacing them with the next promising candidate. This search for the perfect partner is designed to cover up an inner emptiness or alienation.

Others who have weak object constancy become narcissistic, filling themselves with fantasies of grandeur of how they once were or how they could become. They seek their own idealized image in a partner who adores or can be adored as what he or she wishes to be. These efforts usually fail, and the narcissist turns to face his or her own emptiness and aloneness.

Resolving this issue of object constancy is difficult and often takes considerable time for adults. It means learning to accept oneself and others with imperfections. It means being able to hold onto an image of our own goodness even when we are not behaving in good ways toward ourself or others. Even more difficult at times is to be able to maintain a positive self-image when someone close to us disapproves of our behavior. It means learning to tolerate our ambivalence toward ourselves and others and seeing everyone as having both strengths and weaknesses.

Therapy Tools

Because of the tendency to see themselves or others as either over-adequate or under-adequate, clients might be asked to make a list of how they are "special." If the list has any distortions, they can begin, with some help, to develop an awareness of what is "adequate" from their

clients

perspective without any distortions. This is useful in a group therapy setting with others giving feedback and support to the process.

Another tool I use is to help clients begin to focus on similarities, instead of differences, between themselves and others. Because people with object constancy problems are alienated from themselves, they usually manage to alienate themselves from others, commonly by looking for ways in which they are different from others. I have had profound results from teaching clients to practice this "focusing on similarities" exercise. They can do it anywhere: watching TV, waiting in line at the bank or supermarket, attending a sports event, or being with people they meet for the first time. If a person successfully learns this skill, he or she begins to see all his or her experiences as related and connected rather than fragmented and unrelated.

Clients also must be helped to learn to be vulnerable with you in your sessions, and this often generalizes to other relationships. If they can come to recognize that you accept the things they see as bad in them and you still like and respect them, they often can heal splits in their self-image.

Fusion

Fusion with the parental energy represents another devastating effect of failing to complete the psychological birth process. From the initial bonding there is a fusion with mother's energy. As the drive toward separateness increases and functional autonomy occurs, this fusion typically collapses. If it doesn't, the child remains dependent on mother's cues to help him or her decide things. Later, substitute mothers serve to maintain this fusion. As Ken Wilber put it, "The person goes through life never daring to entertain an original idea and never daring to strike out on his own. Fusion reigns: development stops, differentiation stops, transcendence stops." [27]

When dealing with fusion issues, I use a process similar to the one described with recycled development issues in Chapter 6, Developmental Process Work. To get someone who is dependent to take action on his or her behalf, is difficult but that is what I aim for, even in small ways, from the beginning. A great deal of patience and support are necessary to help clients take risks. Helping them make contact with unspoken feelings and teaching them how to express these feelings are important. This learning is a big first step in becoming separate from the parental energy to which they are fused.

THE SPECIAL CASE OF THE INFLATED EGO

One of the common traps that people seeking transcendence often fall into is trying to appear enlightened instead of solving the problems that block true enlightenment. The "inflated ego" seems to be a case of splitting related to poor object constancy.[28] As a transpersonal therapist, I seem to see more people with this problem than any other. Other transpersonal therapists are likely to see a number of clients who have split off their "dark side" and are trying to elevate their higher Self and identify solely with their Godlike qualities. Ken Wilber's entire thesis surrounds this issue. He explained that people make a mistake in not accepting that their core Self is *already God* and, instead, trying to inflate the ego to look like God. This he termed humanity's Atman Project.[29]

People who have fallen into this trap are recognizable in a variety of ways. In general, when individuals are attempting to operate out of some superior attitude, inflation of the ego is probably behind it. Those who are truly enlightened have no need to tell others how enlightened they are or to try to gain power over others. Any power orientation that attempts to define reality for others likely has some omnipotence behind it. An attempt to equate one's own private truth with universal truth (as in writing a book like this one) is likely rooted in ego inflation. Those who come from a context of discovery instead of a context of justification avoid most inflationary tendencies. The more obvious examples of ego inflation are overly critical people who always find others less able or people who use power plays to get their way.

The myth of Icarus from Greek mythology is a prime example of ego inflation. Daedalus and his son, Icarus, were in prison in Crete, and Daedalus made them each a pair of wings so they could escape. Daedalus warned Icarus not to fly too high or the sun would melt the wax on his wings. Icarus became so exhilarated over his ability to fly that he forgot his father's warning and flew too high. The wax melted and Icarus went crashing into the sea. This is the common problem with the inflated ego: a misjudgment of situations.

There is also a *negative ego inflation*, exemplified by the person who believes he or she is a justified victim trapped by circumstances and rendered helpless by others' actions. Ego-inflated people are also capable of inflating their feelings of distrust or guilt. Sometimes a person alternates between the two extremes.

One such client came to me with a rather bizarre set of physical symptoms, as well as an obvious attitude of superiority in her relationships. The initial physical symptoms were an intense burning in the chest, partial loss of hearing, dizziness, constipation, and skin rashes.

She had been told by a series of physicians that they could not find any physical causes for her symptoms. In working with her, I discovered that she had been verbally and sexually abused as a child. She believed she was treated so badly because she was a bad person. Therefore, she identified with the aggressors (mostly her mother and father) to avoid feeling her guilt. Her feelings emerged in physical symptoms. She believed that if she suffered long enough physically, she could absolve herself of the guilt. Of course, that only worked temporarily until the guilt built up again. She actually believed she was so bad that she drove her father away. Because of that, she could not have effective male-female relationships and constantly behaved in ways that drove men away. She was so fused with her mother that when she looked in the mirror in the morning, she saw her mother's face, not her own.

One of the ways I began to help her break down her identification with her mother was by asking her to make a list of the positive and negative ways in which she was the *same* as her mother and the positive and negative ways in which she was *not* like her mother. At first, all her negative traits and most of her positive traits were like those of her mother. With further therapy she began to see positive and negative aspects of herself that were not like her mother. She began to take purposeful action on her own behalf, setting healthy limits in relationships. As her therapy progressed, most of her physical symptoms disappeared. Occasionally they reappear, but they don't last long because she now has learned effective ways to deal with her feelings.

AN EXPERIENCE OF LOVE

No spiritual journey, however high or enlightened, can teach people how to love. Love of self and others comes from an emotional level, and loving God comes from a spiritual level. I usually start working with people on an emotional level to help them experience love coming from within themselves. This can form the basis for experiencing a deeper, more transpersonal love. A transpersonal kind of love can emerge only from acceptance of self and others, true forgiveness of self and others, and with compassion. These are hard things to teach anyone, but I often use imagery, metaphors, breathing exercises, or affirmations to help nurture that experience.

The following is a guided imagery exercise that I use frequently with clients to help them lift the barriers to loving themselves. This is often done in conjunction with breathing exercises to help people relax. Background music is sometimes added to create a receptive mood. My favorite is Pachlebel's "Canon in D."

Ask the client to lie on his or her back and get comfortable. Give the following instructions:

Every relationship begins with your relationship with yourself, and intimacy with yourself sets the foundation for all relationships. In our preoccupation with others, we often forget that the basis of a very loving relationship is our loving relationship with ourself.

It seems to be a paradox of human existence that the degree to which we are enabled to love another human being corresponds directly with our ability to love and affirm ourself. Only when we love ourself can we truly love and risk and be "self-less" in a relationship with another person.

Our society/culture/family/experiences all tell us that to love ourselves is to be selfish. But selfishness is the very opposite of self-love or selfness.

The central goal of this activity is to help you learn to reach and love the self where your love and power are integrated naturally. This starts by asking you to adopt a kindly, accepting, positive attitude toward your core self. Most people feel they really do love themselves, but deep down the exact opposite may be true. We may be afraid to confront/explore, in an understanding/loving manner, those areas of ourselves that we fear. Carl Jung wrote that the "least of my brethren is me."

Imagine for a moment (with your eyes closed) that you are another person, whom you truly love. In your mind's eye, get up and sit down in front of yourself facing yourself. Ask yourself these questions, and then wait for the honest answer: Do I really try to recognize, accept, and respect this person's feelings—honestly? Am I aware of this person's gifts, talents, exciting potential? Or do I only remember/recognize the mistakes, the imperfections? Am I aware of the reality of this person's limitations and willing to learn from the mistakes and failures rather than be crushed by them?

Do I really listen to this person—the feelings, intuitions, insights? Do I listen to this person's body, its needs, and what promotes its wellness? Do I play with this body, and am I aware of ways I can love it? Do I recognize this person as a gift, a cause for celebration, exactly as this person is? Can I accept the holes, the brokenness, and the incompleteness, too? Do I forgive this person, think of this person as gently and lovingly as the others I love?

By asking you to focus on yourself in this way, I am not talking about narcissism or preoccupation with self. This is merely a description of a balance, in which you show the same concern for yourself that you show to a neighbor or to those you love most.

If you do this, you know what it means, don't you? It means you have to continue to look *you* in the eye, and it takes courage to see that you are not whole yet. You have to embrace the truth about you. You're going to see the evil, the impatience, the greed, the jealousy, the pessimism, the unkindness, and the fear. And then, when you get over the horror of it all, you'll have power—the greatest power, really. The truth will set you free because it brings love. Forgiveness gets you high, because if you see you as you really are, and love it all, you can accept and love and affirm that in the other. By denying your faults or limitations, you merely strengthen their hold on you and make yourself feel more powerless. Recognizing your limitations takes the poison away and destroys their hold on you.

The feeling of being in love with yourself doesn't imply that you have risen above all your faults and emotional problems. It merely implies that you refuse to be paralyzed by them. When you realize this, you can love yourself and someone else without strings, games, fear, or exploitation. Then you can truly rejoice in and celebrate your own uniqueness and goodness. Go in peace.

NOTES

1. See Herbert Read, Michael Fordham, and Gehard Adler, eds., *The Collected Works of C. G. Jung: Vol. 9, Archetypes and the Collective Unconscious* (New York: Pantheon Books, 1953), pp. 1–147.
2. See, for example, Michael Fordham, *New Developments in Analytical Psychology* (London: Routledge & Kagan Paul, 1957).
3. Jane Loevinger, *Ego Development* (San Francisco: Jossey-Bass, 1976).
4. Ken Wilber, *The Atman Project: A Transpersonal View of Human Development* (Wheaton, IL: Theosophical Publishing House, 1980).
5. Margaret Mahler, *The Psychological Birth of the Human Infant* (New York: Basic Books, 1975), pp. 1–4. See also Louise Kaplan, *Oneness and Separateness.*
6. Hubert Benoit, The Supreme Doctrine (New York: Harper, 1960), p. 64.

7. See Thomas Verny, *The Secret Life of the Unborn Child* (New York: Dill Publishing Co., 1981), p. 12.
8. Verny, pp. 36–39.
9. Verny, p. 41.
10. Stanislav Grof, *Realms of the Human Unconscious* (New York: E. P. Dutton, 1976), p. 152.
11. Dennis Stott, "Follow-up Study from Birth of the Effects of Prenatal Stresses," *Developmental Medicine and Child Neurology*, 15:770–787, 1973.
12. Lester Sontag, "Somatophysics of Personality and Body Function," *Vita Humana*, pp. 1–10, November 1963.
13. Verny, pp. 47–49.
14. Grof, p. 161.
15. Weinhold, *Developmental Process Work*, unpublished manuscript.
16. Frederick LeBoyer, *Birth Without Violence* (New York: Knopf, 1975).
17. As evidence, see Joseph C. Pearce, *The Magical Child: Rediscovering Nature's Plan for our Children* (New York: E.P. Dutton, 1977).
18. Charkofsky, see Barry Weinhold, *Breaking Free of Addictive Family Relationships* (Walpole, NH: Stillpoint, 1991).
19. Marshall Klaus and John Kennell, *Maternal-Infant Bonding* (St. Louis: C. V. Mosby Co., 1976).
20. Louis Kaplan, *Oneness and Separateness: From Infant to Individual* (New York: Simon and Schuster, 1978).
21. LeBoyer
22. Grof, p. 160.
23. Grof, p. 162.
24. Two books explaining this process are: Leonard Orr and Sandra Ray, *Rebirthing in the New Age* (Millbrae, CA: Celestial Arts, 1977), and Sandra Ray, *Loving Relationships* (Millbrae, CA: Celestial Arts, 1980).
25. Klaus and Kennell, pp. 2, 3.
26. W. Y. Evans-Wentz, *Tibetan Book of the Dead* (New York: Oxford University Press, 1960).
27. Wilber, p. 140.
28. For a full discussion, read E. F. Edinger, *Ego and Archetype* (Baltimore: Penguin, 1972).
29. Wilber, p. 103.

4

Being and Personality

Gay Hendricks

A deep understanding of the concepts of being and personality, and the interplay between them, can be helpful to the transpersonal therapist. Although each of these concepts sounds abstract, they are immediately applicable to the very next session of therapy you do. As your own grasp of these central ideas of transpersonal psychology grows, so will your ability to work with clients.

Philosophers from Socrates to Sartre have made their own attempts to define being and to assess its contribution to life. Even though I studied these philosophers in numerous classes over the years, not until I experienced and practiced psychotherapy did I finally understand what being actually is and how profoundly it affects everything in life. Now I view being as the fundamental element in the whole therapeutic enterprise.

I like to think of being as the amount of space the therapist is willing and able to occupy. If we think of being as space—the space within us and the space without us—it becomes easier to think of *doing* as the things that fill the space. Clearly, doing gets more attention than being.

Space is invisible, hard to talk about, harder still to measure. Doing can be weighed, counted, even agreed upon now and then. Fortunately, in our time we are beginning to have some ways of understanding the rules and characteristics of space.

In therapy, who the therapist is makes all the difference. The being of Fritz Perls as he conducted a two-chair experiment was utterly different from one of his followers, just as the listening of Carl Rogers was qualitatively different from another practitioner of the person-centered approach. I also have seen unknown and unsung therapists who, by the quality of their presence and attention, assisted their clients in "moving mountains." I, too, have come to rely on the observation of being as the crucial factor in keeping my own work alive. For example, every now and then I experience a phenomenon that never fails to move me. I will be working with someone in therapy, and it will be slow going. I may be bored or tired or preoccupied with some issue of my own that has nothing to do with the work at hand. Suddenly (if I am lucky) I will notice the low quality of presence I am bringing to the situation. My attention shifts and I am back to the present, fully there with an open heart. Then the real magic happens: The overall quality of the interaction with my client shifts. An emotion breaks through or an insight appears, whereas the going was sticky and slow before. The air in the room even seems fresher. Only being has changed—but everything has changed.

WHAT IS BEING?

What, specifically, is being? From a clinical perspective, I believe that being is the therapist's *willingness to experience*. How willing are we to experience fear, anger, joy? How willing are we to confront ourselves with unflinching honesty? How willing are we to say the thing that absolutely needs to be said? All of these issues determine being, because to withdraw from them obscures being. I have a beautiful 200-year-old Tibetan bell on my desk. It has a tone as clear and shimmering as a crisp mountain morning. But if I wad up a piece of paper and put it inside the bell, the sound is deadened slightly, corrupting its purity. Another piece of paper dulls it further. Soon there is only a clunk where before there was a clarity that thrilled the space all around it.

So it is with being. If I am open to all experience, I am able to have a permeable relationship with myself and the world around me. For example, if I am afraid and I stay open to it, I can see right through it to the being at my core. But if I withdraw from the fear and push it out of my consciousness by pretending it is The Other, the Not-Me, all my free attention goes into holding it arm's length. Soon it becomes difficult to resonate with my being.

In the therapy relationship, therapists are challenged constantly to expand their willingness to experience. A client may bring a problem relating to the expression of anger. What happens if the therapist also has major unresolved issues with regard to anger? If the therapist has only limited strategies for dealing with anger, the client may not learn (with this therapist, anyway) how to experience anger fully, express it appropriately, and come to love it. As therapists, anything within us that we regard as Not-Me is broadcast subtly to the client: Not Here, you don't. The therapist's willingness to experience feelings, to give them the space to *be*, is the major contributor to the quality of being in the relationship.

In the realm of the mind, a similar principle holds true. The therapist must be willing to hold diverse points of view. Beyond that, the therapist must be willing to let go of points of view, to be free of beliefs and opinions. Therapists enhance the quality of being by allowing space for different points of view and by being willing to jump off into space with no point of view. By modeling these risky moves in the therapy relationship, the therapist sets an example of utmost importance to the client. A singular freedom comes from the willingness to drop attachment to specific points of view. Therapists who can do it themselves are the only ones who can grant that freedom to clients.

In the realm of the body, these issues take on an added dimension, one that only recently has been explored in therapy. The quality of being also is determined by how much space therapists are willing to occupy in their bodies. Therapists are beginning to ask themselves how much body awareness they have. What is my level of tension and relaxation? What are my breathing patterns saying about me? How much love do I feel toward my body? What are my unloved aspects of my body?

One of my students was working with a person who was struggling to open up to some grief she had been holding for a long time. As I watched the videotape, I noticed that my student had his chin pulled down nearly to his chest and was breathing very shallowly. He was unconsciously mirroring his client's posture. I asked him how much of his sadness was stimulated by his client's grief, and he acknowledged that the client's emotion did in fact trigger some previously unexplored sadness of his own. He had not realized it until after the session. I asked my student to focus on his own body-consciousness in his next session. Particularly, I asked him to be aware of his breathing, to notice when it was free and relaxed and when it was shallow or restricted. My hunch was that his body had been working at cross-purposes to his words. He was telling his client verbally that she should deal with her sadness, but he was broadcasting with his body that she'd better not.

The difference in the next session was striking. Instead of resisting her sadness, as she had been doing for several sessions, the client opened up to it and cried deeply. Insights flowed spontaneously from her, and at the end of the session she looked several years younger. When I talked to the student later, he remarked on how easy it all had been. Particularly, he said, he noticed that if he just focused on his breathing, the client seemed to do what she needed to do. This latter finding might be used as a motto for powerful therapy.

Ultimately, the most significant force for creating being in therapy is our willingness to experience and express love. The quality of being in any relationship may depend on the amount of love each person is willing to bring to it. Love is the most powerful force for transformation that I have ever experienced. In my own life I have seen long-disowned parts of myself come into unity only when I loved them. In therapy, I have seen people resist loving something in themselves until all else failed. Then a moment of love brought the painful part of them into harmony. I vote for willingness to give and receive love as the ultimate lesson we need to learn, both in therapy and life itself. In more than two decades of living and practicing therapy, I have never seen anybody go wrong by loving more.

In the realm of being, love is the ultimate creator of space, because it always contains within it what is not loved.

PERSONALITY

I have often puzzled over several related paradoxes in the realm of psychological and spiritual growth. Most of us want to transcend the limitations of our personalities so we can experience our being directly and permanently. In fact, one definition of the word *transpersonal* relates to going through and beyond (trans) the personality (personal) to the essence at the core. Why then do we often seem to encounter the most difficult obstacles in ourselves just before or just after a breakthrough to a new level of awareness on the spiritual or psychological level? Why do we create major upsets in our close relationships just after or just before a period of intense closeness? Why does a time of deep meditation often bring to the surface the most crystalized difficult aspects of our personalities?

The reason is this: Being is powerful, but so is personality. Being is the essence of everything: Personality is the structure in it. Built into us is a strong urge to experience pure being. But personality is what has enabled us to survive in the real world. We all have assembled many layers of persona to relate to people around us as we grew up. All of these personas worked, in the sense that they reduced pain or got us some form of recognition, even though the recognition may have been negative.

The closer we get to pure being, then, the more our personalities will rebel against the process. Personalities develop a life of their own and do not willingly surrender their place in our lives. It is as if our personalities fear being, just as we are deeply attracted to it at the same time. The being part of ourselves is bent on enlightenment and our full development, but personality wants to make sure we will survive. Hence the paradox. To the best of my knowledge, there is only one way out.

Before we discuss the escape hatch, let's be clear on just what we mean by personality. Personality is:

—any ritualized and repetitive pattern of interaction. The tendency to withdraw and sulk when criticized is personality, as are any of Eric Berne's "games," any repetitive style and theme of arguing, or any repetitive manner of getting attention.
—any ritualized or repetitive style of thinking, such as beliefs about the self ("I'm no good") or the world ("It's dangerous").
—feelings that recycle (e.g., being scared in the presence of authority figures, feeling lonely in a crowd, free-floating anxiety or anger.)
—habits and patterns in the body (e.g., psychosomatic disorders, unnecessary muscle tension, imbalances in the posture).

These elements of ourselves make life miserable for us and those around us. Invariably they persist until we see them clearly and learn to love them. Then they drop out or melt into the background. That is the escape hatch.

Barriers to Loving Our Personalities

Some particularly troublesome barriers stand in the way of a loving relationship with our personalities. Chiefly, there are three.

1. *The power of human unconsciousness must never be underestimated.* Sleepwalking is the general characteristic of humanity, so says the Russian mystic Gurdjieff, and a trip through your local mall may confirm his point beyond our worst dreams. So simply waking up and seeing our personality patterns is a courageous act in itself.
2. *Once we wake up, we often seek to "fix" ourselves by pushing hard in the other direction.* A common trap that snares even the best and brightest among us is the attitude that something is wrong with us for having these elements of personality. From the perspective that we are broken, then, we try to fix it. This leads us to push hard away from anger, say, if that is the element of ourselves we are trying to fix. Instead of seeing our anger clearly, noticing what triggers it and the reasons for it, we often try to ignore it or to cultivate an opposite emotion such as compassion. Compassion is a fine thing, but it is ultimately useful only when it grows organically in the field of awareness, not as a transplant to kill weeds.
3. *We resist loving ourselves just as we are.* One of the breathtaking paradoxes of life is that when we can love ourselves exactly as we are, we change. But I have seen people go nearly to the ends of the world to avoid just loving themselves. I notice in myself that when I forget to love myself for something, I tend to push hard to get rid of the thing I can't love. This strategy makes the whole situation worse, because it widens the split in myself rather than healing it. Pushing hard to grow on the spiritual and psychological levels is likely to bring this problem into sharp focus. A commitment to spiritual and psychological growth often has the effect of showing the faults and flaws in the material and relationship areas of our lives. As one of my clients put it, "As soon as my ex-husband started meditating and doing The Course in Miracles, he stopped sending his child support payments." Setting high spiritual goals tends to invite problems in the material world, not as a test, but rather as an opportunity to put into practice what one has

learned on the spiritual level. If a breakthrough in meditation or therapy is followed by a flat tire, fixing the flat can be the perfect place to put the breakthrough into action. After all, if enlightenment can't help us fix a flat, what good is it?

Viewing personality issues as negative perpetuates them, and this is a distorted perception of their role in our lives. A more evolved view is to regard personality and being as equal expressions of an overall oneness. The oneness of ourselves is seamless, and to regard any aspect of ourselves as greater or lesser is to create a fault-line that later must be healed. The emergence of personality can be seen as no better or no worse than anything else. On the way to embracing this spacious point of view, the emergence of personality might be regarded in a positive light, as an antidote to the long-held bleak view of ourselves and our "darker" natures.

The Positives of Personality

We can regard the emergence of personality in several positive ways. One is to see it as a healthy sign of growth. When exploring a room in the dark, we may not see all the places that need dusting. Light a candle, though, and we can see the true extent of the problem. At first we may feel despair about the amount of work to be done. But another way to look at the situation is to celebrate the fact that at least we can *see*. Meditation and therapy are like lights that increase our ability to see what is real. If what we first see is not pleasant, it is not meditation or therapy's fault. We just need to stay with the process until it smoothes out.

I am now approaching my twentieth year of daily meditation, approximately one to one-and-a-half hours a day. The first year or two was not always fun as I looked into some of the dusty corners of my life that I had ignored or denied for a long time. As I settled into the process, however, I became more comfortable with truth than illusion. As bad as it seemed at times, I came to feel that waking up was better than continuing to sleepwalk. Eventually my attitude shifted so I felt good about it all. Then, as if by magic, a lot of the noise and chatter quieted down in my mind. At the same time, the outer circumstances of my life smoothed out, as well.

Another positive way to regard the emergence of personality is to see it as a call for *grounding*. By grounding I mean any process we use to get our feet back on earth and our consciousness back in our bodies after a flight into space. Grounding is both literal and metaphorical. There is nothing better than a brisk walk or a deep massage to center our consciousnesses back where they belong, in our bodies. Metaphorically, grounding means we are integrating the learning we have attained on the mental or spiritual level so these levels do not get out in front of where the rest of our lives are. Nothing is quite so embarrassing as knowing something but not being able to act on it.

A NEW TECHNOLOGY

We need to develop new ways, suited to the times, to handle personality issues that emerge as we work on ourselves through meditation, therapy, and other procedures. An old technology, still in use in some quarters, is to withdraw from the world. Monastic disciplines have existed for thousands of years in the East and over the past thousand years in the West. The Sufis, for example, say that once you open the door to yourself, you should plan to spend twelve years sorting through the material you find that has to be transformed.

These are different times, which call for something different. I suggest that we throw ourselves fully into life, rather than withdrawing from it, while we are seeking our full evolution. In the new technology, instead of pulling back from jobs and relationships, let's use these parts of life as the arenas in which we put into practice what we have learned on the spiritual and psychological levels from hundreds of thousands of hours of careful work by thousands of clinicians over the past hundred years.

One of the major insights of all time is that **what we resist runs us.** *The most efficient way to be rid of something is not to ignore or deny it but, instead, to integrate it into the totality of ourselves. Any technology not based on this principle is out of date.*

The Principles of Integration

What would a process be like that made full use of the principles of integration? It would be a process that celebrated the emergence of personality issues and provided powerful means of transforming them. It would allow personality to reveal itself and be dealt with in a way that did not inconvenience ourselves or those around us. It would allow personality issues to slip through us effortlessly and be cleared up through expression and love. It would involve some or all of the following elements:

- ❑ *Witnessing or noticing the manifestation of personality in the form of thoughts, behavior, feelings, and body sensations.* The more practice one has in the process, the faster one is able to catch the personality in early phases of manifestation. For example, in the early stages of noticing personality, a man may catch an issue only after he has started an argument with his wife by saying, "You flirted too much with Sam at the party tonight." With more practice he may catch the manifestation earlier, when it is a feeling in his body or a thought in his mind: "Honey, I feel afraid of abandonment when I see you talking to other men, like the way you were talking to Sam at the party. I thought you were flirting with him." In the latter statement, he has captured the essence of the issue without criticizing or projecting the issue onto his wife.

- ❑ *Taking full responsibility for the element of personality that is manifesting.* Frequently we do not notice the personality issue until we have projected it onto someone or something in our environment. This tendency causes great amounts of trouble in human interaction and definitely slows down the process of growth. In handling personality issues, it is vital that we notice items before projecting them, and assume full responsibility for them.

- ❑ *Experiencing the element of personality directly rather than thinking about it, analyzing it, dramatizing it, or making an effort to get rid of it.* Insight follows experience. For example, if a person is afraid of heights, the way to treat the problem is to have him or her experience the fear directly. Meaningful insights flow only when they emerge organically from participating directly with the experience.

- ❑ *Communicating clearly about experiences from a position of responsibility.* If a person is in an appropriate position with regard to it, verbal communication can be helpful in integrating personality issues. But if we do not communicate clearly or responsibly, the process of using words can be a massive obstruction in psychological and spiritual growth.

❑ *Loving it.* The quickest way to integrate an element of personality is to live it. As we have said, love can contain its opposite. We can love ourselves for not being able to love ourselves. I have seen literally thousands of instances of difficult elements of the personality coming into harmony by loving these elements.

The Processes of Integration

Let's explore for a moment how these processes might work in three types of personal growth opportunities: meditation, intimate relationships, and therapy.

Meditation

I sit down to meditate in a comfortable, upright position. It is late afternoon, and I am in my office, preparing to teach a class. The day has been a long one, full of interruptions and petty annoyances. I am tired and slightly irritated. After a minute of rest, I begin to let a mantra resonate in my mind. The mantra is a pleasant-sounding Sanskrit word given to me in the early seventies by a meditation teacher, who gave me precise instructions on how to use it. Over the next half hour of meditation, I repeat the mantra effortlessly in my mind, occasionally becoming lost in thought, then returning to the mantra. As the meditation session proceeds, there is less thought. The mantra refines to a subtler level, becoming more of a pulse or a rhythm than a word. Gradually space and quiet come to the fore in my mind. Thoughts melt away, replaced by an all-encompassing pure consciousness. Then the session is over and I resume my work, feeling light, clear, and relaxed. No trace of the tiredness or irritation remains.

A key attitude makes meditation possible and fruitful: *not minding thoughts.* Many of us regard our thoughts in ways that cause us problems. Sometimes we ignore them or are not aware of what is going on up there. As a result, we may not see how they are programming our actions. At other times, we overvalue them, allowing them to dominate us and make us miserable. A third practice, which I have noticed particularly in New Age circles, is to think something is wrong with having thoughts. Before I learned to meditate properly, I had the same attitude toward my thoughts. I had a slightly negative attitude toward them, as if I were supposed to get rid of them. Then when I learned to meditate from a good teacher, he pointed out that most thoughts were simply a symptom of stress releasing. They were positive signs that meditation was working and were certainly not to be dramatized, criticized, fretted over, or taken seriously. They simply *are*. When I was lost in thought, I should simply come back to the mantra with no muss and fuss. After a while, when the current stress was released from my system, the thoughts would quiet down. And that's exactly what would happen, time after time. Over the years of practice, the process deepened so that now it takes very little time to settle into the stress-free state of clarity, light, and relaxation.

An important lesson about life is to be learned here, one that is consistent with the five principles of integration. Personality issues can manifest themselves in all sorts of thoughts, feelings, and patterns. We can simply allow this to occur without attaching unnecessary energy to the process. If we can let what we need to learn slip easily and without censure through our consciousness, the whole process of evolution may be speeded up.

Intimate Relationships

Close relationships are a rigorous proving ground for any process of change, because the very nature of those relationships is to bring up our deepest, most crystalized personality material. Love creates space in us and will cause to rise to the surface any resistance to it. How we handle this resistance determines whether the relationship will flourish or die. Often, when we think a relationship is not working, what we really mean is that it has worked too well. The closeness has brought up more personality material than we can integrate comfortably.

A crisis emerged with a couple I know when the husband had an extramarital affair. The wife, because she was working on developing full responsibility for her life, chose not to view herself as the victim in this situation. She asked herself: What is it in me and in the relationship that is contributing to this painful situation? As she progressed with this courageous inquiry, she uncovered many layers of feeling. She felt hurt and anger at her husband and, even deeper, a fear of abandonment accompanied by a sense of unworthiness. Upon reflection, she realized that most of those feelings had been with her since childhood. The current situation was the trigger that was bringing these issues to the surface. As this happened, her attitude toward her husband shifted. In fact, she thanked him for bringing the fear to her attention. She told him she was willing to deal with this issue and that he did not need to have an affair any more to bring it to her attention.

Shortly after this conversation, he ended the affair, realizing that he had started the other relationship because of some midlife fears about disillusionment and death. In my opinion, the wife accomplished something quite rare in her response to the situation. By choosing not to engage in a power struggle or to approach the situation as a victim, she allowed her own personality issues to rise to the surface, which in turn created the space for her husband's issues to come forth.

Therapy

One of the major functions of therapy is in helping clients learn effective ways of relating to their personalities. I know a man who was working in therapy to clear up a decade-long siege of conflict with his former wife. One day he was sitting at home when he found himself thinking about (in his words) "what a jerk my ex-wife is." Instead of indulging this projection of his mind, he was able to catch his personality in the process of manifesting and to channel the energy into something more effective. He took responsibility for the anger he felt and allowed himself to experience it in his body. Immediately, "a wave of compassion swept over me, the first time I could ever remember feeling compassion for her." Several more feelings came up, and he allowed them to slip through himself without censuring them. Then, spontaneously, he experienced love for both himself and his ex-wife.

Several particulars of his process are worth noting. When his personality began to emerge, in the form of the "she's a jerk" thought, he did not take it seriously. Instead, he saw it as the symptom of something deeper that was happening in him. Rather than indulging in the thought, he opened up to the feelings underneath it, experienced them, and came to an organic resolution.

We are often encouraged to "trust the process" in therapy and personal growth. What this means, in practical therapy terms, is that we as therapists have an unshakable knowledge that all elements of the personality are structured in being, the pure consciousness at the source. If we and our clients fully understand the nature of being, we can rest securely in the knowledge that no matter what manifestations of the personality may emerge, there is unity at the core of everything.

5

Transpersonal Uses of Human Energy Patterns

Barry Weinhold

A s a transpersonal therapist, one of my tasks has been to broaden and deepen my understanding of human behavior and at the same time look for, in all theoretical systems, common elements that provide simple and direct ways to understand behavior. My own life experiences have helped me broaden and deepen my understanding of human energy systems.

My wife Barbara died suddenly. Because she died in an accident, I never got to say goodbye or feel complete by understanding why she had died. The circumstances surrounding her death were strange. She and I were skiing together when we hit an unmarked patch of ice and both fell. When I recovered, I saw her lying unconscious nearby. I also saw that she was bleeding through her ski pants. When the ski patrol arrived, they cut open her ski pants and revealed an eight-inch cut in her upper right thigh, which had severed her femoral artery. She never regained full consciousness and died twenty hours later following an unsuccessful attempt to repair the artery. There was no reason for such a deep cut because her ski pants had no rips. I went over the accident thousands of times in my mind with no possible explanation.

After about six months of grieving, this lack of completion continued to haunt me. Finally an opportunity to complete this came to me. A friend of mine suggested that I ask my spirit guides to arrange a meeting with Barbara. I thought about this and decided it was worth a try. I had practiced bringing Barbara back through my sensory memory of her. I could remember how she looked, sounded, felt, smelled, and tasted. When I used all my senses to bring her back, I found that I could feel her energy present, and then I asked my spirit guides to help arrange a meeting with her. I experienced being led by one of my guides into a rather dark and damp cave. Finally we came out into a large room filled with mist. I waited and eventually heard Barbara's voice coming from the mist. I could not see her, and I asked her to come out where I could see her.

She replied, "No, not now, for you may be frightened by my changed appearance." She said:

> I knew I was going to die. I knew it for about a year, but I didn't want to accept it. I tried not to think about it, and when it was no longer possible for me to block out the thoughts, I tried to talk to you about it. You weren't able to listen to my fears. I am sorry I had to leave you, but I had no choice. I could not stand the pain in my body any longer, and I realized I had to leave my body behind me before I could go any further. Please forgive me for leaving so suddenly with all the unfinished business I left for you to clean up. I wish it could have been done some other way. I was still ambivalent even after the ski accident. I didn't want to live as an invalid after the accident. I will always love you.

I was filled with tremendous sadness and joy. I could hardly speak, but finally I said, "Barbara, I'm so relieved to be able to talk to you and feel complete. I may need to talk to you some more before I'm finished with this. Please forgive me for not wanting to hear your fears. I was too scared of losing you to be of much help. I do love you and release you to go on with your life on the other side. Some day we may be joined again."

Then Barbara laughed in her characteristic way and said to me, "It gives me great pleasure to tell you that you will not have to be alone very long. They are trying to find someone to send to you. Also, you will be happy to know that she will have evolved to a higher consciousness and will not have the same problems that I had."

I was shocked and thrilled by what she was saying. I asked, "Who are *they*?" She replied, "*They* are the members of our soul group."

Then I asked, "How will I find this person?"She responded by saying, "You will not have to look for her. She will find you and you will recognize her by her vibration, which will be much like mine."

Finally I asked, "How long will I have to wait until she shows up?"

She said, "It is not possible to say exactly, but it shouldn't be very long."

We said our tearful goodbyes, and I felt a sense of completion to the first phase of my healing.

The significance of this work became apparent in the year that followed this event. I will discuss that year in the next chapter.

MY WORKING HYPOTHESES ABOUT HUMAN ENERGY PATTERNS

In my work with people, I seek the most direct ways that enable me to understand and predict their behavior at all levels. My search for these common elements has led me repeatedly to the study of human energy patterns. During this study, I have found the following basic working hypotheses useful to me:

1. Human energy is always moving. It is either expanding or contracting.
2. Any resistance to either the expansion or the contraction of human energy causes problems. The flow of energy has a natural rhythm, and when we resist our natural flow, we use up considerable energy and create problems for ourselves.
3. Thoughts are a basic form of energy, and they follow the laws of energy in that they never run out of energy and are eternal. Their form may change after our physical death, but they continue to exist.
4. The quality of our thoughts seems to influence the expansion or contraction of our energy fields. Paranoid or negative thoughts tend to produce contraction, and harmonious or positive thoughts tend to produce expansion of our energy fields.
5. Feelings are another basic form of energy and, similar to thoughts, do influence the expansion and contraction of energy. For instance, fear causes contraction and love causes expansion.

6. Most people are not conscious of their own or other people's energy patterns. They have to be taught and, once aware, can direct their own energy patterns and become aware of the energy patterns of others.
7. The source of all our energy is our "transpersonal core." Contact with this core without undue "noise," or interference of the energy pulsations from our core, allows us free and complete energy flow and energy exchange.

THERAPY USING ENERGY PATTERNS

When doing therapy, I work in six different modes. I may never use all six of these with a single client, although I frequently do have to touch on all six and then focus on one or two. These are:

- Gaining awareness of human energy patterns.
- Releasing blocked energy patterns.
- Creating new energy patterns.
- Protecting vital energy patterns.
- Sharing creative energy patterns.
- Balancing all life energy patterns.

Gaining Awareness of Human Energy Patterns

Most clients, I find, have little awareness of their own energy patterns, or no awareness at all. Generally I do some telling (explaining the basic operating principles) and a lot of showing, helping them to experience their own energy. Usually I have to create a context for this awareness or I can end up wasting my own energy. Brugh Joy put it this way: "I dare to say that the human mind can and does generate force fields that can transmute matter. I further dare to say that an awareness without spiritual foundation is like a stool with only two legs."[1] There are at least four main areas of awareness:

- Energy fields surrounding the body.
- Energy that flows through the body.
- Energy embedding in the surface muscles of the body.
- Energy in the deep muscle structure of the body.

To illustrate these, I sometimes show my clients a number of high-quality Kurlian photographs of human energy fields.[2] In addition, I use some simple energy awareness techniques, such as the following.

Hand Excitation

I ask clients (singly or in a group) to stand in a relaxed position and shake their hands vigorously for about thirty seconds to a minute, then to place their hands about six inches apart, with palms facing each other, and notice the energy flow between them. After doing this several times, I might have them do it with me or another person. They are usually fascinated and eager to learn more.

Changing Your Energy Flow

Another way to dramatically demonstrate the principle of thought energy and how thoughts can change energy patterns involves an aikido technique. I usually demonstrate the use of thought to change the direction of energy flow.

I have clients stand and imagine their energy moving downward through the bottom of their feet, rooting them to the floor. Then I ask them to imagine actual roots growing out of the bottom of their feet and extending deep into the ground. After that, I try to pick them up or ask another person to try it. I then ask them to reverse their energy and imagine it flowing out of the top of their head, making them light and airy. I have them envision themselves actually lifting off the ground as I try or a partner tries to pick them up. The contrast is always quite noticeable, and sometimes striking. I have clients do the same process with me or a partner so they are able to do both ends of the experience.

The Universe Always Says "Yes"

Another of my favorites, this activity helps clients realize that thoughts are energy and that these thoughts manifest into experience. The basic premise is that whatever you are thinking at the moment is always supported by the universe, which is saying "yes" to what you are thinking.

The universe doesn't care about the quality of your thoughts; it is basically neutral. If you are critical of yourself, the universe will support your self-criticism. The same is true when you are loving toward yourself.

---

client

Step 1. Have clients pair off with a partner or with you. One is the universe and is to answer "yes" to everything the other person says. As a way of directing the process, I ask participants to share at least three common negative thoughts they have about themselves. After each one, the universe is to reply, "Yes, that's true," or "Yes, Sam, you are selfish," for example. If you are doing this activity with two clients, have them switch roles so both can experience their self-defining words.

Step 2. Next have clients relate three positive thoughts they have about themselves, using the same procedure as in step 1.

Step 3. Ask them to tell the universe (their partner) something they want to change in their lives. The universe is to reply to that by saying, "Yes, you do want to change _____." Again have the two switch roles.

Step 4. This step is designed to help people see that wanting something is a thought barrier to having it. This time have clients restate each statement in step 3 as if it already had taken place. This would mean changing, for example, "I want to have more friends" to "I have all the friends I want." Again the universe partner is to reply and support this thought energy.

Step 5. Sometimes I go even further and have clients write out their statements of step 4 and then jot down any resistant thoughts that surface. These resistant thoughts constitute "noise" that prevents clear communication of the thoughts with the universe. For example, a resistant thought that might surface from the statement in step 4 is, "What if people don't want to be my friend?" Then I ask them to think of another thought that could dislodge that resistance. In this example, a thought that could dislodge the resistant one is, "The people I choose as friends also choose me." Don't forget to have the universe partner affirm that thought as well.

A variation of the above activity is to simply ask clients to state what they want. Ask them to repeat the open-ended sentence, "What I want is..." Use the same affirming procedure as above.

Releasing Blocked Energy Patterns

Frequently, chronic energy blocks show up in the body. If energy has been blocked in a muscle grouping, for example, there will be a shortening of that muscle or certainly a tightness or tension in that part of the body. Some of the early warning signals may be a stiff neck, tight shoulders, headache, leg ache, or stomach ache. If people ignore these signals, the signals will get stronger, perhaps resulting in an illness of some kind. Through experience, I believe that all illness or disease in the body can be traced to a belief or thought pattern that has interrupted the energy flow in the body.

For example, arthritis can be traced to holding on to long-term resentment or bitterness over not being loved the way we wanted to be. Cancer comes from deep grief and hurt and longstanding resentment. In both cases, the problem is in the *holding on*, so I see my major task in helping people with these diseases to learn how to release whatever they are holding on to.

A variety of techniques can be used to promote this release. I often use stress postures from bioenergetics, yoga, breathing (neo-Reichian or rebirthing), imagery, writing processes, movement and dance, meditation, and even art or music as a way of helping clients recognize and release blocked energy.

To initially diagnose blocked energy patterns, one successful means I have found is to have clients draw a front-view, full-body picture of themselves on a large piece of newsprint. Then I take a Polaroid picture of them. In comparing the two pictures, the photograph usually reflects what they have drawn. For example, if a client were to draw herself with one shoulder lower than the other, the same misalignment probably would show up on the photograph. I go over the photos and the drawings with clients and have them write hypotheses about the drawings. In the case of the lowered shoulder, the client might write, for example, "Right shoulder higher to protect that side of my body." I like this method because it gives the client immediate feedback in a usable form, and it conveys useful information to me as well.

Another good tool is to use videotape to do such diagnoses. This allows reflection of the way clients walk, sit, stand, and move.

The most useful diagnostic tool is simply learning to read bodies. With trained eye, one will get everything needed through simple observation. Milton Erickson, the great hypnotherapist, was an astute observer of nonverbal behavior, as was Fritz Perls. Erickson reportedly once paid a pantomime expert to teach him all the ways he knew to say "no" nonverbally.

Briefly, these are among the things I look for in bodies in order to form hypotheses:

1. *How individuals walk.* Which foot do they start on? Starting on the left foot generally means a person is more passive when stepping out into the world; starting with the right foot indicates more aggressive moves. I then look for problems associated with being too tentative (left foot) or too aggressive (right foot). Check their shoes to see what patterns of wear show up on the soles. If the heels are worn down, it can indicate a walking pattern of staying back on the heels.

2. *Body proportions.* A heavy upper body and thin lower body usually indicates a lack of grounding or more armor or protection of upper body functions. Feelings may be suppressed. A heavy lower body and thin upper body can mean a number of things as well. Generally it means too much grounding and an inability to flow with things. It also can mean repressed sexual material.

3. *Misalignment* left to right side or front to back. A raised shoulder is usually accompanied by a raised hip, with the whole body compensating for one part being out of alignment. A raised left shoulder tends to be used to protect feelings, particularly love feelings. A pelvis tilted back can indicate repressed sexual feelings or sexual fears.

4. *The face.* Puffiness under one eye might indicate problems with thinking or feeling. The left eye is usually an indicator of unresolved emotional problems and the right eye, thinking problems. The eye in which tears form first often provides an interesting clue. If tears form in the left eye, the person may be feeling sad; if they form first in the right eye, the person is feeling angry or scared. In almost every case in which I have verified the feeling, this has held true.

5. *Breathing.* Watching how people breathe can tell a lot. For example, people who seem to hold on to their exhaling breath generally have more trouble than usual in letting go or flowing with things; they tend to be more uptight and anxious, too. People who have a rather weak inhaling breath generally don't let in much of the world and often have impoverished or limited experiences; they tend to exhibit more depressive symptoms.

Creating New Energy Patterns

Many people don't seem to know how to create new energy for themselves when they need it. Frequently, they have learned to compensate for this by "stealing energy" from others. This works for them at times. But it means they have to create co-dependent relationships in order to have someone available when they need an energy boost. The co-dependent relationship itself requires considerable energy to maintain, so they may end up using more energy than they can actually steal.

People can be taught, through a number of methods, how to generate new energy on their own. These methods include a variety of meditative techniques, various yoga forms, the martial arts (particularly the forms that focus on inner awareness), exercise programs such as jogging or swimming, some nutritional and diet programs (particularly if a person is overweight), breathing exercises, writing processes, guided imagery and visualization techniques.

Often I use meditation, yoga, and breathing exercises myself to generate new energy when I am feeling low in energy. Sometimes I can use these while being with clients as well. One such structured experience I call the cleansing breath.

The Cleansing Breath

Step 1. Have clients sit or lie on their back with eyes closed, breathing in and out through the nose. Ask them to pull in the inhaling breath and let go of the exhaling breath, connecting both inhale and exhale with no pause in between.

Step 2. After they have developed a breathing rhythm, ask them to concentrate on breathing in *light* on inhale and breathing out *toxins* on exhale. Have them do this for five or six breaths.

Step 3. Now ask them to breathe in *strength* and breathe out *tension* for another five or six breaths.

Step 4. Ask them to breathe in *love* and breathe out *fear* for another five or six breaths.

Step 5. Finally, ask them to breathe in *light, strength,* and *love* together and breathe out *toxins, tension,* and *fear.* Have them take five or six long, deep breaths, filling their body with light, strength, and love and emptying their body of all toxins, tension, and fear.

This short breathing exercise (five to ten minutes) is useful if clients begin to show signs of low energy during sessions. After teaching it to them, I recommend that they use it when they feel they need more energy during their daily routine.

Meditation

In addition to breathing exercises, I may use meditation as a way of preparing a client and myself for a session. We may take the first ten minutes of the session to meditate or breathe together to harmonize our energies and create a more productive energy field for our work together.

Protecting Vital Energy Patterns

As indicated before, many people try to steal energy from others instead of trying to generate their own when they are feeling low in energy. Most clients who come to therapy tend to want to do that, so, as a therapist, if you don't know how to protect yourself from "professional energy stealers," you will burn out rather quickly. I am convinced that the ability to protect one's vital energy from energy stealers is an important skill for most people and absolutely essential for teachers, therapists, or anyone who works directly with other people.

Crucial to this skill is an awareness of your boundaries when someone is intruding on your space. This is partly behind the notion of giving each other space in a relationship.

When someone is stealing energy from another person, many people don't recognize it until it's too late. You probably have had the experience of talking to someone, and after the person left, you felt drained and didn't know why. One of my favorite ways of helping people learn to recognize when they are letting someone steal their energy is the following structured exercise.

I ask clients to share a recent decision they have made that they feel good about. Then I ask them to pay attention to their reactions and what happens in their body while I deliberately try to talk them out of the decision. Frequently they try to defend their decision (energy down the drain), or they tighten their jaw or other parts of their body (e.g., the stomach—further energy down the drain), or they may withdraw by closing down their breathing, looking away, and the like (all activities that drain energy).

When this type of energy stealing occurs, the best response is to remain centered and either let the intrusion go by or take action to stop the intrusion. One of the concepts I teach my clients is how to restore a sense of connection with their own energy when they encounter professional energy stealers in their lives. No one can remain above all such events. No one can remain centered all the time. The trick is to notice rather quickly that one is off center and then take some actions to get back on center again.

A rather new measure of health considers the amount of time you take to return to a calm or relaxed state after being pulled out of that state as a result of some stress. The quicker you recover, the healthier you are. This can be measured by taking your heart rate and pulse rate at rest and then having you run in place for several minutes. Heart and pulse rates are checked repeatedly until they return to your pre-stress levels. The time required for this to happen is an indication of your cardiovascular fitness level. The same is true with psychological fitness. Any arguments or obsessive thoughts that persist can keep you off center longer.

Sharing Creative Energy Patterns

One of the most persistent problems that often brings people to therapy is their inability to share energy with others. Clients frequently feel cut off from others and don't seem to have any synergistic ways to exchange energy with others. I use group therapy most often with these people because it gives me and the client a living laboratory in which to practice the necessary skills. I can observe directly how the client goes about trying to make contact, and I can make specific suggestions and interventions to assist him or her.

A client who was an artist had withdrawn into his art during adolescence to avoid making contact with others. He was an excellent artist, but his work was also his biggest problem because it served as an escape for him when he became fearful of sharing energy with someone. He actually believed he could make himself invisible when he was around people— and thus avoid having to face his fears of closeness.

He wasn't in the group long before this pattern began to show up and other group members began to react to his attempts to become invisible. This led him to an agreement with the other group members to make contact with each one of them during the therapy session and then make a report near the end of the session and get feedback from other group members. Gradually he began to shine and open up in the group so that making contact with others was much easier for him.

Sometimes I do mirroring exercises with clients to promote energy sharing. I also use more subtle exercises such as the "sticky hands." This involves two people standing facing each other with one wrist touching the opposite wrist of the other person. The two take turns, with one leading the movement and the other attempting to follow, always keeping their wrists in contact. After a while, if energy flows between them, they can do this with neither one leading or following.

Balancing All Life Energy Patterns

After spending some time studying the various energies and energy centers in the body, I have gained an appreciation for the art of balancing all our energies. Many different energies flow through the body. Some, like sexual energy and the protective energy coming out of the adrenal stress reaction, are stronger and more dominant. Others, like the psychic energies and more spiritual energy, are often softer and more subtle.

The Chakras

The most effective way I have found to understand and utilize these energies in balance is to use the *chakras*, or energy centers, as a grounding for awareness.[3] Figure 5.1 shows these centers and the kinds of energy that emanate from them. Each center can have too much energy or too little energy. The optimum condition is a balancing of all energy in the body. Some people overfocus on their sexual or power energies and have little or no awareness of higher, more subtle energies. Others, through meditation and other spiritual practices, may have learned to make contact with their higher energies but have little or no grounding energy to counterbalance these other energies. They may have trouble functioning in the everyday world.

The ways I locate blocked or excessive energy at each of the chakras are numerous and often involve intuitive processes. One simple way is to do a body reading, which can tell much and gives clues to follow up on through other methods. For example:

Physical groundedness (root chakra) is easy to check. Ask the client to stand relaxed, as he or she might usually stand. Then push the person slightly from the front, back, and both sides. Some people will attempt to stay where they are and resist you, trying to remain grounded. Others will move with you and ground themselves in the spot they moved to. Still others have little or no physical grounding and literally can be pushed across the room.

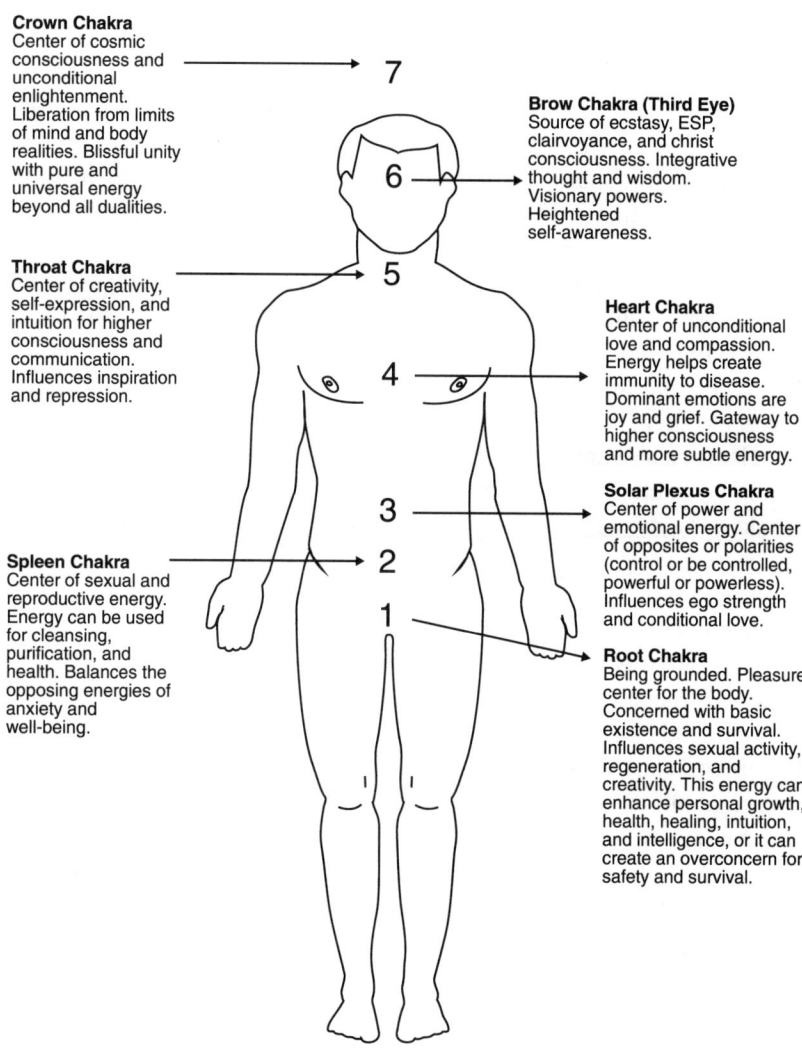

Crown Chakra
Center of cosmic consciousness and unconditional enlightenment. Liberation from limits of mind and body realities. Blissful unity with pure and universal energy beyond all dualities.

Brow Chakra (Third Eye)
Source of ecstasy, ESP, clairvoyance, and christ consciousness. Integrative thought and wisdom. Visionary powers. Heightened self-awareness.

Throat Chakra
Center of creativity, self-expression, and intuition for higher consciousness and communication. Influences inspiration and repression.

Heart Chakra
Center of unconditional love and compassion. Energy helps create immunity to disease. Dominant emotions are joy and grief. Gateway to higher consciousness and more subtle energy.

Solar Plexus Chakra
Center of power and emotional energy. Center of opposites or polarities (control or be controlled, powerful or powerless). Influences ego strength and conditional love.

Spleen Chakra
Center of sexual and reproductive energy. Energy can be used for cleansing, purification, and health. Balances the opposing energies of anxiety and well-being.

Root Chakra
Being grounded. Pleasure center for the body. Concerned with basic existence and survival. Influences sexual activity, regeneration, and creativity. This energy can enhance personal growth, health, healing, intuition, and intelligence, or it can create an overconcern for safety and survival.

Figure 5.1
CHAKRAL ENERGY CENTERS

This activity can tell me whether the person is too grounded and has considerable energy tied up in security and survival issues. These people are highly resistant to change and generally work more slowly in therapy. The ungrounded person, in contrast, is likely to bounce off the walls when he or she starts to change, and may need additional help to stay grounded.

Sexual energy (spleen chakra) can be assessed by the way people walk and how they carry themselves. If the pelvis is tilted forward when they walk or just stand, this indicates strong sexual energy. On the other hand, a pelvis that is tilted back to protect the genital area may be an indication of repressed or low sexual energy.

The third (or so-called power) chakra can be detected by upper body posture and build. People who slump over slightly and have rather shallow breathing are usually closing down the power chakra, which is located behind the solar plexus. Heavy upper body build could indicate excessive energy devoted to power and control of self and others.

Heart chakra energy can be detected by breathing and body posture. Shallow breathing in the upper lobes of the lungs and a shallow inhale would indicate some blockage. Rounded shoulders and caved-in chest are also indicators of blocked energy. Open, overexpanded upper body shown by a strong inhale could suggest too much heart energy not in balance with other energies.

The throat is the center of the fifth chakra. Listening to the quality of sounds made during normal speech can provide some clues. A light, high-pitched voice can indicate tension and blockage, for example. Listening to and watching breathing patterns also can yield much information about the energy at this chakra. The throat has to open to allow free passage of air to the lungs as we breathe. By observing how easily this occurs, you can assess the energy levels. The throat chakra also controls verbal communication and expression of the other energies. If it is too open, the expression is often scattered and confusing. These people talk too fast and too much and don't know what they are expressing. Hesitant and halting speech patterns may indicate low energy in this chakra.

Usually more subtle and harder to read through observation is the energy of the third eye. Generally I look for the extent of self-awareness and how that is balanced with the awareness of others. Too much focus on self might indicate excessive energy, whereas too much concern for what others think and do can indicate blocked energy.

Crown chakra energies are detectable by holding your hand palm down six to eight inches above the person's head. The stronger the energy, the more tingling you will feel in the palm of your hand. This energy is weak and undetected in some people until the blocks at the lower chakras are removed.

Energy-Balancing Techniques

After I have assessed where energy is out of balance either by being blocked or being too strong, I begin to employ various energy-balancing tools. In this work a wide variety of therapy tools is helpful. The therapy tools used in the psychodynamic, behavioristic, and humanistic schools can be valuable in dealing with imbalances involving the first three chakras. The higher chakras are served best by more spiritual, meditative, and non-Western therapy tools.

Quite often breathing can be used as a basic energy-balancing tool. Upon locating blocked energy centers, I may have the client breathe into those areas and learn to release the blocked energy. Placement of the breath is a way to focus energy. In addition, I sometimes use a small, hollow, rubber or plastic play ball (four to five inches in diameter). I have the client place it on the spine at the point of blocked energy and lie on the ball while breathing into that area. This can cause a release to occur quite quickly.

Bioenergetic exercises and stress postures are often useful to increase the tension and force a rebound release in the muscle that may have contracted around a blocked energy center. I sometimes have clients kneel and slam a tennis racket on a pillow. I have them grip the racket with both hands and swing it back over their heads as far as they can, then slam it down, making a sound. This often opens up the third chakra and enables clients to make contact with their feelings. Gestalt and neurolinguistic programming (NLP) work on polarities is suggested in dealing with blocked third chakra energy.

Breathing can also be useful for contacting the higher, more subtle energies. I also incorporate guided imagery, meditation, and movement activities to deal with blocks at the higher centers.

Alignment of Energy in Relationships

Another area for energy balancing is the alignment of the chakral energies between partners in a relationship. This alignment at all energy centers seems extremely important but not well understood. I have often heard couples say, "When he (she) didn't understand, I felt betrayed by him (her)." The word *betrayed* reflects being out of alignment with someone or having done something to break an alignment that previously existed.

The obvious example of betrayal in relationships is having sexual intercourse with someone other than the person with whom you are in alignment by being married, living together, which violates a monogamous agreement between the couple. Betrayal can occur at any of the other energy centers as well. Verbally sharing intimate thoughts and feelings with someone other than your partner in a committed relationship can be felt by the partner as a betrayal of your alignment at the throat chakra. By trying to exercise power and control over the thoughts or behavior of a partner, you may be betraying an alignment at the third chakra.

To promote alignment of energies, I introduce an exercise to enable the partners to spot areas where misalignment is present. They utilize the chart shown in Figure 5.2.

Step 1. Have both partners rate themselves and their partner on the perceived level of chakral energy (high, medium, or low) at each of the energy centers using the chart in Figure 5.2.

Step 2. Have the partners compare the ratings of each other, without trying to determine who is right or wrong if the perceptions disagree. The purpose is mostly to enable each to learn more about the other's perceptions. They should note where they have about the same level of energy and where they appear to be discrepant.

Step 3. Have the partners look at areas in which both noticed a discrepancy. For example: One partner may see himself or herself as low in sexual energy and the other may see this the same way; both might agree that the other partner is high in sexual energy. These perceptions point to possible areas where a misalignment might be present, indicating a direction for therapy or problem solving.

In another activity to promote the awareness of alignment of energies at each chakra, I have partners sit facing each other, eyes closed, holding hands. I give the following instructions:

1. Imagine a white light starting at the base of your spine. Breathe into that area.

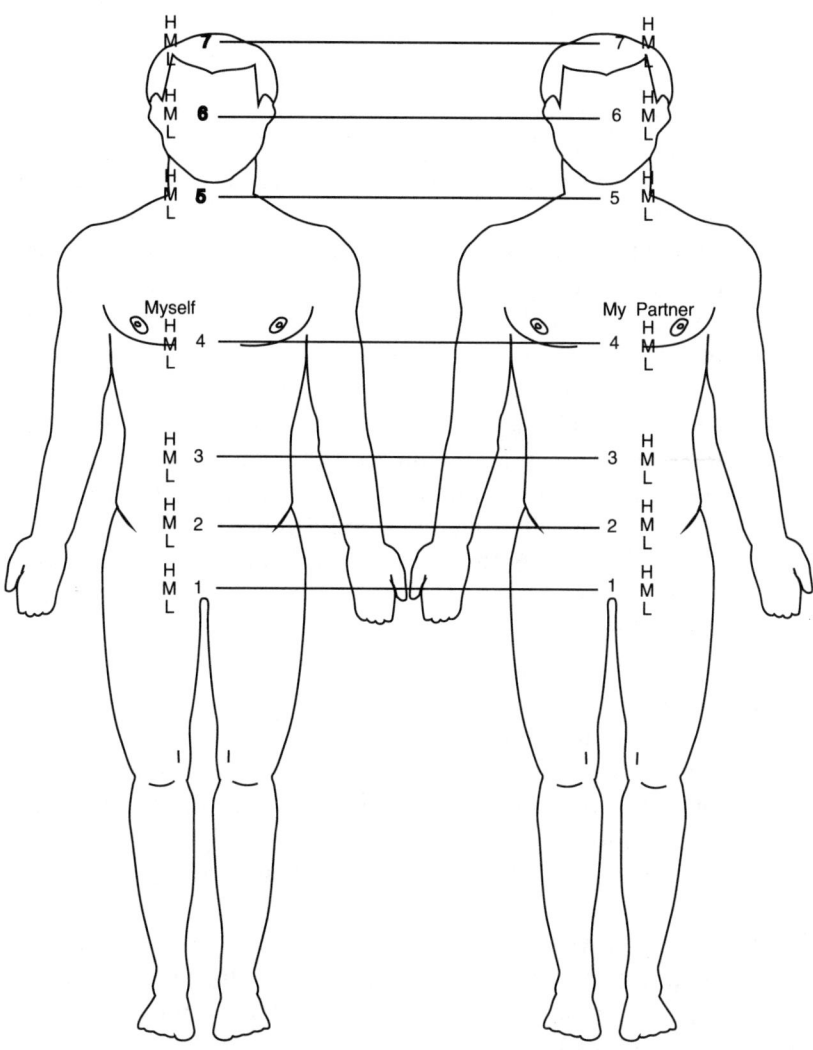

Figure 5.2
CHAKRAL ENERGY AWARENESS FOR PARTNERS

2. Visualize the light beaming out toward your partner's root chakra.
3. Make an energy contact between you and your partner. (Pause thirty seconds.) Now say "lah" and see if you can feel the vibrations at the base of your spine.
4. Move the white light up to your navel, and again visualize the beam of light extending out to your partner's second chakra. Make contact and hold that contact. (Pause thirty seconds.) Now say "bah" and vibrate the sound into your second chakra. Notice any thoughts or feelings that come up for you while doing this.
5. Move the white light up to your solar plexus, the hole in the center of your upper abdomen just below the rib cage. Make contact with your partner, and again notice any thoughts or feelings. (Pause thirty seconds.) Now say "rah" and vibrate into your third chakra.
6. Move the white light to the fourth chakra, in the middle of your chest. Make contact with your partner. Feel this area opening up to receive energy from your partner. Watch your thoughts and feelings emerge and dissolve. (Pause thirty seconds.) Now say "Ya-Mm" and allow the sound to fill your upper chest.
7. Move the white light to your throat chakra just behind your larynx. Visualize the contact with your partner and notice your thoughts and feelings. (Pause thirty seconds.) Now make the sound "hah" and vibrate your throat.
8. Move the white light to your third eye. Feel the contact with your partner. (Pause thirty seconds.) Make the sound "ah." Feel it coming from your third eye. *Optional:* Open your eyes slowly and focus your attention on a single point in the middle of your partner's forehead. Let that one point become figure while everything else fades into the background. (Pause five minutes.) Close your eyes again.
9. Finally, move the white light to the top of your head. See/feel the contact with your partner and notice your thoughts and feelings (Pause thirty seconds.) Say "om" several times and feel the energy releasing off the top of your head. *Optional:* Open your eyes, keeping them very soft. Focus your attention to a point several inches above your partner's head. (Pause thirty seconds.) Just focus and empty your mind of thoughts. See and feel the energy emanating from your partner's crown energy chakra.
10. Stay in eye contact with your partner and experience the openness that now exists between you.

At the present, practical uses of chakral energy awareness require much more study and experimentation. The activities in this chapter give you suggestions for beginning that exploration. I am cautious about drawing any definite conclusions from these activities, but at the same time I encourage couples to allow any meaning to flow from their experiences.

NOTES

1. W. B. Joy, *Joy's Way: A Map for the Transformational Journey* (Los Angeles: J. P. Tarcher, 1979), p. 129.
2. Thelma Moss, *The Probability of the Impossible* (Los Angeles: J. P. Tarcher, 1974).
3. The term *chakra* and the systems of energy centers in the body are taken from Hindu philosophy and medicine. Reference to energy centers in the body is also found in ancient Hebrew, Buddhist, and Chinese cultures.

6

Developmental Process Work in Marriage and Family Therapy

Barry Weinhold and Janae Weinhold

A transpersonal theory of marriage and family therapy goes beyond the psychodynamic, behavioral, humanistic, and family systems models of therapy. It draws from all of these approaches and then moves beyond their scope to include metaphysical and transpersonal elements. An emerging transpersonal model clearly attempts to treat the "farther reaches of human behavior" (which Maslow called the "transpersonal realms") as they appear in relationship problems in marriages and in families. Using our developmental process work approach, we found many transpersonal elements in family and relationship problems. Once we learned to follow the relationship and individual processes as they emerged out of these problems, we often encountered spiritual abandonment, demonic forces, intrapsychic holes, transcendent experiences, and other transpersonal phenomena.

We have learned through these experiences to trust the "rightness" of whatever process is emerging. We believe that this openness to and acceptance of a wide range of psychological and spiritual experiences is necessary to do this kind of work.

A couple came for therapy in the midst of an intense crisis. The woman had just discovered that her husband was having an affair with another woman. She was angry enough to kill him. She claimed that a demon inside of her was telling her to kill him and that she was afraid this demon would take over her behavior. We asked her to draw a picture of her demon and to then dialogue with the demon.

Much to her surprise, she discovered through dialoguing with this demon that he served a useful purpose in her life. When she asked him what it was, he replied, "I have been waiting 900 years for you to work on this issue." When she asked what the issue was, he said, "You need to learn how to give up control. It was your need to control that led your husband to have an affair." He added, "I'm here to help you let go, and I am very patient."

Eventually she asked the demon to help her work on her control issue, and she began working on this issue in therapy. She also saw that her husband's affair provided her with another opportunity to learn to give up control over him and other people as well.

We wonder how more traditional therapists might handle a client who is, in effect, having a spiritual emergency. Medically oriented therapists probably would have medicated and even hospitalized the client in the example to get her through her emergency.

To work with people at these deep levels does require spiritual courage on the part of both the client and the therapist. This kind of work also can produce a spiritual emergency in therapists if they have not done their own deep work. We have been challenged by our clients to do our own deep work, from which we sometimes emerge only to find clients waiting for us to help them with a similar issue. We trust that our clients will bring us exactly what we need and that only those clients who are ready for our help will appear for therapy.

OUR PERSONAL CONTRIBUTIONS TO DEVELOPMENTAL PROCESS WORK

Barry

My contribution to the developmental process work approach to marriage and family therapy has grown out of my own experiences. The first set of experiences occurred when I entered outpatient reparenting therapy in 1974. I seemed stuck in the marriage relationship I was in. I couldn't get out of it, and I couldn't improve it.

I had been involved in a training program in transactional analysis (TA) when I first met Jan Vanderburg. Jan reminded me of my mother, because both were large women and both seemed to be able to see through me. Because of these similarities, I was both attracted to and scared of Jan. Jan was one of my trainers, and as I watched her supervise and teach, I became impressed with her skills and her information about reparenting. She conducted outpatient reparenting groups, in which people contracted to complete some of their unfinished business from childhood. I began to fantasize what it might be like to have her as a contract mother. I was aware of my early bonding issues and knew that my chronic overeating and indigestion following a meal was a result of my not knowing when I was full. This seemed to relate to when I couldn't get enough to eat when my mother tried to nurse me during the first six weeks of my life. She had trouble producing milk, and by the age of six weeks, I weighed less than when I was born. Finally Jan agreed to be my contract mother to help me heal my early bonding issues and the eating problems these issues produced.

My first therapy session with her was in a weekend therapy marathon. Everyone went around and made an initial contract to work on some problem during the weekend. When it was my turn, I started to make a contract, but Jan interrupted by yelling at me, "Knock off your goddam professor shit and make a contract." I sat stunned, wondering why I had created another abusive mother. I wanted to run out of the room and never come back again, but I swallowed hard and made a contract to lie near her, covered with a blanket, and to just listen. She accepted this, and I spent the whole weekend plus many of the weekly groups lying under a blanket near her. I gradually moved closer to her and eventually was able to bond with her. After three years I found that I had healed many of the early bonding issues and closed many of the bonding gaps in my developmental history, so I terminated therapy. This work also allowed me to separate from and divorce my first wife, Fran, from an "I'm okay, you're okay" place.

The second set of experiences that expanded my awareness about developmental issues occurred after the sudden death of my second wife, Barbara, in April of 1983 and my subsequent marriage to Janae in November of 1984. Janae and I had many things in common, and we were both full of love and dreams as we started our new life together. As we got closer to each other, I found myself dealing with new and unexpected issues related to my early developmental traumas.

After getting married in late November, we went to Greece and Egypt on our honeymoon in January with a group led by Jean Houston. This was an intense experience for both of us, which seemed to bring us even closer together on spiritual levels. When we returned, we also participated in a five-day Native American dance ritual that opened us up even more spiritually.

Late in the spring of 1985, I began to feel ill. I experienced low energy and pain in my left side. I finally went to the doctor and found out I had an early stage of colon cancer. I was totally shocked and terrified. To me, cancer meant death, a slow, horrible death.

As I began to recover from the shock and looked at my treatment options, I was determined to get to the source of the problem using a body-mind approach. With Janae's support, I selected to begin with the most noninvasive physical treatment I could locate. This meant starting with drastic changes in diet and nutritional balancing. Next I began to look for any unfinished business related to the cancer. Because the cancer was on the left side, at the top of the descending colon, I looked at the feminine side of my unfinished business. (The left side of the body is often associated with the feminine and the right side with the masculine.) Several contributing factors were immediately apparent.

At that time I was under tremendous stress at the university because I was appointed as the faculty advocate for a female junior colleague who was applying for reappointment. What I realized in meeting with various personnel committees and administrators was that the university system was set up to "kill" feminine aspects of faculty members. The only things they wanted to focus on were the number of works this female colleague had published, the quality of her publications, and what line of research she had developed in the less than three years she had been at the university. No one was interested in the fact that she was a single parent who had to spend lots of time with two very sick children during her first two years at the university. Also, no one was interested in the fact that she was hired at a salary far below what most male assistant professors made and that she had to teach extra classes to provide for her family. No one was interested in knowing that she received almost no mentoring from any senior colleagues about what she needed to do to prepare for her personnel review.

When all my attempts to present a balanced perspective fell on the deaf ears of my colleagues who were sitting in judgment on this case, I finally began to understand. I realized that the university system of which I am a part is designed to kill the feminine aspects of its faculty members. It was killing me as much as it would try to kill anyone who attempted to be a whole person.

Because I knew I was going to be gone for six months on a sabbatical in Switzerland, I immediately resigned as chairperson of my department and put off resigning from the university. I knew if I didn't get to the bottom of this problem, my resignation from the university was inevitable.

I worked further with the theme of the "killer of the feminine" to see where else that was true for me. As I was growing up, I certainly never felt any support for my feminine qualities. They were either killed or put down. As an adolescent I loved to read, to write poetry, and to listen to classical music, but none of that seemed of value in my culture. To be "one of the boys" in junior high school, I pretended not to study or be interested in reading books. I became a "jock" and played basketball and baseball in high school so I could "belong." All my adult life I had been fighting to recover my feminine side. After Barbara's death, I worked hard to reclaim it, only to find people trying to kill it again.

Barbara's death, I knew, also symbolized the killing of my feminine ideal that I had projected on her. By the time the cancer appeared, I began to wonder if I had completely reclaimed my feminine ideal. Finally I did some more therapeutic work to uncover the source of this illness, and what I found blew my mind.

In my daily meditations I began to get images of being killed by someone stabbing me with a long spear in my left side. The more I worked with these images, the more I realized they were not from this lifetime. They were Egyptian in nature, and eventually, in a waking dream, the whole story came to me. I remembered that Janae and I were part of an Egyptian Mystery School. I had threatened the power structure of that school because I wanted to integrate the feminine and masculine aspects of their teachings. Specifically, I wanted to have more attention placed on the earth and the shadow aspects of human behavior, whereas those in power wanted the school to focus on moving toward the transcendent qualities of the light and away from the dark side of human beings. I wanted a balance between these two, and apparently they decided I was dangerous and had to be killed. Janae (a man in that lifetime) was to be my killer. What to do with this awareness would soon become apparent.

In early July 1985, we went to California to attend a week-long therapy workshop with Dr. Arnold Mindell, the Jungian analyst whom we were planning to study with in Switzerland the following January. Dr. Mindell had developed a new approach that he called *process-oriented psychology*, which we were eager to learn more about. By the end of the second day, I decided to work on my cancer in front of the group and asked Arny to help. He suggested a psychodrama so I could reenact the death scene and learn what wasn't finished with it that I was still trying to complete.

I reenacted the whole scene with Janae stabbing me in slow motion with a fireplace poker. When she pressed the poker against my side where the colon cancer was, I fell on the floor and screamed in agony. I reexperienced the physical and emotional pain of being betrayed and abandoned by my friends and loved ones. The pain subsided after a while, only to be replaced by intense anger and rage. I raged on the floor while eight or ten people held me down to protect me from hurting myself or others.

When this subsided, I got up and faced Janae. I knew there was something else to finish with her. I grabbed her, and we began to wrestle. I felt as if I were fighting for every man who had ever been betrayed and abandoned, and later Janae confided that she felt she was fighting for every woman who had been attacked by a man. It was an intense struggle between two strong opponents. Finally I wrestled her to the ground and ended up sitting on top of her. She looked up at me and said, "Aren't you getting lonely up there?" Obviously I was, because all the energy immediately went out of the fight for me. I rolled off of her, and I knew that what I really wanted was full partnership with Janae. We ended our battle of the sexes that July day in California.

I still wasn't out of the woods with the cancer. With additional psychological and nutritional work, however, my cancer went into remission and I was symptom-free by August 1985. Since then, I have continued a vegetarian diet and taken various nutritional supplements and kept myself from being overstressed.

In July 1989, after one of my periodic check-ups, my nutritionist said to me, "I have some good news and some bad news for you." I said, "Give me the good news first." She said, "The good news is that your body is perfectly balanced nutritionally, and the bad news is that you will have to devote two hours a day of spiritual work to keep it balanced." What she was referring to was prayer, meditation, yoga, and just taking time to be with myself and to do unto myself. She said she believed the next challenge was for me to focus on myself for a minimum of two hours a day.

My first thoughts were on how easy and nice that would be for me. What I found out in the ensuing months was that this was the most difficult prescription I ever had to fill. It brought me up against my deepest beliefs about not being worthy of two hours a day devoted to myself. Now, after a year and a half of dealing with these issues, I still can report success only about sixty to seventy percent of the time. My oldest program of taking care of others first is really difficult to change. So I continue my journey to reach and maintain my two-hour goal on a consistent basis.

Janae

My contributions to developmental process work have come from my own experiences in healing deep psychological wounds from my early years in a highly dysfunctional family. My mother and father were locked in a deadly struggle that was never spoken out loud. Their struggle ended when I was twelve years old. At that time she committed suicide by asphyxiation while she held my five-year-old brother on her lap. My own place and role in this family system created experiences of abandonment, covert incest, caretaking, and confusion. Not until age thirty-seven did I realize my need for therapy.

When I finally opened myself up to comprehend the damage that had been done to me in my childhood, I began to understand the destructiveness of my family environment. Not until I married Barry when I was forty, however, did I begin to feel at a deep level the extent of my childhood losses. The love and freeing environment of our relationship provided a safe place from which I began to plumb my own depths.

In 1986 I was living in Switzerland studying process-oriented psychology with Dr. Arnold Mindell as part of my doctoral studies at the Union Institute. Union's program requires its learners to follow their own inner process while they create their doctoral learning experiences. I was excited at the idea of being able to learn process-oriented psychology in a self-directed way that would complement my studies at Union.

During the second week of a six-week intensive course in Switzerland, I was shocked to discover that most of the classes offered would not allow me to learn in my own way. Instead they were taught in a rather formal European style in which the instructors were highly authoritarian and scientific. These classes accorded no opportunity for me to learn by following my own process. When I confronted the instructors (primarily male) about the incongruency between the content of their classes and the structure of their teaching, my feelings and ideas were not received. They made it quite clear that if I wanted to participate in the course, I was the one who would have to adapt.

When I realized the finality of this dictum, I began to pull away from the classes to assess my options. At the beginning of the third week, I decided that I would not participate in any classes taught by authoritarian instructors. I attended two classes taught by women instructors who focused mostly on application of theory and I had the freedom to learn in my own style. I also began studying on my own and working privately with a woman tutor who understood my need for congruency between the theory and its practical application. Taking these actions resolved my problems with the intensive course, but the situation also stirred something deep inside me.

As I pulled away from the group involved in the classes and went more inside myself, I began to experience a deep hurt and sense of wounding. I tried to use the tools and paradigm of process-oriented psychology to work myself through the feelings of abandonment, despair, and fear of death that were coming up. Even with Barry's support, for more than a month I floated in an anxiety that seemed to have no bottom. At one point the pain became so strong that I decided it would be easier to exist if I were to enter a deep catatonic state and never come back. At almost the same time I was making this decision, an old friend from Hawaii visited us at the site where our classes were being held. His timely support brought me back from the chasm and helped me move back into life again.

For several months after this crisis, I experienced a sense of childlike helplessness, memory loss, and general confusion. I was aware of some similarity between my experience in Switzerland with the intensive group and my feelings of being unreceived in my family of origin, but I could not completely understand the relationship or see the pattern that connected them.

Gradually I pieced myself back together again by immersing myself in my doctoral studies, building a new home, building a larger practice as a therapist, and starting a nonprofit institute. These external activities helped me also restructure my inner self and find new strengths from the Swiss experience.

I began to use the tools I had learned in Switzerland with my clients in my private practice. I noticed, especially when Barry and I worked as co-therapists, how the tools never worked quite the way we saw them demonstrated in our Swiss classes. Barry and I discussed this interesting circumstance, and I also reflected a lot on how those classes hadn't helped me really complete work on some deep aspects of myself during my breakdown there. We began to look closely at the discrepancy between the theory of process-oriented psychology as we had learned it and the experiences we were having using it.

About this time the addictions and recovery movement began to emerge in our therapy work. I could see how many addictions were related to the "inner child" and the importance of experiences in the first years of life. At this point I realized that in all the Swiss classes I had attended, no one had demonstrated an inner-child process. Everything was presented so that the mythological, global, or theoretical aspects of the process-oriented paradigm emerged.

When it became clear to me that process work was going to function differently for Barry and me as we used it, I began to work from my own experience to revise the model. I studied all the early developmental resources I could find, to understand my own early needs and the effect of two traumas in my first year of life. With this information as a map, I began to collaborate with Barry on creating a different map for working with clients and ourselves. We called this *A Map for Breaking Free from Dysfunctional Family Patterns.*

As I used the map to heal my own wounds, the wounds seemed to open up new pieces of the map. Sometimes I began to feel as though I were the map. I began to examine the pattern of manic-depressive behavior that appears in my family, looking at my own propensity toward it. This brought up new areas of personal research. I looked at how the release of early patterns shifts the biochemical balance of the body. I explored the effects of early separation at birth and how that affects the infant's adrenal stress response. My mother's suicide during menopause and my own menopause made me interested in the relationship between biochemical shifts and the propensity for psychotic behaviors. In each of these areas, I examined the developmental components of the problem. I also delved deeply into the psychosis in my family, which drew me into cultural research about the way in which relationship patterns between men and women get expressed also as global conflicts. In each level of exploration, the map grew more complete, more detailed, and more grounded in my personal experience.

When I decided to repair an old injury to my coccyx that had happened at age five, it opened up in our map another level of self-exploration that reemphasized the significance of bodywork, biofeedback therapy, and nutritional support. I found myself using almost every therapeutic modality I knew to heal the physical, emotional, mental, and spiritual wounds connected to this injury. I hesitated to mention to many people the depth of my personal work, for fear that they would regard it in a state-oriented matter rather than understanding that I was in a process of healing. I held tightly to this tenet of our philosophical foundation, for I knew that I would ultimately emerge more whole, more individuated, and more able to be my full Self.

For almost four years we have researched this map, first with ourselves and then with many clients. We continue to use this research to refine our model into what we now call *developmental process work.* At times I have felt ashamed that I had such a dysfunctional family and that I had so much unfinished business to bring into my adult relationships, especially those with my two children. I also feel grateful for finding the resources that have allowed me to finally complete this old unfinished business and that now allow me to guide many others through similar kinds of issues.

A MAP FOR BREAKING FREE FROM DYSFUNCTIONAL FAMILY PATTERNS

1. *Become aware of your addictive and dysfunctional patterns.*
   - ❑ Identify the betrayals, abandonments, rejections, abuses, and other traumatic events in the first five years of your life.

- ❑ Identify your recurrent Trauma Drama based on these traumatic events.
- ❑ Identify the addictive and dysfunctional patterns of behavior you learned in your family of origin.

2. *Identify the unfinished business from your Trauma Drama.*
   - ❑ Learn about the healthy developmental needs and stages of relationships.
   - ❑ Identify the unmet developmental needs that are recycling in your current relationships and in adult behaviors.
   - ❑ Identify appropriate activities necessary to fill the developmental parenting gaps.
   - ❑ Begin to make contact with your inner child.
   - ❑ Identify narcissistic wounds.

3. *Do your "original pain" work.*
   - ❑ Create a system of committed friends to provide external support for your feelings during this period.
   - ❑ Develop intrapsychic structures such as "protector" or "nurturing parent" to provide you with internal support for your inner child.
   - ❑ Understand the role and range of feelings.
   - ❑ Make contact with your wounded inner child and the child's unexpressed feelings.
   - ❑ Learn how to express these feelings appropriately.
   - ❑ Feel your feelings connected to the early childhood traumas and have them supported by another caring person.
   - ❑ Receive validation of your childhood experiences and feelings.

4. *Complete the unfinished business of your Trauma Drama.*
   - ❑ Decide where, when, and with whom you will contract to complete work on your developmental needs.
   - ❑ Create corrective parenting experiences for yourself to get your unmet developmental needs met.
   - ❑ Develop daily activities to provide nurturing parenting for your inner child.

5. *Become an autonomous person.*
   - ❑ Set limits and develop healthy boundaries.

        ❑ Take back the parts of yourself that you project on other people.

        ❑ Reclaim your personal power.

        ❑ Complete your psychological birth by separating emotionally, mentally, physically, and spiritually from your parents.

        ❑ Confront and change your self-limiting beliefs.

        ❑ Commit to asking directly for what you want.

6. *Take charge of your body.*
   - ❑ Eat more consciously.
   - ❑ Exercise regularly.
   - ❑ Do structural bodywork that helps dislodge old patterns from the body and also realign it with your new patterns of thinking and behaving.

7. *Develop your spiritual life.*
   - ❑ Use prayer, meditation, and other forms of spiritual practice to help you reach deeper spiritual levels.
   - ❑ Understand your life's purpose and your place in the world.
   - ❑ Discover and live out of your True Self.

8. *Live interdependently.*
   - ❑ Create functional relationships with people and the planet alike based on the principles of partnership, co-creation, flexibility, and intimacy.
   - ❑ Develop vocations and avocations that support the unfolding of your highest potential.
   - ❑ Express your life's purpose through forms of high service.
   - ❑ Create a support system that enables you to live in a partnership society.

THEORETICAL FOUNDATIONS OF DEVELOPMENTAL PROCESS WORK

The theoretical foundations of developmental process work are a synthesis of material from a broad psychological spectrum. Both synthesizers by nature, we tend to use theories that work effectively in practice. The theoretical roots of developmental process work come from the Jungian-based *global process work* approach of Arnold Mindell, from the psychoanalytic work of Alice Miller, from the transactional analysis reparenting theory, from the developmental theories and research of Margaret Mahler, Eric Erikson, Robert Havighurst, and Jean Piaget, and from various transpersonal and metaphysical theories, including rebirthing.

Contributions from Transactional Analysis

In 1970, Jacqui Lee Schiff published a book titled *All My Children*, which described a revolutionary new therapy approach called reparenting,[1] which grew out of Eric Berne's[2] work on transactional analysis. The book reported the work she and her husband did with schizophrenics no one else wanted to work with. Their treatment approach involved a residential treatment program that required twenty-four-hour-a-day care. Most of the people who went through their program went on to become highly functioning adults, many becoming therapists themselves.

Their methods, highly controversial at the time, encouraged the client to regress to an infant stage and work there to heal the developmental deficits from that age. This included diapering clients, and holding them and feeding them from bottles, as well as structured anger and rage-reduction techniques. Their methods were designed to reconnect clients with the sources of their original trauma, to allow them to express any unexpressed feelings related to the trauma, and then provide them with support, nurturing, and new information that would help them heal their early wounds.

As the practice of reparenting grew in the 1970s, many practitioners began to experiment with it in an outpatient format. From this early experimentation practitioners were able to detail the kinds of interventions that produced lasting changes in their clients. Jacqui followed with a sequel book, *The Cathexis Reader*[3] which described a set of passive or discounting behaviors that keep people stuck in symbiotic or co-dependent relationships.

Jacqui also outlined effective methods for confronting these dysfunctional behaviors. For example, she found that passive people often discount their own needs and focus on the needs of others, hoping to win some attention or approval from them. Passive people, she also found, discount their ability to ask directly for what they want. Being forced to ask directly to get their needs met was found to be an effective confrontation for dealing with this problem. As the Schiffs studied passivity and discounting, they discovered that it wasn't just part of the pathology of

[margin note: PASSIVITY & DISCOUNT]

schizophrenics but also was very much a part of the everyday life of most people. They estimated that as many as two of every five "transactions" or interactions between people involve some evidence of discounting or passivity.

TA practitioners Dorothy Babcock and Terry Keepers combined the passivity/discounting information with script analysis in a book for parents called *Raising Kids OK*.[4] Robert and Mary Goulding adapted this material into other types of TA therapy such as *redecision therapy*.[5]

During this period Jacqui Schiff became embroiled in political and ethical battles within the International Association of Transactional Analysis, and the organization eventually censured her. This effectively stopped the progress of this treatment modality except with a few of Jacqui's former students who continued to develop the theory. I (Barry) continued using some reparenting techniques with my clients in private practice as a psychologist but had gone on to explore other, more transpersonal approaches by the time this had happened.

With the onset of the co-dependency movement, the reparenting treatment modality again began to appear in the recovery literature. In their book, *Recovery From Co-Dependency*, Jon and Laurie Weiss[6] describe corrective parenting techniques they use in treating co-dependency. Jean Illsley Clarke and her colleagues wrote several books applying this evolving theory to parenting.[7] Pam Levin also wrote several books that further developed reparenting theory.[8] Our own books *Breaking Free of the Co-Dependency Trap* and *Counter-Dependency: The Flight From Intimacy* further developed aspects of this theory.[9] *Breaking Free of Addictive Family Relationships* describes the process of breaking dysfunctional transactions in present relationships, using many concepts from reparenting.[10]

Clarke and Levin added much to understanding the use of developmental affirmations that help people heal early developmental deficits. They also organized helpful lists of the developmental needs of early childhood.

The Psychoanalytic Contributions of Alice Miller

Much of the revival of our own interest in the reparenting approach grew out of the work of a Swiss analyst, Alice Miller. Her pioneering books, *Prisoners of Childhood, The Drama of the Gifted Child* and *For Your Own Good*,[11] helped rekindle our interest in how early narcissistic wounds affect later development. Miller's work showed clearly some of the adverse effects of what might be called "standard parenting practices," and it documented how the same dysfunctional patterns of behavior repeat from one generation to another.

The Developmental Contributions of Eric Erikson, Robert Havinghurst, and Jean Piaget

The work of Erikson, Havinghurst, and Piaget[12] was quite helpful to us in identifying the normal stages of physical development and the cognitive and emotional tasks that have to be mastered at each stage. We learned the most, however, by reading the research of Margaret Mahler.[13] She and her colleagues were able to chart the course of development from the early bonding stage of the infant (birth to nine months) through the separation stage (nine to twenty-four months). Louise Kaplan's book *Oneness and Separateness*,[14] based on Mahler's research, provided us with a clear narrative description of these two stages, including what might prevent the successful completion of each stage.

The Global Process Work Approach of Arnold Mindell

These contributions were all coming together in 1985–86 when I finished writing a book called *Breaking Family Patterns*.[15] At this same time we met Arnold Mindell, a Jungian analyst who was developing a new adaptation of Jungian theory now called *global process work*, formerly known as *process-oriented psychology*. Earlier in this chapter we reported our first meeting with him.

While working as a Jungian analyst in Zurich, Switzerland, Dr. Mindell became ill with a life-threatening disease. After unsuccessfully attempting to cure himself using the standard analytic tools he had in his Jungian tool box, he began to investigate the connections between body symptoms and dreams. He realized that he knew much less about his body than he did his dreams, so he began studying various body-oriented therapies in an attempt to heal himself. He studied yoga, bioenergetics, breath work, rolfing, massage, movement therapy, psychodrama, neurolinguistic programming, Gestalt therapy, and meditation. In the process, he not only healed himself but also began to find threads present in all these approaches that he could weave together into a totally new body/mind therapy that he called the *dreambody approach*.

Mindell also expanded Jung's ideas about dreams and began to realize that most people are dreaming all the time. Their waking dreams are often ways to avoid unpleasant realities or unpleasant memories, and their sleeping dreams provide an outlet for unconscious material to emerge.

The real genius of Mindell's theory, however, is his expansion of information theories such as neurolinguistic programming (NLP) into six main channels for inputting and outputting information, and the use of Taoist principles. This information theory allowed a mechanism for the therapist to track information as it presented itself through client symptoms and problems. His uses of Taoist principles provided a context of "rightness" of all symptoms and problems as well as the use of client-centered techniques for "following" the client. In addition, he drew upon the principles of unified field theory from quantum physics to show how problems move from one "field" or system to another. According to his theory, for example, an internal conflict that is not resolved at the individual level will move out into the relationship field and emerge there as a conflict. If not resolved at that level, it will move out into the next level of system, the family. Using this theory to examine national and international conflicts, one can see how they can be the collective manifestation of many unresolved individual, relationship, and family problems.

When we studied with and were in therapy with Dr. Mindell in 1986, he was still evolving his theory.[16] Since then he has become interested in and involved with global conflicts, so he changed the name of his theory from process-oriented psychology to global process work. We have adapted many of the concepts from his theory in our developmental process work approach.

The Transpersonal and Metaphysical Contributions

The more we synthesized the various theories, the more we realized a need for a solid spiritual foundation. We saw that a spiritual component was necessary both for helping clients move directly into their core issues and for moving through them permanently. Here we found the work of Ken Wilber[17] helpful in describing the transcendent and spiritual aspects of developmental psychology. His concepts of the *trans-egoic* stages of human development, as well as the superconscious levels of awareness, helped us integrate the spiritual and transformative elements of human development into our own emerging model. His work led us to study other transpersonal approaches including the teachings of spiritual masters from Eastern philosophies such as integral yoga, Taoism, Hinduism, agni yoga and other teaching of ageless wisdom.

Leonard Orr, the founder of rebirthing, helped us understand the power of the breath in helping people reconnect with and heal early childhood traumas, including the birth trauma. We trained as rebirthers, which helped us experience and understand the importance of natural childbirth techniques that respect the sanctity of the birth process and the child's need to be in charge of his or her own birth.

The work of Frederick LeBoyer, the French obstetrician, and Igor Charkofsky, the Soviet physician, plus the work of the American midwifery movement, helped us develop therapeutic methods to assist people in recreating an ideal birth. Our study in the birthing area helped us develop a variety of ways to link adult problems to the trauma of birth.

APPLIED FOUNDATIONS OF DEVELOPMENTAL PROCESS WORK

Our individual searches for a transpersonal relationship with ourselves, with each other, and with our spiritual parents provided the laboratory to synthesize, research, and apply these theories. The theoretical foundations of our approach require that we work first on ourselves as individuals, then in our relationship with each other, and finally in our relationships with our families, before we feel solid enough to use the approach with clients. As transpersonal marriage and family therapists, we believe it is important to "walk our talk" and teach by sharing our own journey to wholeness.

This belief in the importance of teaching from our own wounds has been supported through our work with teachers who have been willing to do so, most recently John Bradshaw and Robert Bly. From them we have seen the power of removing the teacher from the pedestal and finding human connection through our common wounds.

As we apply our approach with clients, we continue to discover more about ourselves and use this to do more work in our personal laboratory. This interactive process keeps us refining and expanding both ourselves and our model.

The transpersonal aspect of developmental process work also emerged from the discovery of how unfinished business with our parents interfered with our being in a healthy relationship with our spiritual parents. As we surrendered more and more of ourselves and our life together to be guided by spirit, the obstacles to spiritual intimacy emerged. We began to see how we projected the faces of our human parents onto our spiritual parents. Our inner children believed that Father/Mother God would respond to our prayers, ideas, dreams, and feelings just like our human parents had. We could see that we expected to be abandoned, judged, abused, and shamed as we had been as children and that we would have to do everything ourselves by working hard. The moment when we saw how the developmental issues of our early childhood were creating a dysfunctional relationship with our spiritual parents was one we will long remember.

We have personally experienced developmental process work as a highly effective treatment modality. It has helped us heal our narcissistic wounds and complete the developmental tasks necessary to recover our True Self. We have used our approach with hundreds of clients and found it to be as effective with them as it has been with ourselves. We also have trained many therapists who have used our approach just as successfully with their clients. As we continue to work personally and professionally with our model, we see people experiencing the transpersonal part of themselves and of others. We regard developmental process work as a sacred technology to be used in "midwifing" people through their psychological birth, which we consider just as sacred and important as the physical birth.

OPERATING PRINCIPLES OF DEVELOPMENTAL PROCESS WORK

Developmental process work builds on the transpersonal paradigm presented in Chapter 3 and the various assumptions outlined there. It adds numerous principles that apply directly to the therapeutic process and support the client in emerging from therapy with a more whole, more individuated process. The main operating principles are as follows:

1. The goal of developmental process work is to help people develop an intimate relationship with their own soul and with spiritual realms.
2. To develop this spirit/soul intimacy, people have to reclaim the parts of themselves they split off during childhood. At the core of

each split-off part is also some unmet developmental need that must be met before that part can be integrated.

3. The process of reclaiming split-off parts includes the need for doing core feeling work (examples: experiencing fear of abandonment/engulfment, shame, rage, grief, ecstasy, bliss, unconditional love). Unexpressed core feelings help keep dysfunctional patterns recycling.

4. Developmental deficits occurred in our primary relationships from childhood and healing these developmental deficits in adults requires safe primary relationships. These may be therapeutic love relationships between friends who are committed to helping each other get their unmet developmental needs met.

5. Every person has an innate desire to be whole and is always working in his or her best way (though usually unskilled) to become whole. Every behavior, whether effective or not, is an effort to find the wholeness.

6. Each client enters therapy carrying a "healing process in progress." This healing is expressed in behaviors and body signals. The therapist has to discover this self-healing process and help the client become aware of it so he or she may do it more consciously. The client always has to be seen as evolving in this process rather than as someone who is stuck in a particular psychological state. This requires process-oriented thinking rather than the state-oriented thinking associated with most medically oriented psychological models.

7. The client is always in charge of the therapy and dictates the rate at which his or her process moves. This puts the power back in the client's hands and removes the therapist from a role that can be invasive or abusive.

8. A client's progress can be slowed down but not speeded up. Clients truly move at their own pace. Hurrying them along often makes them skip important pieces of their learning process, which then requires them to cycle the issue again.

9. Unmet developmental needs are carried along as "excess baggage" until they get met. They recycle again and again in different ways in our relationships with different people, always pressing to be met.

10. All current conflicts and problems are the result of unmet developmental needs from childhood. By following the client's proc-

ess, we can discover the family-of-origin sources of these unmet needs.

11. Therapists attract clients who have the same issues they have. This mutual attraction can help both complete their unfinished business.

12. All problems and body symptoms have a "rightness." Looking for the rightness of all problems and symptoms is a way of helping clients reframe their experiences. This removes judgment and avoids shaming.

13. It is never too late to get childhood developmental needs met. Human development is a life-long process that can get stunted or have gaps, but it never stops.

14. The therapist is seen as a protector. The therapist's first and foremost task is to provide a safe and sacred space in which the client may open up his or her most vulnerable parts. Invasion, perpetration, and abuse of any kind in such a space might justify the label of "sin."

15. Developmental process work is a transpersonal approach that acknowledges the presence of both soul and spirit elements in the healing process. It acknowledges that the true power of healing comes from transpersonal realms. The therapist's role is to access these realms and to facilitate the client in also accessing them. Developmental process work must be used with the utmost respect for the divine nature of both the client and the unseen forces that create the healing process.

APPLYING THE THEORY AND PRINCIPLES IN THERAPY

In developmental process work the goal is to help the client gain access to the unconscious material carried by some aspect of the split-off inner child. Any therapeutic doorway can open to the client's unconscious to discover parts of the psyche that were closed off during childhood because of trauma or developmental disruptions. These split-off or unintegrated parts usually exist in opposition to other parts of the psyche that are "owned" or more integrated. Discovering these conflicting parts of the psyche, which usually operate at an unconscious level, is the first step in applying the principles of developmental process work. The second step is to help the client discover how the conflict between these two different parts contains unmet needs from childhood. The third goal is to help the client get these needs met and integrate this new learning so that the client become more whole, more individuated, and more able to access transpersonal realms.

How to Follow the Client's Progress Using Developmental Process Work

To discover the conflicting parts of the psyche, to identify the unmet developmental needs that are keeping them split off, and then to help the client get these needs met, it is necessary to follow the client's signals. Each client is seen as a system that constantly emits information through verbal and nonverbal signals. Following these signals can be a challenge for therapists because the signals may take therapists through a confusing maze that can make them feel lost and out of control. Following the client through this winding journey of signals requires a guiding structure. The following concepts help create a structure that allows the therapist to follow the client more effectively.

The Primary Process

This is what the client is identified with at any given moment. It may be called the "ego self" (e. g., "I am unemployed"). Statements that begin with "I am" are indicators of the client's primary process.

The Secondary Process

This is what the client is not identified with in the given moment. The client usually describes it as something that is "happening to" him or her. The secondary process of the client who is unemployed might be, "No one wants to hire me." The secondary process is often associated with an unwanted or unintegrated aspect of the personality that often carries repressed feelings such as shame. As moving into the secondary process with its unconscious material is often a frightening experience for a client, it is important to move slowly and respectfully into this material.

The Edge

This is the point of conflict between the primary and the secondary processes. It is also the edge of awareness between the known and unknown parts of the psyche. The edge often can be identified by statements that begin with "I can't...." In our example, the edge might be, "I can't get a job." Because moving into the secondary process is often frightening, it is important to work as long as necessary at the edge of it. At the edge, the client will learn many valuable things. He or she may learn about unmet developmental needs, about dysfunctional behavior patterns, or about spiritual lessons. The edge is also the place that stores old feelings that have to be released. And the edge is the place where people can build important intrapsychic structures needed to close the developmental gaps and ultimately repair the damage to the soul.

Channels

Channels are the ways in which information passes through a person's system. The channels we use are auditory, visual, kinesthetic (movement), proprioceptive (a combination of emotions and body sensations), relationship (between two people), and family (among three people or more). The therapist's task in developmental process work is to follow the flow of information as it winds its way through the client's information channels without interrupting, perpetrating, violating, or disturbing the client and his or her process until it is appropriate to make an intervention. When the information is flowing through a channel, it is described as "occupied." When a channel has no information or has unconscious information in it, it is described as "unoccupied." Terms such as these are simply tracking mechanisms for the therapist while watching the information flow.

When information flows simultaneously through two channels and the information is not congruent, it is described as a "double signal." An example of this would be a woman saying, "I'm in love with my husband" while she is also shaking her head side to side, which may be saying, "I don't think my husband loves me." Double signals offer a quick way to help the therapist identify the primary process ("I'm in love with my husband") and the secondary process ("I don't think my husband loves me") so the work at the edge of the secondary process can begin ("I can't face finding out that he may not love me").

Amplification of Signals

This involves deliberately increasing or decreasing the strength of a signal to help the therapist and the client determine the actual meaning of the signal. For example, a therapist might ask a client who is shaking a foot while talking to shake it more or to stop shaking it altogether. Either approach may open up some new information that could be hidden in the movement.

Mirroring

In mirroring, the therapist shows the client how his or her behavior looks from the outside. This technique can be useful for clients who cannot see their own behavior. To do this, the therapist must be good at observing and then acting out the observation.

Taking Over a Signal or Part

This requires that the therapist act out, or role play, an unwanted part that exists in an unoccupied channel so the client can learn more about it. The therapist has to give the part back to the client during the therapy so the client can integrate it and so the therapist does not continue to carry it after the session is over.

Interpretation

Little interpretation is done in developmental process work. Again, it is up to the client to determine what is meaningful and useful. Intervening and interpreting are only appropriate when the client needs cognitive information, mirroring, or help in completing some developmental task.

Resistance

In developmental process work, the concept of resistance does not exist. If you as a therapist suggest an intervention and the client doesn't respond favorably, this is considered negative feedback. The client is indicating that this is not the correct approach or it is not the right timing for the intervention. The client should never be forced to follow the therapist's agenda or program.

Doorways to the Unfinished Business of the Inner Child

A client entering a therapy situation will already be exhibiting verbal and nonverbal signals that present the therapist with a number of doorways through which unconscious material can be accessed. These doorways, identified as "channels," are: visual, auditory, proprioceptive, kinesthetic, relationship and family.

Visual

Dreams are a visual doorway to the unconscious. Dreams can be analyzed for their symbolic content, and for their feeling content, and for their spiritual content, and ultimately they can be acted out in the form of a psychodrama. Through this analysis and enactment the client can determine what opposing parts of the psyche are showing up in the dream and what in the dream has to be completed.

Auditory

An internal conflict many times offers an auditory doorway to the unconscious. The conflict often is experienced as a conversation between two opposing parts of the psyche. In this case the client might be asked to work through the dialoguing techniques that help him or her discover what is not finished about some old pattern in the internal conflict. Once this is determined, it may be possible to construct Gestalt or psychodynamic processes in which the old pattern can be completed, allowing the client to construct a new pattern.

Proprioceptive

Body symptoms, both acute and chronic, are another useful doorway to the inner child through the proprioceptive channel. Amplifying the pain of the symptom, such as an ulcer, often helps the client remember some incident from the past representing unfinished business. The incident, long forgotten and now somatized, can be examined to determine what the opposing parts of the psyche are and what in the process remains to be finished. Once the client completes a process and integrates the two parts, the pain or symptom usually disappears. If the pain reappears at some later date, we may advise clients to consider it as an ally that can help them uncover even more unconscious patterning. Emotions also provide a doorway to the inner child. Expressing emotions often opens memories that may emerge as physical pain, pictures, conversations, or movements.

Kinesthetic

Unconscious movements offer a doorway to the inner child from the kinesthetic channel. Incomplete or abrupt movements, in particular, allow the body to reveal the opposing parts. Asking the client to consciously repeat a movement in slow motion will often shift his or her awareness into some memory of a forgotten childhood event that reveals the opposing parts. At this point the client is encouraged to look for what in the event is not complete, and he or she begins to create a plan for bringing the opposing parts together in an attempt to complete it.

Relationship

Relationship conflicts provide a doorway to the inner child from the relationship channel. Relationship problems, usually a reflection of some internal conflict that has not been resolved, can reveal the split-off parts each partner is projecting onto the other. When each person identifies his or her projected parts and reclaims them, each can locate some event or problem from the past that is trying to complete itself. By reclaiming the projected parts and completing the old event or problem, the two people are often able to resolve their conflicts.

Family

Group conflicts are a route to the unmet needs of the inner child using the family channel. In this case we would assume that each participant involved is individually projecting some split-off part or unresolved family-of-origin issue onto a group of people organized by some collective perspective. The first step in resolving such a conflict would be to help each person identify both the personal aspect of the psyche being projected and the old issue (probably family-of-origin based) from which it originates. The second task would be for each to create ways in which his or her issue could be completed within the group setting.

Reconnecting Split-Off Parts

Channels are essential in helping the client gain access to a split-off part, for they help identify the place in the client where the splitting process may have occurred during a childhood trauma. For example, a sensitive man who was shamed by his mother when he was a child because she saw him as effeminate often splits off his feminine part. To reconnect with this part, the boy must go back into the proprioceptive channel to access the feeling of shame. Here he can remember the incident or incidents in which his receptive or innocent nature was ridiculed, feel the shame and express his old feeling of shame. In hearing the shaming messages from his parents, he would also tap into the visual and auditory channels.

To reclaim his feminine part, this client would need to use all three channels. First, he would have to access the feeling channel where he would discover his old shame. Then he would need to have his shame identified as a feeling, have his experience of feeling shamed validated by the therapist, and have his feelings supported. In the visual and auditory channels he would need to see some nurturing person (perhaps the therapist) looking at him in a caring manner while speaking words acknowledging the client's sensitivity, innocence, and receptivity. (The client also would need to understand how he has to have this feminine part to function as a warm and compassionate person.) He then can integrate his femininity into his psyche to be more whole, more individuated, and more able to have functional relationships with women and with his spiritual mother.

Constructing Intrapsychic Structures

Channels are also critical in helping clients construct intrapsychic structures that are missing, particularly in individuals who had severe trauma from neglect, abuse, or abandonment. These people often split off vital parts of themselves so severely that the parts may be almost impossible to find. If the parts are split off to an extreme, they may develop "personalities" that have names. Individuals with such severe intrapsychic gaps often lack inner structures that can help protect and nurture them. Without these intrapsychic structures the client may have difficulty in problem solving during a crisis. The man mentioned above, for example, might regress into a childlike state if someone accuses him of being a "sissy." Without an intrapsychic structure to serve as an inner protector, he may fall into an intrapsychic "hole" where he feels crazy.

The process of creating missing intrapsychic structures is a delicate one. It requires the therapist to follow the client's signals astutely, for somewhere in the flow of information through his or her channel system, the doorway to the part will appear. The therapist's task is to be gentle and supportive, for most likely the client is in a regressive state, perhaps one that is preverbal.

For children to survive early trauma requires that they also receive some kind of nurturance and protection from another person. Those without such care either die young or become psychotic very early. It is assumed, therefore, that adults who begin to heal such trauma must have had some positive experiences to balance the negative. The therapeutic task is to recover these experiences in the channel where they occurred and to use them to create the missing intrapsychic structures. A computer-based analogy might explain from a more technical angle how this process works.

If, for example, the missing intrapsychic structure is a "nurturing parent," we would insert into the computer a new disc that we name "NP." Then, using channel theory, we would scan all the files (people from the client's past) to look for experiences. An older sister with whom the client slept as a small child might carry a proprioceptive memory of nurturing. An incident with a warm-hearted kindergarten teacher might carry a visual memory of nurturing. The voice of the client's grandfather reading a story to him might carry an auditory memory. The movement the client's mother made when she blew him a kiss good night might carry the kinesthetic memory. Once the client becomes aware that all the parts of a nurturing parent are already stored on the "hard drive," he or she can imagine "copying" the nurturing memories onto the new disc. This allows the client to assemble the missing structure from his or her own experience.

Once copied and assembled, the new structure can be experienced piece by piece, as the client remembers and then reenacts these old memories with the other person or persons. This grounds the structure physically, emotionally, and psychically within the client. It also allows the client to access the self-nurturing structure by remembering the nurturing component stored in each channel. If a channel contains no nurturing memory, the therapist can help the client fill that gap through reparenting experiences.

Using such a precise psychological technology allows the therapist to identify exactly where the developmental gaps are. With such precision the therapy can be much quicker, much easier, and much more effective. This technology also relieves the therapist from some of the client's intense transference. The therapist will no longer feel the client demanding that the therapist become the "ideal parent" who can supply all the client missed in childhood.

This technology allows the therapist and the client to work more cooperatively without the intensity often involved in client/therapist transference. Clients find it highly empowering and therapists find it highly freeing.

Steps in Following the Client's Process

Step 1. Begin therapy by asking for a contract with the client. This may entail both a general therapy contract—regarding number of sessions, cost of sessions, and goals for the therapy—and specific goals for each session. This is important for two reasons. First, as much of the power as possible should be placed into the client's hands. Reclaiming personal power and making clear and healthy agreements are important parts of the therapy process. Second, having a contract enables you and the client to have some measure of outcome both for the therapy contract and for the session contract.

Step 2. Support the client's primary process by using reflective listening, by using clarifying statements, by supporting the feelings (expressed directly or indirectly), and by validating the experiences (often by naming—e. g., "That sounds like abuse"). We also use warm, empathic verbal tones, attentive body language, and direct eye contact. These basic counseling skills help develop rapport and a sense of safety for the client. This creates the security needed for the client to reveal any hidden or secondary material to the therapist. This step may take several sessions with a new client or only a few minutes with a client with whom a relationship already has been established.

During the first few minutes or hours of rapport building, the client will reveal through the conversation a number of doorway opportunities: movements in the hands or feet, lowering of the head, eyes looking up or to the side, or the client describing a strong relationship or group conflict. Many simultaneous signals can confuse the therapist. Patience is the best tool for the therapist, to wait for a signal that has a lot of energy in it or recurs several times. At this point it is safe to assume that this strong signal is a doorway through which to seek access to the unconscious material. Again, the therapist should watch closely for the client's feedback. If it is negative, the therapist should wait for another strong signal indicating another doorway to the unconscious.

At this point the spiritual component of developmental process work must be kept in the forefront. When the unconscious material (i.e., the wounded inner child) appears, the therapist absolutely must assume a position of protector. When some aspect of the inner child appears after a long period of hiding, the therapist can assume that some abuse or trauma is associated with its disappearance. When meeting this reemerging part, it is appropriate to assume an attitude of reverence, of sanctity such as that associated with an infant's birth. There can be an urge to want to take the client into the unconscious material too quickly in an attempt to get him or her through it rapidly. The therapist should guard against moving too fast for the client. Rather, the therapist should find the client's rhythm and then follow it.

Urges to move quickly can be ego-directed on the part of a therapist who sees himself or herself as director of the therapy. In developmental process work the client is the director of therapy and the therapist is following almost all the time. Interventions are appropriate only when the therapist sees a gap in the client's development that requires new information, options, or directions to help the client live more functionally. Even then, positive feedback from the client is necessary before continuing.

Step 3. Look for a signal that identifies the secondary process. When a strong signal appears in another channel, the therapist can offer feedback to the client such as, "I notice that you keep rubbing your left ring finger when you talk about your ex-husband" (kinesthetic channel), then notice how the client receives the feedback. If the client responds with, "I have an itch on this finger today, that's all," the therapist would not follow this signal. The client has given negative feedback. If the client says, "I was thinking about how sad I am not to be married to him any more," the therapist can assume that the finger-rubbing is a safe signal to follow.

Step 4. Amplify the signal at this point by asking the client to do it more or by forbidding the signal at all. For example, with the previous client, you might say, "Just close your eyes and let yourself feel that sadness" or, "What would happen right now if you stopped rubbing your finger?" Either statement could help the client change channels (from kinesthetic into proprioceptive).

Step 5. Facilitate the client in changing channels as many times as needed to help him or her access new information or release old feelings. Changing channels usually brings a release of information from the unconscious to the client. If the change involves moving into the proprioceptive channel, it can also lead to a release of old feelings.

Information theory can clarify the different body signals that indicate which channel is carrying the important information about the client's process. When the eyes look up, it usually signifies that a client is in the visual channel. When the eyes look sideways, it tends to indicate that the client is accessing information in the auditory channel. Lowering the head or looking down is usually a sign that the client is in the proprioceptive channel. Movement of any kind indicates that information is flowing in the kinesthetic channel. Direct eye contact between client and therapist and congruent or mirroring body postures can be signs that the client is in the relationship channel with the therapist or with a partner who also has come to therapy. Multiple relationship issues indicate that the client is in the family channel.

Step 6. Work at the edge if a client is not able to change channels. Here the client will learn valuable emotional, mental, physical, and spiritual lessons that indicate the real nature of the problem as well as the course of action needed to remedy it. Working at the edge is a sacred space and requires the most respectful and attentive attitudes. Letting the client work at the edge without pushing him or her over takes patience. Most of the therapy time in developmental process work involves working at the edge. Some techniques for working at the edge are:

- ❑ Have the client explore options about going over the edge to make sure he or she has adequate intrapsychic structures for going over the edge without creating a psychic break or psychotic episode. This is particularly important in working with clients who have a history of borderline behavior.
- ❑ Amplify or forbid the act of going over the edge.
- ❑ Have someone else (or you) go over the edge for the client by role playing.
- ❑ Have the client fantasize what going over the edge might be like.
- ❑ Help the client find a way around the edge.
- ❑ Have the client ask for the kind of support needed to go over the edge.

Step 7. Apply therapeutic interventions in developmental process work when unmet developmental needs emerge in the client's process. These needs may be related to incomplete bonding, separation, autonomy, or cooperation issues from the first five years of the client's life. The therapist must be able to recognize the nonverbal signals that indicate the wounded inner child may be emerging in the therapeutic process. Rocking movements, a childlike tone of voice, curling up, lying down, and crossed feet are some signals.

The therapist has to know the specific developmental needs and tasks of each of the four stages of development: co-dependence (bonding), counter-dependence (separation), independence (autonomy), and interdependence (cooperation). Each stage leaves characteristic adult behaviors that indicate exactly what must be completed. For example, an adult with incomplete bonding will have addictions to substances (food, drugs, alcohol), sex, and people. Adults with separation issues will have addictions to work or compulsive activity.

We have developed a series of skill-building exercises designed to help the client complete these developmental stages. These include:

- ❑ Identifying unmet developmental needs.
- ❑ Discovering ways to get these needs met as an adult.

❑ Learning to express feelings appropriately.
❑ Validating the client's experiences as real.
❑ Identifying early developmental traumas that create life patterns.
❑ Completing unfinished business with members of the client's family of origin.
❑ Resolving conflicts in win/win ways.
❑ Developing a vision of life beyond dysfunction.

We find that therapy proceeds more rapidly and effectively if the client is willing to work at several levels simultaneously. We recommend that they work alone by reading books, attending workshops and seminars, and following spiritual practices such as meditation and prayer. We also find that working cooperatively in committed relationships and in support groups or therapy groups accelerates the therapy process. This broad approach supports the clients in taking more and more charge of their healing process, which helps them reclaim their personal power. This quickly shifts the therapist's role into one of facilitator and consultant and helps prevent co-dependency between client and therapist.

Step 8. Help the client find ways to integrate the new information, insights, perceptions, and awarenesses gained during the session. The most effective way for a client to anchor the new learnings is to help him or her return to the channel that was occupied at the beginning of the session.

For example, if the client's presenting issue or problem emerged in the form of a dream or in a series of internal pictures, the occupied channel was visual. To integrate the session's learnings, the client would return to the visual channel. The therapist can help the client do this by asking, "How do you see yourself using what you learned in this session, especially with regard to the issue you began with?" The client then would have to create a new series of pictures related to the presenting issue that he or she would use to develop new behaviors that are congruent with the new learnings.

This aspect of developmental process work is important for several reasons. First, it provides a vision of the next steps in the client's process. Without a vision, we have found, it is almost impossible for people to develop new behaviors. Second, it asks the client to take information and experiences that may be of a transpersonal nature and translate them into practical, day-to-day behaviors or goals. Third, it returns the client and therapist to the goal stated at the beginning of the session. This aspect of integration provides a sense of completion and also sets up closure for the session. It further offers an opportunity for both the client and the therapist to evaluate the therapy experience and can provide productive feedback to the therapist.

CONCLUSION

The maps, charts, and tools needed to travel the mystical and mysterious roads of the transpersonal world have begun to reach over into the realms of the scientific. Technologies such as those used in developmental process work allow one to identify, track, retrace, and recover the flow of transpersonal energy as it moves through individuals, couples, and families. The technologies, however, are there to support the mystery of spirit and the mystical nature of humans. In such an environment, in which humans can begin to join with their own true transpersonal nature, co-creation becomes possible.

NOTES

1. Jacqui Schiff, *All My Children*, (New York: Pyramid Books, 1970).
2. Berne is perhaps best known for his book, *Games People Play* (New York: Grove Press, 1964.)
3. Jacqui Schiff, *The Cathexis Reader* (New York: Harper & Row, 1976).
4. Dorothy Babcock and Terry Keepers, *Raising Kids OK* (New York: Grove Press, 1976).
5. Mary Goulding and Robert Goulding, *The Power Is in the Patient: A TA Gestalt Approach to Psychotherapy* (San Francisco: TA Press, 1978).
6. Laurie Weiss and Jon Weiss, *Recovery from Co-Dependency* (Deerfield Beach, FL: Health Communications, Inc., 1989).
7. Two of these are: Jean Illsley Clarke, *Self-Esteem: A Family Affair* (Minneapolis: Winston Press, 1978); and J. Clarke and C. Dawson, *Growing Up Again: Parenting Ourselves, Parenting Our Children* (Minneapolis: Hazelden, 1989).
8. Pamela Levin, *Becoming the Way We Are* (Deerfield Beach, FL: Health Communications, Inc., 1988) and Pamela Levin, *Cycles of Power* (Deerfield Beach, FL: Health Communications, Inc., 1988).
9. Barry Weinhold and Janae Weinhold, *Breaking Free of the Co-Dependency Trap* (Walpole, NH: Stillpoint International, 1989) and *Counter-Dependency: The Flight From Intimacy* (unpublished manuscript, 1992).
10. Barry Weinhold, *Breaking Free of Addictive Family Relationships* (Walpole, NH: Stillpoint International, 1991).
11. Alice Miller, *Prisoners of Childhood* (New York: Basic Books, 1981) and *For Your Own Good* (New York: Farrar, Straus & Giroux, 1983).
12. Their works are represented by: Erik Erikson, *The Psychoanalytic Study of the Child* (New York: International University Press, 1946); Robert Havinghurst, *Developmental Tasks and Education* (New York: David McKay, 1972); and Jean Piaget, *The Child's Conception of the World* (New York: Humanities Press, 1951).

13. Margaret Mahler, *On Human Symbiosis and the Vicissitudes of Individuation* (New York: International University Press, 1968) and Margaret Mahler, *The Psychological Birth of the Human Infant* (New York: Basic Books, 1975).

14. Louise Kaplan, *Oneness and Separateness: From Infant to Individual* (New York: Simon & Schuster, 1978).

15. Barry Weinhold, *Breaking Family Patterns* (Colorado Springs, CO: Author, 1987).

16. A work published about that time is: Arnold Mindell, *Rivers Way* (Boston: Routledge & Kegan Paul, 1985).

17. Ken Wilber, *The Atman Project: A Transpersonal View of Human Development* (Wheaton, IL: Quest Books, 1980).

7

A Transpersonal Approach to Working with Feelings

Gay Hendricks

As I think of what the most important issues are in being effective as a therapist, so many of them relate to how to deal with *feelings*. Learning to deal with feelings—my own as well as clients'—was my first major step in becoming a transpersonal therapist.

A REVELATION

One autumn day in the early 1970s, I was taking a walk in the Colorado Rockies. I had been wrestling with a number of difficult issues in my life. I was at a juncture in my personal life—I had just moved from California to take a new job—and I felt at a crisis point professionally. I had done all the things I was supposed to do to become an expert in my field, and I still did not feel like I knew anything that resonated deeply in my own heart about what brings about change in ourselves. I had learned a thousand facts and techniques, but none that I had personally discovered to be true about life and transformation. I was looking for the central problem, the one thing that makes life difficult, the one thing we needed to do or not do to smooth out all of life. I had not found it.

On my walk I paused to consider these things, and I realized I had been looking outside myself for the answer to these questions. I had chased around the country seeking books, professors, and gurus, and it had not occurred to me to ask *myself* these questions. Until that moment, I had not been willing to trust my own experience.

So I asked myself what I most wanted to know for myself and my clients. How can I stop seemingly uninvited feelings from recycling through me over and over again? What can I do on a moment-to-moment basis that will enable me to let go of the past and greet each moment anew? How can I turn each moment, even the dreary ones, into an opportunity for spiritual and psychological growth? How do I get some quiet in my mind?

Within seconds the answers began sweeping through me in a way I had not expected. Instead of being logical thoughts, the answers came in the form of rushes of electric-like energy that seemed to leave the answers behind in their wake. This stunned me. I had not expected to receive answers in the form of an *experience*. The answers themselves were equally amazing to me because they spelled out an entirely different way of thinking. I would now characterize it as thinking with my body as well as my mind.

To the question of how to stop feelings from recycling through me, again and again, the answer, experienced in my body, was: Let yourself feel them completely. The feelings had recycled because I had not let myself experience them completely. Instead, my mind had tried to talk me out of them, to resist or ignore them. It was a revelation to me that a negative experience, such as anger or fear, could be dissolved by allowing myself to experience it. What had kept my negative feelings recycling was my own unwillingness to experience them!

This remarkable (to me) answer spilled over as part of the answers to the next question. I realized I had held onto the past because I was resisting what I was experiencing in the present. I would, for example, replay tapes in my mind of an argument from the day before because I was unwilling to get in touch with the anger I was feeling *right now* in the present moment.[1]

The glue that keeps us attached to the past, I saw, is our resistance. We resist what is going on right now in ourselves and others, and it binds us tightly to old ways of being. I realized that at the bottom of all our problems was our resistance to love. When we resist our love for ourselves and others, we create endless dramas in our lives. When we drop our resistance, we open up space to love ourselves for who we are. By doing this, we also can love others for who they are.

I saw also that the way to peace of mind is through total participation in the present moment. Until we become willing to experience the truth of the present, our minds must restlessly ruminate about the past and the future. At the moment we become willing to see, feel, and hear what is *right now,* the mind becomes quiet and attentive. Meditation and other practices can help, but our willingness to experience the present is what brings about the moment-to-moment peace we seek.

These realizations led me to a totally new way of living my life and to a different way of practicing therapy. The day after I had the experience of these things, I saw a client who was deeply afraid. Instead of trying to talk her out of her feelings, I invited her to surrender to them fully. She underwent a deep experience of shaking and sobbing, followed by a period of quiet. In this period of quiet, several solutions to her problems appeared spontaneously to her.

I had heard the proverb, "The answer lies within," a number of times, but I had not seen it unfold before my eyes so dramatically. Here was a person who had moved from a state of confusion to a state of clarity by dropping her resistance and experiencing what she was experiencing. I was moved. Now, though I have since seen the same process a thousand times, I continue to be moved by the ability of people to discover their inner wellspring of creativity by becoming willing to experience how they are feeling right now.

BASIC ISSUES OF FEELING

Several basic issues are involved in learning to work with feelings. Among these are learning how to greet our feelings, learning how to express feelings, and learning how to greet the world so that it does not trigger unwanted feelings in us.

Learning to Greet Feelings Effectively

Feelings are a natural human heritage. Our feelings themselves are not the problem, but our ways of greeting and handling those feelings often are.

There are only a handful of basic feelings, such as fear, anger, sadness, happiness. If we greet those feelings with acceptance and if we express them clearly, they do not cause problems for us. Only when our strategies for experiencing and expressing our feelings are faulty do we have difficulty with them. Clients do not consult therapists because they are scared or angry but, rather, because they do not know effective strategies for relating to fear and anger or for expressing them.

How, then, do we relate most effectively to feelings? Early in life many of us experience a split between emotion and reason so these two aspects of ourselves are in conflict rather than harmony. The mind, because it is the repository of our history of conditioning in regard to feelings, frequently tries to talk us out of the very feelings we most need to feel. To relate effectively with feelings, we must develop mental strategies that enable us to greet feelings with acceptance rather than resistance.

Rather than resisting our inner experience, we must greet it warmly. Rather than hating the way we feel about things, we must open up to those feelings, explore them, and ultimately come to love them.

Because of childhood conditioning, we frequently come to a confusing conclusion regarding whether our feelings are appropriate. In their zeal to have us be able to interact well with the outside world, parents want very much to get us to express only certain feelings, and those only in socially appropriate ways. Parents confuse expression with experience, so we think something is wrong with our feelings themselves. The message that parents fail to give is: Your feelings are okay, but how you express them has to be fine-tuned. In regard to certain feelings, such as anger and sexuality, strong, confusing messages can be implanted, and these can be uprooted later only with great effort.

For example, parents do not want their children to express their sexuality in ways that have negative consequences. In building a strong taboo to prevent this, parents frequently communicate that something is wrong with sexual feelings themselves. This sort of message puts children in an intolerable bind, because to make it in the social environment, they must feel bad about something that feels good (albeit strange and confusing) to their organisms.

Thus, those in the helping professions have to tell people that their feelings are perfectly all right but that they must learn effective ways of expressing those feelings so that positive consequences result for all.

Part of learning to relate to our feelings is to be willing to feel them deeply and completely. To use a metaphor from theatre: When we deny feelings entirely, life becomes a tragedy. We die to our own inner experiences; life loses meaning; we cannot respond to others; illness and misery ensue. When we do not feel our feelings completely and deeply, life becomes a soap opera, full of recycling melodrama in the form of incomplete communications, silent suffering, untold truth, tawdry conspiracies, and other staples of afternoon TV.

What are we afraid of? Why do we mute our feelings so we feel them only superficially? In the conditioning process we incorporate inaccurate beliefs about our feelings, based on what people have told us and what we have seen them doing. Some common, unfortunate beliefs I have picked up from clients over the years are:

- ❑ If I let myself feel my anger fully,
  I will explode.
- ❑ If I let myself feel as sad as I feel,
  I will never stop crying.
- ❑ If I let myself feel scared,
  I will not be a real man.
- ❑ If I let myself feel as sexual as I feel,
  I will become promiscuous and insatiable.
- ❑ If I let myself feel as depressed as I feel,
  I will die.

Sometimes these types of beliefs can be dissolved by awareness. Often, though, we must experiment personally with allowing ourselves to experience each feeling so we can know for certain that feeling it is all right. In the realm of our feelings, there is no substitute for certainty.

Once, during a period of solitude in a cabin in the mountains, I began to experience boredom. Rather than submitting to the boredom and looking for something new to do, I began to experience it. Soon it dissolved and I got to the deeper feeling beneath it, which was a fear of being alone.

This is truly one of the most primal of human feelings. I began to let myself experience it, feeling as if I were lowering myself into a maelstrom of unexplored stuff. For several hours I kept at it, feeling the sensations of the fear in my body, losing it, then getting back to it again.

Suddenly I burst through to the deepest experience of fear I had ever encountered. I began shaking and shuddering uncontrollably. I put on some music and began to dance, to have some outlet for the vibrations that were pouring through me. I kept dancing and experiencing the fear, with the intention of letting myself feel it to completion. Then, without warning, the fear dissolved and was replaced by a warm sense of quiet joy, which persisted for days afterward. Now, after many similar experiences, I know for certain in my body that all I need to do when I feel fear is to let myself experience it deeply.

One of the most life-enhancing messages we can communicate is that at the bottom of all our feelings, there is peace, bliss, and a deeper, more creative relationship with ourselves.

Learning to Express Feelings Effectively

In my own work with clients over the past decade, I have been most interested in finding what types of communication allow people to get off recycling patterns on which they are stuck. For instance, a couple may be stuck on a pattern in which they argue about who is right and who is wrong. The pattern may repeat itself in a thousand intricate variations on the same theme. Is there a certain style or mode of communication that will stop these patterns and get to the resolvable issues at the bottom?

To use another example, let's say a woman has a recycling pattern of conflicts with her mother. What depth or intensity of communication is required to get away from the old pattern and come to a clear, possibly satisfying resolution? Asking these kinds of questions has led me to some ideas about what brings about a type of communication that dissolves problems rather than perpetuates them.

Most of us are afraid of communicating clearly. The reasons are simple. When we told the truth early in life, we got in trouble. Also, we saw people around us couching the truth in crooked terms. Generally, people do not do this maliciously. These mistakes are simply symptoms of a vast area of human unconsciousness and lack of skill in communication. Although we get twelve years of grammar and math in school, how much time is spent teaching us how to get in touch with our feelings and communicate them clearly? Acknowledging that most of us are first graders in the art of communicating clearly about our inner experience, what are the essential lessons about communication that we should deliver to our clients?

Learning How to Greet the World Effectively

Problems clear up when one or more parties express a deeper level of feeling. I have witnessed the following scene many times: Two people are locked in an argument. They recycle the issues over and over. Nothing happens—no resolution, no agreement. Then one person risks a deeper level of communication. The person says, "I'm angry about. ..." or, "I'm scared that..." or, "I need this from you." Something shifts, and the situation moves toward resolution. It is as if the entire argument rested on a deep feeling that had not been expressed. When finally expressed, the situation could clear up.

Deep expressions of feeling almost always begin with *I*, as in *I* am scared, *I'm* angry, *I* need, *I* want, *I'm* hurt. And the clearest communications seem to require the fewest words. People unknowingly try to make statements of feeling more complicated than they actually are, but the greatest movement occurs when one or more of the people in the situation are willing to risk being simple and to speak clearly, economically, from the heart.

Frequently in counseling I ask clients to look me in the eye and tell me the deepest level of feelings they are experiencing. I may give them examples of what the deepest feelings are, or I may ask questions designed to get them to tell me what they are scared, angry, or sad about. Not until the words actually come out of their mouths, though, does the real movement take place.

There seems to be something liberating about speaking the deepest truth about ourselves in the simplest possible terms.

People need to learn to take responsibility for their feelings. Blaming others for our feelings and our problems is one of the greatest barriers to effective living. Most people who consult counselors, however, are not prepared yet to assume full responsibility for their own experience, so counselors must begin with people where they are. Only when people have had their point of view acknowledged do they become willing to move off it to a position of greater responsibility.

I find myself going through several stages in helping clients get to a place of responsibility in regard to an issue. Frequently I begin by listening carefully to the client's present point of view. For example, a man complains that his wife does not understand him. We explore how he feels when he is not understood, and we discuss recent examples of the problem.

When I feel he has had a chance to express his position clearly, I begin the second stage by introducing the idea that it is *his* issue, that he may want to consider that he is using the present situation with his wife to work out some past issue. I ask him if the present situation reminds him of anything from the past.

Then the third stage begins, in which we look at any past issues or any present resistance to taking full responsibility. Some people become upset at the idea that they are totally responsible for their lives, so we have to work on that before we can go further. In the case I am referring to, the man quickly saw that his present issue with his wife was actually a replay of an old issue with his mother. His mother was one of those people who needed to be right all the time, and his feeling of being wrong and misunderstood dominated his childhood. When he saw he was replaying that issue with his wife, he relaxed and was able to ask his wife clearly for what he wanted. As if by magic, she started listening to him in ways that he liked better.

Not all present problems refer back to an earlier problem, of course, and a person need not necessarily find the historical roots of a situation. All that is required, I have found, is that clients be *willing* to consider that the present issue is something of their own creation.

Something about the act of being willing to take responsibility frees up energy that moves the present situation to a new place.

Clarifying Intentions

In working with clients on their ability to communicate their feelings, a great deal of attention goes into helping them get their intentions clear. So often in communicating, our intention is something other than communicating clearly. We let a past issue interfere with our ability to communicate the information we want to say in the present.

For instance, a woman may want to tell her husband that she needs a few days to herself to meditate and be alone. Suppose her intention is muddled by a belief that she never can get what she wants from men. She has a whole history of experiences that confirms this point of view. If her intention is not clear, she may pick a time or circumstance that does not favor his listening to her. She may tell him when he's upset, or in a place that does not support a dialogue on the subject. She may tell him in a tone of voice that triggers an argument rather than an effortless resolution. She may tell him in a way that activates a fear that she is going to leave him.

Many times I have asked clients (and myself) questions like:

- ❏ What is your intention in communicating this information?
- ❏ Is it to make the other person wrong?
- ❏ Is it to prove some belief you have about the world? (e.g., "See, I told you I can't get what I want from men!").
- ❏ Can you present the information simply in a way that brings positive results?

Clarifying intention is in itself a valuable activity, because it gives clients an opportunity to examine their way of acting upon the world in getting their needs met. The results of communicating with clear intentions are often quickly manifested and readily apparent.

Fine-Tuning the Mind

If you have ever driven a car in which the front wheels are out of alignment, you know what an unpleasant vibration can result from such a small needed adjustment. In the same vein, the smoothness of our clients' trips down the road of life can be enhanced by relatively small adjustments in their style of thinking. Certain mental maladjustments can result in a rough trip. For this reason, I give considerable attention to helping clients look at their beliefs, to find out if their minds are serving them or enslaving them.

It is an odd paradox that the same mind that can write symphonies, cure polio, and build bridges can also make us miserable, sick, and commit suicide. The big brain of the human can use its awesome power for great leaps of liberation and imagination, and it can turn on itself and others with acts of oppression and destruction. At the center of the problem is the mind's tendency to generalize and form beliefs.

Some beliefs are formed under stress, when our minds are casting about in a storm for some mooring to hang on to. Others are the result of deliberate or unconscious inculcation at the hands of the people around us as we are developing. For example, a man could get the belief that "people can't be trusted" from being abandoned himself or from hearing that belief from his grandfather, who heard it from *his* grandfather. Regardless of the source of beliefs, they seem to generate unpleasant feelings far out of proportion to their size. One of the most satisfying aspects of working with beliefs in therapy is often seeing clients make enormous changes in how they feel by clearing up even one inaccurate belief.

Some beliefs I have seen clients uncover, which, when dissolved, significantly enhanced their feelings about themselves, are:

- ❑ I am unlovable.
- ❑ The world is an unsafe place.
- ❑ In a conflict I must always lose.
- ❑ Nobody can be trusted.
- ❑ If I go out into the world, I'll get in trouble.
- ❑ I shouldn't be too successful.
- ❑ I have to let boys be smarter and win.
- ❑ If I can't get ahead, at least I can get revenge.

These are all examples of inaccurate views of reality. Because beliefs are made only by mindstuff, they do not actually exist. They are illusions and can be changed quickly through awareness and accurate information.

Asking clients to examine their beliefs, to see whether they hold mental positions that generate unpleasant feelings, has a powerful effect. First, the process uncovers areas in which the mind is being used against itself. And second, the very act of examining beliefs empowers clients by letting them know that the same mind that has been strong enough to limit their freedom and cause them pain is also powerful enough to transform itself, liberating untold energy and creativity.

8

Transpersonal Uses
of Prayer

Barry Weinhold and Dawson Hayward

Except at those times of personal crisis, I had not thought much during my life about the healing powers of prayer. I remember riding in an ambulance, about eight years ago, on the way to Vail Medical Center with my critically injured wife Barbara lying unconscious in the back. She had been injured in a skiing accident and was in shock from the loss of blood. I could hear the beep-beep of the EKG machine that was monitoring her heart rate when all of a sudden the beep-beep turned into a constant, high-pitched whining sound, indicating that her heart had stopped beating. I prayed to God that she would not die and asked that she be saved. As I was doing this, I could hear the medics administering CPR to Barbara. Within what seemed like a lifetime, but what probably was only twenty seconds, her heart began to beat again.

Barbara lived for another twenty hours, and following surgery she died. During that last twenty hours I also prayed constantly for her recovery. At first I thought my prayers had no effect and I thought God had turned a deaf ear to my desperate cries. Now I look differently at my prayers of that time. I understand that my prayers may have been for the wrong reasons and that I cannot change what was in the divine order of things that are going to happen. I believe that Barbara's time to die had come, and in my fear and panic and with my limited self-oriented view, I could not see any divine order present; nor could most people in my situation. I now know that had Barbara lived, her brain probably would have been damaged because of the loss of oxygen when her heart stopped. She also would have lost a leg and would have had to be on a dialysis machine because of kidney damage. She would never be able to live life the way she had prior to the accident. I wanted to "play God" and have her live and if she had lived, God only knows what that would have been like for her and for me.

My only other memories of prayer were in church on Sundays as a young adult when the congregation was asked to recite the Lord's Prayer or to pray silently. I remember that I prayed silently for the health and welfare of others I knew and always prayed for wisdom and under-standing for myself. Perhaps that was because life seemed confusing to me when I was young (now I have given up trying to figure it all out). I certainly have received lots of help throughout my lifetime, and I do believe that many of my prayers have been answered.

RESEARCH FINDINGS ON THE EFFECT OF PRAYER

Since Barbara's death I hadn't thought much about prayer until several years ago, when I heard Larry Dossey speak about new research that confirmed the healing powers of prayer. Dossey spoke of a study done by cardiologist Randolph Byrd[1] which Byrd described as "a scientific evaluation of what God is doing." Byrd used a clinical double-blind study in which he randomly assigned 393 coronary-care patients at a San Francisco hospital to "prayer" or "no prayer" groups. Neither the patients nor the doctors or nurses knew which patients were being prayed for. He then contacted various established prayer groups in different parts of the country and asked them to pray for patients in the "prayer" groups. These groups were given the patient's name and some information about the patient's medical condition and were asked to pray each day. They received no instruction on how they should pray or for how long each day. Between five and seven people prayed for each patient.

The results surprised even Byrd. The prayed-for patients had:

—five times less need for antibiotics (three, compared to sixteen in the non-prayer group).

—three times fewer cases of pulmonary edema (six, compared to eighteen patients).

—no need for mechanical breathing assistance (eighteen of the non-prayer group required this procedure).

—fewer deaths.

From a transpersonal perspective, the most interesting finding was that the distance between the prayer group and the patients being prayed for did not matter. The prayer groups that were around the corner from the hospital had no more effect than the prayer groups that were thousands of miles away in Miami or New York. Therefore, distance was no factor.

This finding suggests that whatever "energy" is involved in prayer does not behave according to the laws thought to govern energy flow in science. This may suggest several interesting hypotheses. First, if people were praying to God to intercede in the medical treatment of these patients, the prayer could not be to some place called Heaven, where God lives, and then beamed back to earth to these patients in San Francisco. It suggests that what we call God may exist everywhere and may even reside inside as well as outside of us. It asks us to consider that we may have a "non-local" self that transcends the local or ego self. This is the very basis for transpersonal psychology, and certainly these findings support the presence of the non-local or transpersonal self. Although this finding runs counter to all the standard medical healing practices, it presents an interesting alternative. Much more research has to be conducted to verify these results before any changes will likely occur in standard medical practices.

I was so intrigued by Dr. Dossey's report of this research that I purchased his latest work, *Recovering the Soul,*[2] to see if he had found any more interesting research on prayer. Much to my surprise, he had uncovered a unique organization in Oregon that has been researching for more than a decade the effectiveness of prayer. Spindrift, as this organization calls itself, has been testing the assumption that all humans have within them divine qualities and possess a oneness with God.[3]

One of the more basic experiments was designed to answer the question: Does prayer work? People who were trained in prayer were asked to pray for one batch of germinating seeds and not another. Using rye seeds divided into two groups and placed in trays with a soil-like substance, they prayed for one side of the tray, divided only by a string down the middle, and did not pray for the other side. When the seeds sprouted and pushed through the surface, there were significantly more rye shoots on the prayed-for side of the tray than the other side. This simple test was replicated again and again with the same results each time.

Reasoning that prayer is often used on sick or unhealthy people, Spindrift deliberately stressed the rye seeds by adding salt water and keeping the rest of the experiment the same. Prayer had an even greater effect on the stressed seeds, and they actually grew faster than the control seeds, and better than the normal seeds that were prayed for in the other experiments.

Using other kinds of seeds and other stresses, such as temperature and humidity, Spindrift found that the effects of the prayer increased with the increased stress on the seeds. They also found that the amount of prayer had a positive effect. Twice as much prayer produced twice the effect. When the person who was praying was not informed of the effects of his or her prayers, the effectiveness of the prayer was drastically reduced. The researchers concluded that it was important for the person who was praying to know the effect of his or her prayers. They also found that people who were experienced at prayer were more effective than others who were not.

One of the most important findings of the Spindrift researchers was that nondirectional prayer worked better than directed prayer. This means that when a person prayed for a specific outcome, such as more rapid seed germination, he or she was less effective than when the person prayed for "what's best" for the seeds. It was better to let the seeds decide what was best for them.

This finding has strong implications for the use of specific directed prayer and visualizations on the treatment of cancer and other specific illnesses. The Spindrift researchers refer to nondirectional prayer as genuine spiritual healing and see directed prayer as "psychic" healing or "faith" healing. It is difficult not to want to use directed prayer if someone is ill or is dying, but we cannot know what the best outcome would be for the person and for the universe. If every person who is prayed for lives instead of dies, we might face massive over-population problems. The laws of the universe dictate that there is a time when physical death is natural and in harmony with these laws.

We cannot play God, but we can assist God, if we so desire, through prayer.

Dossey writes this about prayer: "When we go beyond the local definition of ourselves to an awareness of our non-local self, the situation changes. Aware of our infinitude in space and time, we are then free to contemplate the divine qualities that each of us contain. Within this awareness we are poised to understand the wisdom of the norm, even though it may mean the extinction of the physical body or the progression of incurable illness"[4] (p. 62). He suggests that we pray "Thy will be done" instead of "my will be done." This takes us out of our ego self and allows us to connect with our non-local or transpersonal self.

WHAT IS PRAYER?

Prayer seems to differ from other transpersonal tools such as meditation or psychic healing. First, prayer usually involves *asking*, whereas meditation usually involves *receiving*. Both are important, but they clearly require different kinds of energies. Prayer is part of what I call the "masculine form of surrender," which involves taking charge without guilt. In prayer you are asking for what you want, which means you have to be active and know clearly what you want. The research on non-directional prayer, however, cautions us not to ask specifically for some outcome. I usually pray that whatever happens will be in my highest good or the highest good of the person I am praying for.

Meditation is more passive energy, and I call this practice part of the "feminine form of surrender." The feminine form is a willingness to receive without resistance. In almost all forms of meditation, the object is to quiet the surface mind to allow the person to receive the deep levels of thought that emerge. This also relaxes the body, which puts up with the "chatter" of the surface mind and resists the effects of this chatter, perhaps because the body knows that the chatter can have harmful effects on its functioning. Prayer also has a "receiving without resistance" part because when you ask, you also have to be ready to receive what you ask for. If you think you don't deserve it, you may feel guilty and then resist receiving what you have asked for. To be effective, prayer does require both masculine and feminine aspects of surrender.

Prayer in this context can be seen as:

—personal two-way communication with God;
—personal communication with other beings within the spirit realm, such as angels, ascended masters, or spirit guides;
—communications with fellow humans or deceased ancestors or relatives;
—communications with other Earthly realms, such as the mineral, plant, or animal realms; and
—communications with higher spiritual aspects of ourselves.

MY PERSONAL USE OF PRAYER

Several years ago I met a young man (three years younger than me) who taught me much about the use of prayer. His name is Dawson Hayward, and he will tell some of his story later in this chapter. Dawson is a white man, but he has lived a Native American Indian lifestyle for the past fifteen years. A former corporate executive who dropped out of the corporate world, Dawson has been permitted to study with some of the most powerful Native American shamen alive today. Because of his work, he was "adopted" into a Lakota Sioux family.

I asked Dawson to teach me how to make better use of prayer in my life and how to integrate it into my daily spiritual practices. I have incorporated much of what he has taught me. For example, when I meditate, I ask for the loving presence of the angels to be with me and to bring me their gifts that serve my highest good. This prayer has greatly improved the quality of my meditations and has helped me use meditation as a "sowing" tool to bring me what I most need to know and understand.

In addition, Dawson offered to direct an "earth orientation" ceremony for me that spring. It was an excellent time for me, as the spring is always a time of rebirth and new awareness. The purpose of this earth orientation was to bring me back into proper relationship with the spiritual forces of the universe. I knew I was out of alignment in a number of areas of my life. I was suffering from hay fever, which had been worse than usual that spring. I also was considering some major life decisions about my career. Finally, I was out-of-relationship with my parents, who had not spoken to me for more than a year and a-half. They became angry with me when I told the truth in a book I had written about how I experienced growing up in a dysfunctional family.

The ceremony, scheduled to take place on the full moon, began with drumming, chanting, and singing. Dawson gave me my instructions according to the native traditions about the six major directions: east, west, north, south, below, and above. He helped me understand the psychological and spiritual issues each direction symbolizes. He also used a Tarot deck to help me determine the core denial I might have to face in each direction.

I was then directed to find a "power spot" in the nearby Garden of the Gods, where I was to spend one hour in prayer and one hour in meditation in each of the six directions. Following that twelve-hour ritual, I was instructed to sleep under the full moon and dream any healing dreams I might need. The whole ceremony took about twenty-four hours.

I found my spot in the Garden of the Gods, which was upon a ridge of red rocks where I could see in all four directions. I set up my own medicine wheel by positioning rocks in a large circle with a small rock circle in the middle.

Beginning in the south, the place of innocence and the inner child, I prayed for the first hour that my core issues and core denial that was "dullness" be revealed to me so I could heal them. I asked that these things be granted if it were in my highest good. In the second hour as I meditated, some new awareness came to me. I realized that adults often see the innocence of the child as dull. My child was wise beyond his years and was called dull by adults who didn't understand this wisdom. I realized that I adopted their definition of me when I was a child, and now I had to embrace my dullness and reclaim the wisdom of my child. I realized that I can ask "stupid" questions and let others see my dullness. I was never able to do this as a child. I was told not to ask stupid questions. At some later time, I think in college, I began to realize that I might be smart. I saw that by hiding my dullness, I was hiding a vital curious part of myself. I saw that my truth and my light will shine brighter when I fully embrace my dullness.

Also in the south, I worked with my mother. I entered my innocent child and asked that the part of her that knows the truth be present with me. I gave back to her all the things she gave me that were not mine. I gave back her fears of the earth and its creatures, her fear of water, her anger at men, her shame and guilt, and her insecurities that she projected on me. I sent all this back to her and through her to its source without harming anyone it passed through. I asked that all these things be transmuted into love and light.

By not contacting her, I also realized that I was buying into her definition of the relationship and being reactive. I decided to follow my heart and send her flowers for Mother's Day. I had no expectation of what this would bring, only that it was coming from my love and I hoped it would be received this way.

Then I moved to the west, where my core denial was "the achiever." The west is also the place of introspection and intuition. Again I prayed for help as to the true meaning of this issue in my life. For most of the two hours, I struggled with this concept until finally I saw that I deny my achievements in my personal and spiritual work. I saw that I have learned to play down and even deny my personal and spiritual growth when talking with others because I am afraid they might shame me or ridicule what I have done. I know this happened to me as a child, and I could see how I still react the way I did then.

I went deep inside myself and began to appreciate my achievements. I really felt the growth I had made over my lifetime, and I really felt and honored the personal clarity I had achieved.

Then I moved to the north, where the spiritual issue was worldly wisdom and the mind. My core denial was "the devil's play," which was the Tarot card I had drawn. I did not know what that meant. The Tarot card had a flute on it, so I decided to play my Native American wooden flute. The wind had shifted and was blowing in my face from the north, making it impossible for me to play the flute. I felt as if I were doing battle with the powers of the north as I attempted to play my flute. Finally I was able to play the flute, and the wind calmed down again.

As instructed by Dawson, I placed on the ground just outside the north entrance to my medicine wheel a triangle made of sticks and stones. I asked any demons or shadow figures present to show themselves in the triangle. I waited, and none appeared except the wind, which swirled around me. Then I used a gourd rattle to call them. Again nothing appeared, and I accepted that I couldn't make these forces appear before they were ready to show their face. I prayed that they would appear when they were ready.

I began to realize, however, that I now had sat for six hours in the midst of wind-blown pollen and had no symptoms of hay fever. I had to urinate about this time, and I stepped outside of my circle. Immediately I started to sneeze, and I realized that I was being protected from pollen only as long as I stayed inside the circle. I realized that I needed to pray for this same protection all the time.

158

I was fasting and drinking only water and tea, so I took a long drink before moving to the east. The east is the place of illumination and the place of spirit where mature male wisdom resides. My core denial in the east was "the feeler." The issue that came up for me was taking charge of my spiritual growth without guilt (masculine surrender). I saw how I still felt guilty when I took time for myself. So much of my life I was programmed to take care of others, and now I wanted to change that. I saw that my spiritual growth is often squeezed in after I have taken care of others. I vowed to schedule this into my day to prevent me from slipping back.

While sitting facing the east, I witnessed the moon rise. It was a full moon on a perfectly clear evening. I felt overwhelming love for the earth. It was truly wonderful to be alive and enjoy the daily rhythm of the earth's rotation with each hour bringing changes and new awarenesses.

It was almost dark when I turned to the below, where the key issue was my relationship with the earth as a living being. The core denial for me was "the emperor." I prayed to Gaia and asked her help in getting through my allergies. These allergies have interfered greatly with my relationship with the earth. I asked her to become my protector so I could bond more fully to her. I believed that the messages from my mother and others in my family about the "earth is a scary place" had prevented me from bonding more fully with mother earth.

By the time I got to the above, it was completely dark and I could see the stars shining through the moon glow. The core denial was "the priestess," and the key issue was to honor my teachers, guides, saints, and avatars, as well as the sun, the moon, and the stars. It was easy to honor the moon and the stars as they lit up my campsite. About one o'clock in the morning, I heard an owl screech, and that woke me up as I had started to drift off. I didn't get much more from this position except a full experience of being alive and an appreciation for the support I had received and was continuing to receive. I prayed a prayer of thanks to all who had assisted me in my life.

The final instruction was to build a fire just before dawn, tend it until the sun came up, and allow the fire and the sun to be united again. As I did this, I remembered all the wonderful things I had learned in the past twenty-two hours. I felt full of new energy and realized I had received much to nourish me in the months ahead. I vowed that I would do this ceremony again when I felt the need for it.

I returned to my home to find Dawson drumming and chanting. I helped him close the ceremony and had some breakfast. He mentioned that at some point in the evening, the tone of the drum changed. According to his system, it had moved from denial to transformation, which is certainly what I experienced.

After breakfast I ordered flowers sent to my mother and began to gear back into my daily routine. Concentrating on "doing things" was difficult so I decided to just take it easy and allow time for the experience to settle into my body.

The next morning I was still feeling open and somewhat vulnerable when I received a call from my mother. She was crying as she thanked me for the flowers. She asked me to "come home" and expressed a desire to resolve the differences that had separated us. I too cried as I experienced the love between us in that moment.

I also experienced an end to my allergies. From that day until the present, I have not had the allergic reactions I used to have in the spring and in the fall.

DAWSON'S STORY

The following is Dawson's account of how he integrates prayer into his life. It illustrates some of the barriers to overcome before prayer can be used effectively.

"I was first encouraged to take up the daily practice of prayer by a Native American elder. I experienced immediate resistance to the idea. After attempting the practice, my ineptitude, my discomfort, and my inarticulateness were of such a magnitude as to discourage me from praying altogether, and I returned to my familiar and practiced disciplines of contemplation and meditation.

"However, I chose to persist in my prayer practice. I had been deeply touched by the prayers of my mentor. The ease with which he communicated with the Creator, the "Sacred Space" that was generated through that communication, and the resulting sense of connectedness with God, Spirit, Earth, and all other beings were compelling reasons to follow his instructions.

"As my mentor perceived, and I have come to understand, the practice and art of prayer is a developable skill, which, like any other learning, requires commitment, discipline, and persistence. I committed myself to daily practice and began by praying for guidance and assistance that I might develop my ability to commune and communicate in ways that Grandfather had so clearly demonstrated to me. My request for guidance was received, and my first task was to examine my resistance to the process. This resistance persisted even in the face of my initial success in receiving clear direction and response to my prayers for guidance. I clearly had my work cut out for me.

"I began a personal inventory of all my experiences that related to prayer in any way. This included who was praying, what was being prayed about, to whom the prayer was addressed, the results, when and where the prayer was deemed appropriate, and my responses and feelings at the time. Some of the attitudes and beliefs and conclusions drawn as a result of my experience were: Only certain individuals are allowed to pray; prayer is restricted to Sundays and certain holidays except in the case of an emergency and/or at times of dire need; it is selfish to pray for one's self; you can give thanks for certain things at certain times, like turkey dinner and pumpkin pie when certain family members are present. But it isn't necessary at other times when those people aren't around.

"Sunday School provided some opportunities to pray, but I never was clear how to do it. I also remembered the feeling that God and Jesus were probably too busy to pay attention to me anyway, and I didn't deserve it besides. I tried out a few prayers and, as far as I could tell, they didn't work. I concluded that prayer must have been invented for someone else, and I gave up. From that point I remember sitting quietly wondering when it would be okay for me to open my eyes or what I was going to do when I got out of Sunday School. No wonder I had resistance.

"As I restructured or released my old prejudices and limitations, I began to envision new realms of possibility. My daily practice became easier. The resistance ceased, changing into motivation.

"The practice of prayer has added immeasurably to the quality of my experience of myself as a human being and the quality of my life. When I use prayer every day, my life is smoother and I make better choices. I feel more self-assured, calmer, and can stay centered most of the day. From a centered place I know better who I really am, what my boundaries are, and how to make choices that support my happiness, growth, and well-being. Prayer also helps me create a new reality for myself, a Higher Self from which to know and transform my old patterns of behavior."

HOW TO PRAY (DAWSON'S IDEAS)

Skeptics generally have a difficult time with prayer. It is not God's or anyone else's responsibility to prove to us that prayer works. We are responsible to demonstrate that for ourselves. Belief in it is not essential, but the suspension of nonbelief is extremely helpful to establish a ground for practical experimentation. For all the doubt, skepticism, disbelief, and even cynicism that we might hold consciously, a part of ourselves knows and is already in communication with God. The law is: Ask and you shall receive. There is no intercession or assistance without request. Rescuing is not permitted. The question of co-dependency does not arise: We will not receive anything unless we are willing to ask for it directly.

There is an enormous amount of assistance and energy available to teach each and every one of us: Ask and you will receive. Ample scriptural, historical, and testimonial evidence supports the efficacy of prayer. There is no substitute for personal experience that comes with practice. The use of prayer in times of extreme need and emergency is well documented.

The integration of prayer into our daily lives as an ongoing process of connecting and communicating with God, our family of spirit, and ourselves will have a profound effect on the entire ground of our being. The dimension of prayer is of a different order of reality than that to which we are habituated. Practice increases the ease with which we can access the different realm, our ability to be conversant in it, and our capacity to receive the benefits of our practice without resistance.

THE ELEMENTS OF PRAYER

Let us look at the elements of prayer and how we can incorporate them into our ongoing experience.

Setting

One of the wonderful things about prayer is that it can be used anytime, anywhere, and under practically any circumstances when initiating your practice. It is often helpful to create a special place that facilitates it. Prayer is an effective means of generating sacred space in a room or a house. You also may create sacred space in your room to attune your mind and being to the act itself. Whatever produces a feeling and sense of the sacred and the presence of Spirit is appropriate. Religious articles, pictures of the saints and sages, incense, smudge, music, chanting, drum and gourd, soft lighting, breathing deeply, relaxing, being in nature, watching a sunset, sitting by a river, climbing a mountain, going to your favorite "power spot"—these are a few of many possibilities. Prayer is a developable skill. Start by selecting a setting that supports and encourages your practice. Once you have mastered the basic skills, these externals will be less significant, although always enjoyable and enriching to your experience.

Creating Your Prayer

Choose the subjects of your prayers. Clarity is important. Be specific. Vague prayers generate vague outcomes. Remember that you are seeking assistance or establishing communication on a high level of being. Honor yourself and who you are praying to with clarity, directness and sincerity. The subject of your prayer could include a request for a specific thing, occurrence, ability, outcome; assistance to facilitate a specific result; thanksgiving and expressions of appreciation; guidance and instruction; clarity and increased knowingness in a specific area; increased awareness; facilitation of process; generating options; narrowing options; discernment and discrimination. You should add disclaimers such as "if this prayer is in my highest good" or "I ask for this or something better that is in my highest good." These disclaimers allow you to apply the information about the power of nondirectional prayer.

Clarifying Your Intentions

Again, clarity is important. An important guideline for developing clarity of intention is to consider the effect over time if your prayer were to be answered. Is it what you really want? Is it in your highest good? Will it benefit yourself and all other beings? Do you fully understand the implications of your request and the projected results? You also may pray for assistance to generate answers to these questions. This step is extremely important, especially if you have evolved to the point of taking responsibility for your actions or hold beliefs around the concept of karma. Remember the law: Ask and you will receive. Prayer helps you develop your ability to ask clearly for what you want. Be sure that what you are asking for is what you want and you are aware of any potential consequences related to getting what you want. It is far easier to adjust things before they are a manifest reality.

Languaging

Because languaging is the medium of prayer, attention to the details of your languaging is extremely important. Consider writing out your prayers and examining them for clarity, accuracy, intention, consistency, integrity, specificity, appropriateness, and alignment. As you develop your facility with the language and clarity of thought in articulating your prayer, you probably will choose to discontinue the writing. Additional benefits of this activity are to deepen your understanding of your thought processes that improve your communication skills and to increase your ability to express yourself more fully and accurately. You may ask some questions about your languaging as you did about your intention: Is it what you really want? Is it in your highest good? Will it benefit yourself and all other beings? Do you fully understand the implications of your request and the projected results? You may pray for assistance to answer these questions.

To Whom?

Most prayer is addressed to God, Creator, Great Spirit, etcetera, depending upon the individual's beliefs and the cultural/social setting in which the prayer is made. The choice is always appropriate. In my practice of prayer, all prayer is opened in that way, and all further or additional communications or requests are made through and with the guidance and supervision of the God channel. As indicated in the definition of prayer here, a number of options are available. Some of those possibilities are:

- ❑ Communication with other beings in the realm of spirit such as guides, teachers, avatars, enlightened beings, angels.
- ❑ Spirit and soul communication with our fellow humans, other sentient life forms, ancestors, and relatives.
- ❑ Communication through the dimension of spirit with other earthly realms—the mineral realm, the plant realm, the animal realm—and the spirits associated with those realms.
- ❑ Communicating with the "higher" spiritual/soul aspects of oneself. This is a way of developing spiritual self-reliance, competency, inner strength, personal responsibility, and self-trust.

I highly recommend that you enter into any or all of these dimensions with and through the assistance, guidance, and protection of God. This is important for your personal well-being on all levels and assures that your prayers and communications are in alignment with your intention and for your "highest good." Ask God to assist you in establishing these criteria as the basis of your prayer practice.

Delivery

When you have determined to whom the prayer is going to be delivered, you are ready to take the next step. Delivery of prayer is practiced in many modes in the various cultures throughout the world. If you are familiar, comfortable with, and currently practicing a certain modality, by all means continue. The most widely practiced delivery is through silent or vocal articulation of the prayer. Silent delivery is most appropriate in many situations. Whenever possible, I prefer to speak my prayers aloud. This allows me to hear them with my outer as well as inner ear and provides the opportunity for editing and additions. Also, for me, speaking my prayers aloud and producing the physical vibrations of speech give a dimension of reality and an affirmation of my commitment to that for which I am praying. To put my prayers out to the universe in that way feels good. It is also good practice for those times when you may be called upon to share your thoughts and prayers with others. I am a singer, and expressing my prayers through song is one of my favorite and most fulfilling means of delivery. Probably the most important thing is this: Whatever the means of delivery of your prayers, let them come from your heart and soul filled with love and feeling.

Receiving

For me, asking was difficult enough, and receiving was even harder. Preparing for this step provides the opportunity to examine your attitudes, willingness, and ability to receive. Much of this has to do with your feelings of deservingness, and self-worth. If these are issues in your life, pray for assistance in finding and releasing the denials and the conditioning associated with them. An enormous amount of energy and assistance are available to each and every one of us all the time.

Ask and you will receive. Develop your ability to ask through the medium of prayer and increase your capacity to receive.

Prayer is one of our greatest gifts. My prayer is that you will use this information to develop and deepen your understanding of prayer and its effective and beneficial use in your life. May God guide and bless you on your journey.

NOTES

1. Randolph C. Byrd, "Positive Therapeutic Effects of Intercessory Prayer in a Coronary Care Unit Population," *Southens Medical Journal* 81:7 (July 1988), pp. 825–829.
2. Larry Dossey, *Recovering the Soul* (New York: Bantam Books, 1989).
3. Write Spindrift at 2407 Lafolla Dr. NW, Salem, OR 97304.
4. *Recovering the Soul*, p. 62.

9

Meditation in the Art of Therapy

Gay Hendricks

Meditation is an important tool in the practice of therapy. What meditation is, why it works, and how it can be useful in therapy are the major subjects of discussion in this chapter.

WHAT IS MEDITATION?

Meditation refers to an array of techniques, predominantly mental, designed to help practitioners dissolve mental, physical, and emotional blocks to unity within themselves, with others, and with the universe. The techniques often consist of mental practices that tend to obstruct, turn down the volume on, or render transparent the workings of the conscious mind, to facilitate the growth of other faculties such as intuition, as well as transpersonal values and experiences such as being, bliss, oneness, compassion, and self-realization.

I first meditated in 1969. In my first meditation I had such a powerful experience that I did not do it again until 1973. Using a meditation practice that I got from a yoga book, I sat down and began mentally repeating the mantra. Within seconds my mind, usually teeming with thoughts, fell utterly silent, as if I were seeing myself clearly for the first time without the intervening fog of thoughts. I felt as if I had removed for a moment a raccoon coat I had been wearing all my life.

Until that moment, everything I had experienced had been filtered through my thoughts. For the moment, the filter was removed and I saw myself, and the world, as I was. Scared by this insight, I stopped meditating immediately. Looking back on the incident, I do not feel as if I were ready to see things the way they actually were.

In 1973 I was properly instructed by a qualified teacher in how to meditate. Since then I have meditated twice daily, for about twenty minutes each session until 1979, when I increased the time to about forty-five minutes per session. The changes meditation has brought about in my life and work have been profound. I would like to describe some of them.

First, how does meditation feel? I begin by sitting in a quiet place, either in a chair or on a cushion on the floor. I use a mantra meditation, so after a minute or so of sitting quietly with my eyes closed, I begin to gently think the mantra. Thoughts come and go. When I find myself lost in thought, I gently return to the mantra. As the meditation deepens, I usually encounter periods of no thought, when all is quiet save the rhythm of the mantra. Then, often, the mantra fades away, leaving behind a quiet, light space of silence. During meditation the typical experience is one of silence. Occasionally, waves of bliss pass through my body and mind, and sometimes solutions to problems pop into my mind. The experience during meditation is generally unspectacular. The results of meditation in my life *are* spectacular.

First, I feel vastly more relaxed in all areas of my life. Twenty years ago one of my friends described me as "a very uptight guy." I chain-smoked two to three packs of cigarettes a day, bit my nails to the quick, and was fifty pounds overweight. I also had an incipient case of ulcers. All those problems cleared up during these years of regular meditation.

A direct benefit of meditation in my counseling work has been that I can more easily pay attention, with a quiet mind, to my own feelings. By learning to listen to my own inner experience, I have also learned to listen to deeper levels of what my clients are saying.

I have also noticed a marked upsurge in intuition and telepathic communication. I believe that these processes occur naturally in us all the time but that other thought processes are so noisy they obscure the subtler levels of thought. Of course, the challenge in identifying intuition and psychic processes is learning how to discriminate them from thoughts generated by fear. For example, on your way to the airport you may have a thought of the airplane crashing. Most often, thoughts such as this are just surface noise from underlying fear.

In my experience, I have found two ways to discriminate intuitions from ordinary thought. An example will illustrate. As I was meditating one morning, a picture of a person I was to see later in the day appeared in my mind. I had not seen him in fifteen years. In my mind I heard him say, "My mother died of cancer about a year ago." The thought had a certain quality to it that somehow made it different from other thoughts. Later, when I saw my client, I asked him how his family was. Fine, he said, except that "my mother died of cancer about a year ago."

One way, then, I have learned to tell intuition from ordinary thinking is to notice different qualities that intuitive thoughts have. A second way is to notice whether any fear is present at the time of the thought. This observation may help you in determining whether the thought is fear-based. Above all, of course, is the need to check out empirically whether the thought has any relation to reality.

SOME VARIETIES OF MEDITATION

We have information, either through writings or through the transmission of students who have studied under qualified teachers, on a substantial number of meditation techniques. Just as many, if not more, techniques probably exist on which we have no information, largely because they are intended for use only within a certain cultural context or because they are intended to be used with the time, place, and nature of the student in mind. An extended listing of meditation practices is beyond the scope of this chapter, but I would like to describe a few techniques in sufficient detail to acquaint clinicians with the use of meditation in therapy. Readers who wish to explore classifications of techniques more thoroughly should see some of the excellent books on this subject.[1]

The three forms of meditation that I describe here are the ones with which I have most experience in therapy: Vipassana meditation from the Theravadan Buddhist tradition, bare attention, and transcendental meditation.

Vipassana (Insight) Meditation

The Vipassana meditation, from the Theravadan (Southern) Buddhist tradition, is practiced primarily in Burma, Sri Lanka, Thailand, and parts of India. In recent years Vipassana meditation has expanded in Europe, the United Kingdom, and the United States.

Joseph Goldstein, a Westerner who has studied in the East for many years, began offering workshops and retreats some years ago in which he taught the fundamentals of the Vipassana meditation. His book, *The Experience of Insight,* contains meditation instructions woven among insights, stories, and observations about the nature of the mind and spiritual unfoldment. Here are several quotes from that book:

> It is important to make thoughts the object of mindfulness. If we remain unaware of thoughts as they arise, it is difficult to develop insight into their impersonal nature and into our own deep-rooted and subtle identification with the thought process.

> It is helpful to make a mental note of "thinking, thinking" every time a thought arises...The thought is the thinker. There is no one behind it. The thought is thinking itself. It comes uninvited...Some people may find it helpful to label the thinking process in a more precise way, to note different kinds of thoughts, whether "planning" or "imagining" or "remembering."

> Awareness of the breath can be practiced in one or two ways. When you breathe in, the abdomen naturally rises or extends, and when you breathe out, it falls. Keep your attention on the movement of the abdomen, not imagining, not visualizing anything, just experiencing the sensation of the movement...

> The alternative is to be aware of the breath as it goes in and out of the nostrils, keeping the attention around the tip of the nose or the upper lip...

> Simply be aware of the in and out breath as it passes the nostrils. It is helpful in the beginning of the practice to make mental notes either of "rising, falling" or "in, out." This aids in keeping the mind on the object.[2]

The essence of the Vipassana practice, as illustrated in the preceding quotes, is the observation and mental labeling of all the events that enter the practitioner's field of consciousness. The observation and labeling eventually give way to a state of bare attention, a pure awareness of everything that is not contaminated with even the most innocent of concepts (such as labeling). The labeling, then, is seen as a helpful process designed to point the practitioner toward the purer process of bare attention.

Bare Attention

Bare attention refers to a quality of mind that is nonevaluative, noncomparative—simple observation of things as they are. This quality of mind, in both client and therapist, can be highly useful in therapy. Many teachers have spoken of the value of bare attention. Again, to quote from Joseph Goldstein:

> This quality of bare attention is well expressed by a famous Japanese haiku:
>
> > The old pond.
> > A frog jumps in.
> > Plop!
>
> No dramatic description of the sunset and the peaceful evening sky over the pond and how beautiful it was. Just a crystal clear perception of what it was that happened...Bare attention; learning to see and observe, with simplicity and directness. Nothing extraneous. It is a powerfully penetrating state of mind.

The Buddhist Walpola Rahula described a similar process.

> Another very important, practical and useful form of meditation (mental development) is to be aware and mindful of whatever you do, physically or verbally, during the daily routine of work in your life, private, public or professional. Whether you walk, stand, sit, lie down or sleep, whether you stretch or bend your limbs, whether you look around, whether you put on your clothes, whether you talk or keep silent, whether you eat or drink—even whether you answer the calls of nature—in these and other activities you should be fully aware of the act performed at the moment.[3]

Krishnamurti, the Indian spiritual teacher who has been talking and writing on meditation and related subjects for the past seventy years, described the meditative state of mind as one of choiceless awareness." By this phrase, he seems to mean a constant state of nonevaluative attentiveness to all life processes. In the same vein, a Zen master was once asked to divulge the key to enlightenment. "Attention" was his answer. When asked to say more about this cryptic reply, he said, "Attention, attention, attention." Yes, but what does attention mean? asked the bewildered disciple. "Attention," replied the master, "means attention."

In the context of therapy, bare attention can be applied during the therapy session as a formal technique, or informally in the client's daily life. Bare attention may be applied to behavior, thoughts, feelings, sensation, intentions, perceptions, beliefs, opinions, or any other experience. Bare attention is simply the practice of using the natural observational powers of the mind.

Transcendental Meditation

Transcendental meditation, commonly known as TM, is a technique from the Indian tradition going back several thousand years. It was brought to the West by Maharishi Mahesh Yogi, who credits his teacher and long succession of spiritual masters with preserving the technique in a pure form for dozens of generations. TM is probably the most widely practiced meditation technique in the West and has been the subject of several books.

After studying the effects of TM through observing its effects on clients, personally experiencing it, and reading the research literature that has grown up around it, I began several years ago to recommend its practice to clients who seemed interested in it.

TM is a simple technique that requires no special postures, diets, clothing, or lifestyle. The technique is performed twice daily, usually before breakfast and dinner, for twenty minutes each time. After initial instruction, which takes place over four days, participation in activities sponsored by the local TM center is purely voluntary. One such activity, which in my opinion is easily worth the instruction fee, is called "checking." This consists of a procedure to verify the correct practice of TM and allows the practitioner to get answers to questions or advice for dealing with any difficulties that emerge from practice of the technique.

Mechanics of this technique, which must be learned from a teacher, include repetition of a mellifluous syllable(s) in a relaxed, attentive manner, a few technical instructions on how the mantra is to be used, and little else. The practitioner does not have to adopt any particular attitudes or beliefs or do anything special aside from the twice-daily period of meditation.

WAYS OF USING MEDITATION IN THERAPY

My method of using the types of meditation just discussed varies from client to client, but it usually consists of one of three procedures. I teach many clients the Vipassana technique and bare attention over several sessions as part of the counseling. Frequently my procedure is to leave ten to fifteen minutes open at the end of several sessions to teach the basics of the techniques.

Another procedure, which I incorporated more recently, is to put the instructions for the techniques on cassette tape recordings so the client can listen to an instruction and practice a phase of the technique either before or after the therapy session. For the Vipassana technique and bare attention, the instructions are recorded on eight to ten separate cassettes, to be listened to on as many separate occasions. For example, the client may learn to apply bare attention to thoughts on one occasion, then return the following week to learn and practice the observation of sensations. With TM, clients make their own arrangements to learn the technique.

After initial instructions, clients practice the techniques in a variety of ways. In my work, clients are asked to practice at home once or twice daily for ten or fifteen minutes, or to follow the instructions for TM, which specify that the practice should be done twice daily for twenty minutes. Sometimes I ask clients to meditate with me for a while, particularly at the beginning and end of sessions.

EFFECTS OF MEDITATION

Various explanations for the effects of meditation have been set forth. The discussion begins with those that are most consonant with prevailing scientific views, then ventures afield into explanations that rest on spiritual or metaphysical underpinnings.

Meditation as a Relaxant

The current interest in meditation can be traced to publication of a condensed version of R. K. Wallace's doctoral dissertation in *Scientific American,* February 1972, which presented data attributing changes in a number of dependent measures to transcendental meditation. The variables studied were oxygen consumption and blood lactate concentrate, which are related to states of deep relaxation. Wallace and his coauthor, Herbert Benson, called the meditative state "wakeful, hypometabolic," because meditation seemed to bring about a condition of the organism that was as relaxed as, and sometimes more relaxed than, sleep but that let the meditator remain in a wakeful state. Following the pioneering work by Wallace and Benson, many other studies confirmed and extended these initial findings.

Meditation might be expected to bring about a decrease in physiological arousal for several reasons. One theory, proposed by Dr. Bernard Glueck of the Institute of Living in Hartford, Connecticut, is that the mentally repeated sound (mantra) used in some forms of meditation may set up resonant derivatives that enter the limbic system of the brain at the proper frequency to dampen limbic hyperarousal. In addition, one body in the limbic system, the hypothalamus, is known to regulate activities of the hormone system and the autonomic nervous system.

Meditation may bring about a state of quiescence in the hymothalamus, fostering a more efficient tone of the parasympathetic branch of the autonomic nervous system.[4] Further, quiescence of the hormonal system could be expected to bring about lessened alarm reactions, thus increasing the meditator's ability to tolerate stress. The authors ventured further afield to suggest that meditation may bring about a hypersynchrony of brain waves between the cortex and the lower, visceral brain centers such as the limbic and the brain stem, thereby healing the age-old split between emotion and reason.

This viewpoint is close to my own theory of meditation's effects. In my view, we experience a conflict between essence—that which we truly are—and the functioning of the ego, including emotion and reason. Essence is that part of us that is free from conditioning, and ego is that part of us that has been adopted for survival and safety reasons. The conflict between ego and essence may keep us in a state of autonomic hyperarousal.

Because many forms of meditation offer the opportunity to alternate between being aware of essence and being lost in ego, the practice may bring the conflict to the level of awareness, enabling the meditator to transcend the conflict. In addition, experiencing essence, which is usually overshadowed by ego, may give the individual a basic sense of self that can heal the split, allowing the meditator to lessen and dissolve the tension that theretofore had accompanied the split.

Meditation as Discrimination Training

Most forms of meditation involve an alternation between a state of attentiveness and being identified with the contents of consciousness. Anyone who has meditated for even fifteen minutes recognizes the constant alternation between the object of meditation (e.g., breath, or a mantra) and being "lost in thought."

Most of the esoteric disciplines consider thought to be one of the major barriers to the harmonious and holistic development of consciousness. These disciplines teach that attachment to and identification with thought prevents us from attaining an ego-free state of nonattachment. The esoteric disciplines have developed many meditative practices designed to correct this situation by detaching the practitioner from thought. Patanjali, for example, wrote 1,500 years ago that "yoga is the control of thought waves in the mind." Don Juan, the Yacqui Indian sorcerer, instructed Carlos Castenada to "turn off the internal dialogue," and the Zen discipline features not only meditative practices but also *koans*, or questions with no logical solution, to disrupt the flow of ordinary thought.

The mechanics of most meditation techniques involve a process of moving back and forth between being "lost in thought" and a state of attentiveness. To illustrate, transcendental meditation makes use of a mentally repeated Sanskrit word or phrase (a mantra). The key instruction in TM is to return to the mantra whenever the practitioner notices himself or herself thinking. Thus, the meditator is continually alternating between periods of thought and repetitions of the mantra. Diagrammed, a sequence of meditation might be experienced as shown in Figure 9.1.

Similarly, one of the instructions in the Zen discipline is to count breaths from one to ten, starting over when the meditator loses attention.

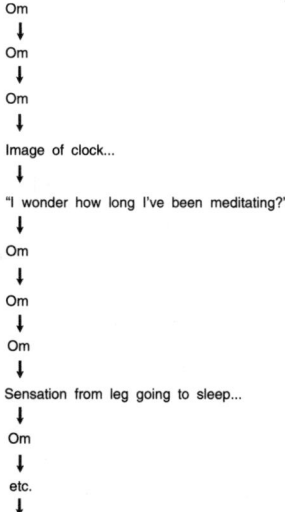

Figure 9.1
A MEDITATION SEQUENCE

The point is that both TM and Zen, along with other techniques, use a process of alternation between thought and attentiveness.

In physiological psychology and learning theory, the phrase *discrimination training* is used to describe the process by which an organism acquires the ability to differentiate between and among stimuli. In one hour's meditation, a practitioner may have hundreds of experiences of being identified with thought, then returning to a more attentive state. This process can be regarded as discrimination training, because the meditator is learning to discriminate thought from other stimuli.[5]

Being skilled at discriminating thought from other events puts the meditator in a particularly strong position of mental health. Thoughts are prominent components of most mental health problems such as depression, anxiety, and schizophrenia. In fact, one could argue that, because nearly everyone has a certain number of neurotic thoughts, mental health is dependent upon the ability to recognize that they are "just thoughts." The depressed person is so identified with thoughts (e.g., "I'm no good") that he or she takes them for fact rather than realizing that they are just products of his mind. Clinically, I have found that clients who are given meditation experiences to learn to discriminate thought characteristically regard the outcome as a revelation. As one client said:

> I would carry on long conversations in my head. I would fantasize future possibilities and base my actions on them. After Dr. _____
> trained me to see my thoughts, I felt a tremendous sense of liberation. My God, there was nothing to worry about—they were just thoughts.

Once this individual could observe her thoughts and was no longer identified with them, she was free to choose whether to base her behavior on them.

In addition, most people agree that being in the here and now is a positive goal from both a psychological and a spiritual perspective. Thought is what usually takes us out of the here and now, so discrimination training through meditation is helpful when we are thinking. This clarity increases because it clarifies the freedom of choice of whether to remain in the thinking state or to return attention to the here and now.

One of the major goals of meditation is to see things as they are. The discrimination training function of meditation makes the contents of consciousness more visible, allowing the meditator more choice as to whether to identify or not identify with them.

Meditation as Training in Becoming Disidentified with One's Point-of-View

Our point-of-view is a subtle perceptual state that literally means the point from which we view the world. It is a screen through which we see the world, a screen that can be dense or porous depending on our history of conditioning and our previous attempts to gain awareness. Do we see the world as a frightening place full of hostile people? A competitive place with not enough to go around? These are examples of points-of-view that I have seen clients recognize and give up during the course of therapy.

Point-of-view is difficult to dissolve because when we are seeing the world from a certain perspective, that is the way we think the world is. By penetrating to the subtler levels of conditioning, meditation affords an opportunity to observe our point-of-view. Once seen, it can be dropped.

The process of dissolving identification with the point(s)-of-view is basically the same one discussed for discrimination training. By alternating back and forth between being stuck in the point-of-view and being in an attentive state free from the conditioned perceptions of the point-of-view, the meditator gains an ability to see how his or her point of view colors the world.

Meditation as Deautomatization

Arthur Deikman, a San Francisco psychiatrist, has advanced the theory that meditation is a process of deautomatization. The concept is meaningful in terms of the approach to therapy described in this book.

Some mystical traditions regard humans as being unconscious or "asleep" while they are responding out of their conditioning. Gurdjieff, for example, based his work upon the idea that conscious effort must be exerted to stay awake and "remember oneself." He and others regarded the asleep state as not making full use of the human capability at this stage of evolution.

Deikman performed some experiments on meditation in which meditators contemplated a vase for several sessions. Afterward, some of the meditators responded that their perceptions of the vase had changed as a result of the meditation. To some it appeared fresher, as if they were continually picking up new aspects of it. Others reported that it became more vivid and meaningful. Based on these data, Deikman proposed that the process of meditation somehow revivified the perception that had become automatic. He suggested that the brain tunes out stimuli as it habitually responds to the world, thus restricting our awareness. Meditation breaks up the automatic responses, cutting through conditioned perception to uncover a fresher, more direct grasp of reality.

This view fits with the view of meditation held by some of the spiritual disciplines. In the Christian tradition, the Scriptures say that unless we see through the eyes of a child, we cannot enter the kingdom of heaven. This can be taken to mean that mystic perception is reserved for those who can cut through their layers of conditioning to see the world as freshly as a child. Similarly, many of the Zen teachings explore the theme of learning to see the world each moment as new and fresh. We have the story of the Zen master who is chased over the side of a cliff by a tiger. He grasps at the branch of a bush growing out of the side of the cliff. From beneath he hears the roar of another tiger. There he hangs, unable to go up or down. Suddenly he sees a juicy-looking berry growing from the bush. He plucks it and eats it with great enjoyment.

Physiological research on Zen meditators supports the idea of meditation as keeping the perceptions fresh. Several accomplished Zen meditators took part in a study that subjected them to a repeated "click" stimulus as they meditated. Normally, the EEG reflects a response to the stimulus for the first few times; then the response decreases as the person habituates to the stimulus. In the Zen meditators, however, habituation to the stimulus did not occur; the brains of the subjects continued to respond to each "click" as if it were the first.

Physiological studies and the verbal reports of meditators alike seem, then, to suggest that meditation can alter our perceptual processes. The benefits in therapy are quite obvious. Most people who come to therapy are there, in part, because they have created unproductive cycles of thought, action, and feelings in their lives. The problem is one of automatic responses of a negative nature to situations in which those responses are inappropriate. Furthermore, many clients are in therapy because they cannot free themselves from events of the past; others are there because of existential crises concerning the meaning of life (the usual responses to life have lost meaning). In all cases I can think of, meditation, with its effects of dissolving automatic responses and freshening perceptions of the world, could be of value.

Meditation as an Aid to Holistic Brain Function

One of the most exciting areas of research has been the effort to understand differences between the left and right hemispheres of the brain. The left hemisphere generally specializes in speech, logic, and linear thought, and the right hemisphere is the domain of intuition and a more holistic type of knowledge. Western culture generally has favored and thus reinforced the left hemisphere type of knowledge, to the neglect and possible underdevelopment of the right hemisphere type of knowledge. A whole person is one who has an integrated mind with logic and intuition working in harmony.

Meditation may have the effect of systematically blocking the linear function of the brain so that intuition is allowed to develop. An example is a form of meditation that uses a mantra. Repetition of the mantra, although it could be considered a left hemisphere operation, is not done for the purpose of logic or meaning. Rather, the mantra is repeated for its sonant or vibratory effects. Meditators are usually advised to disregard thought, to go back to repetition of the mantra, whenever they find themselves lost in thought.

During the course of our development, the brain's linear, logical function may be reinforced to the extent that it overshadows the intuitive function. By putting the linear on "hold," meditation may allow for growth of right hemisphere functioning and thus lead to a more integrated brain function.

Meditation as Quieter of Surface Noise

Most meditators would agree that the practice of meditation has the effect of quieting the surface noise of the mind. Early in the practice of meditation, considerable noise is present in the form of memories of the recent past (e.g., things that we have forgotten to do), plans for the future (e.g., what we will have for dinner that night), and the idle chatter of talk, to ourselves, to others, to no one in particular. As meditation continues, the noise dies down, giving us access to subtler levels of the mind.

One of the subtler levels that becomes accessible is feeling. With a quiet mind one is able to watch thought emerge from feeling. In addition, we can tune in more easily to the physical sensation associated with certain feeling states so we can learn the differences between sadness, fear, anger, and other feelings. This is important because many people confuse feelings. They report anger, for example, when the deeper feeling beneath the anger is fear.

Another level of the mind that emerges as surface noise dissolves is desire or want. Most of us go about wanting things unconsciously, but the desire is buried beneath the surface so it cannot be seen. In meditation one can often spot desires so they can be made public. While the desire is buried beneath the surface, it causes a tension, as if we are straining toward some unidentified object. As we make our desires conscious, we can decide whether they are worth putting energy toward. If not, they can be dropped.

Meditation as Facilitator of Self-Realization

A final view of the effects of meditation that we will consider here is meditation as a facilitator of self-realization. This traditional Hindu view holds that a permanent, unchanging part of us is identical to and part of the absolute. The realization (making real) of this self is the goal of spiritual growth.

The basic human problem is seen as a split between awareness of the relative and awareness of the absolute. The relative world is ever-changing. Problems arise and fall, desires ebb and flow, feelings come and go. Our thoughts are rapidly alternating among the positive-negative aspects of memory, fantasy, and chatter. Our problems stem from our identification with these unstable elements of ourselves. For instance, when we are in the grip of anger, we lose contact with the self, our common element with the absolute. One moment we are identified with the negative thought ("I'm a bad person"), and the next moment a positive thought crowds in ("No, that's wrong, I'm a beautiful child of the Universe"). We become so identified with the comings and goings of the relative world that we lose touch with the awareness of our own divinity within.

Meditation provides an opportunity to realize the self because it makes clearer the impermanent nature of the relative. In a half-hour's meditation we may experience the rising and falling of dozens, perhaps hundreds, of thoughts, feelings, opinions, points-of-view, physical sensations. When the elements of the relative are observed and experienced, they tend to dissolve, so what is left is something that can be experienced of the self.[6]

The foregoing represents some varieties of meditation, what might account for its effects, and how it can be used in therapy. My personal recommendation is that we as therapists should meditate regularly, not only to experience the benefits cited earlier, but also to lay an experiential groundwork for any practices we might recommend to clients. Also, just as the practice of hand-washing between patients has both symbolic and practical value to the healer who works with the body, meditation may offer to healers of the mind an opportunity to begin and end each day afresh, uncontaminated by either our self-generated psychological "germs" or the ones our clients heap upon us. In my opinion, the practice of therapy is the most demanding of vocations, and we need to take advantage of as many tools as possible to further our own evolution, as well as to protect ourselves from the stresses placed upon us by people with troubled lives. I have found meditation to be a valuable tool in my repertoire.

NOTES

1. Some of the most informative books available on meditation are Robert Ornstein's *The Psychology of Consciousness* (New York: Penguin, 1975); Claudio Naranjo and Robert Ornstein's *On The Psychology of Meditation* (New York: Viking Press, 1971); and John White's *What Is Meditation?* (New York: Anchor Books, 1972).
2. Joseph Goldstein, *The Experience of Insight* (Santa Cruz, CA: Unity Press, 1976), p. 176.
3. Goldstein, p. 40.
4. H. Bloomfield, M. Cain, R. Joffe, and R. Kory, *TM: Overcoming Stress and Discovering Inner Energy* (New York: Delacorte Press, 1975).
5. C. G. Hendricks, "Theoretical Note: Meditation as Discrimination Training," *Journal of Transpersonal Psychology* (1975), pp. 144–146.
6. The self itself as permanent or as another impermanent feature constitutes a major difference between Hindu and Buddhist beliefs.

10

Transpersonal Movement Therapy

Kathlyn T. Hendricks

L ife is movement, from the motion of the tides to the life cycle of the human being. The way we move broadcasts our relationship to life. It is the bridge between what goes on inside and what we show the world. The way people move together reveals more about their relationships than anything they could possibly say in words.

Dance and movement rituals have formed the core of community life for thousands of years. Dance has demarcated the major life cycle experiences, the rites of passage, and acts of war. Healers were movers until the age of the mind-body dichotomy and ancient communities recognized and honored the healing power of movement.

In the twentieth century, movement therapy has developed as a specialty in the field of psychology. Since its reemergence with the work of Marian Chace at St. Elizabeth's Hospital, Washington, DC, in 1942, dance/movement therapists have acknowledged the intrinsic life force in all people, the healing power of shared rhythms and expressed feelings. Dance/movement therapists work with all ages and populations—in psychiatric hospitals, prisons, geriatric residence programs, adolescent halfway house settings, special education programs, and private practice.

Movement is a universal language, and dance/movement therapists are trained to use that language to heal and enhance the quality of life.

THE LIFE OF THE BODY

When a person moves, his or her total psychological process emerges. A trained therapist can see the life script, style of encountering the world, major problem areas, all in the way these phenomena are lived out in movement. Movement conveys truth. Because the body essentially fleshes out one's concepts and attitudes and has no mechanisms for lying, it reveals directly one's willingness to see and be the truth of moment-to-moment experience. Movement is the direct printout from the unconscious. When we move, we recreate the self. Movement is therefore the image of our continuity. What we tell ourselves about ourselves becomes embodied. One client, for example, was always told she had "mousy brown" hair. Eventually she came to see her hair that color instead of the blond it actually is, and to become her image of a mousy brown-haired woman.

When people move, their investment in life becomes visible, as does their relative degree of aliveness. The basic rhythm of life is expansion and contraction; all movement is rhythmic, its cadence arising out of the omnipresent pulsation of life energy. Transpersonal movement therapy allows the movement experience to represent the individual's personality and also to move through and beyond the individual's shell of defenses to a deep connectedness with the complete cycles of existence.

The process of the mover *(how* the mover moves) is the focus of movement therapy. The transformation point is upon encountering the unknown, the void before one risks the unexperienced, that juncture between the familiar pattern and the unimaginable. One client wrote a short poem about his experience of that edge:

> *To Move Without a Reason*
> *Action that does no violence to the actor.*
> *"Just move without any particular reason."*
> *She said.*
> *"Okay," he said with the confidence*

of one who found it easy to
follow directions.
...without a reason?
Frozen on hands and knees
Struck by a ray of paradox
in a place no thought can change.
Waiting.
The bubble of expectation pierced.
Waiting.

In movement, the therapist sees the client's willingness to choose and to change. As we grow up, most of us grow in. We limit ourselves to what works, what is functional, what takes less time. We gradually turn ourselves into shells where the inner life becomes dissociated from expression, conflicts with expression, or is denied entirely. For example, one client, while lying on the floor in an early therapy session, was responding to the suggestion to stretch and release. She raised her straight arms above her head slightly, then craned them back to her side, extended her arms directly sideward like one of those wooden Christmas dolls on a string, stretched her toes down momentarily, and stopped. That was the extent of her inner sense of "stretching and releasing—no three-dimensional movement, no whole-body stretch, no real surrender into contact with the floor.

The body is not just a vehicle to carry the head around. The collective late-twentieth-century human body contains large areas that are internally invisible, not felt, sensed, or imagined. This body literally feels less, interacts less with the environment, takes up as little space as possible, and moves only when the task at hand requires it. Expression and creativity have become obsolete or imbued with vaguely sinister overtones. Bertherat, a physical therapist and author, has outlined the problem clearly:

> At a very early age we acquire a minimal repertory of movement that we never think about any more. All our lives we repeat these few movements without questioning them, and without understanding that they represent only a very small sampling of our possibilities. The majority of us make use of a few variations of only about a hundred of the more than two thousand movements that the human being is capable of. But we'd never take seriously someone who suggested that we're physically deficient.[1]

A young, very troubled woman discovered while lying down that she could suspend her leg in the air for nearly twenty minutes (try it!) before she could sense where her thigh was, what muscles were holding her leg in the air, and what could release that holding.

The reasons for this movement atrophy are manifold but are generated primarily in the conflicts created by trying to become what we are told we are as children: "You'd be so pretty if you'd…"; "You're not really hurt"; "Don't be too smart" (…pretty, successful); "Be still; don't be so loud"; and so on. The major signal that internalized conflicts are present is the word "tension."

Tension is the expression of separation from life, from the ground of being. Tension is the label for the process of rigidifying, withdrawing, withholding from life. Our bodies reflect that illusion of separateness: the stiff necks and knotted shoulders, immobile diaphragms and shallow breathing, the face-front march through life with no knowledge of the back, the shadow.

One can manipulate and squeeze and exercise the tension away, but whatever supports tension will recreate it until its deeper meaning is felt, understood, and expressed. Tension, resistance, and stuckness are the same, all signals of the need to experience more deeply.

Tension in all its manifestations emerges throughout the therapy process, and in fact may be the significant presenting problem. The client's assumptions about tension should be addressed before inner sensing can even be approached. I frequently hear people say, "Oh, that's just a tense place," "I'm just tense today," or, most often, "I'd sure like to get rid of this tension," as if tension were an "it," outside experiential, body awareness, somehow correctable by the remedies we use for other disorders (e.g., take a pill for a headache). As one man, totally dominated by keeping an eye on things and keeping up with things, and with frequent headaches, said to me, "If I calmed down, I'd be boring."

People live their tensions and become their conflicts. Polarization, the pervasive either-or, supports much of the unhappiness and life-emptiness that I see in clients. The dichotomies of win-lose, love-hate, up-down, controlling-collapsing, and so forth fight for dominance within the person, eventually immobilizing not only the structure but the life force as well.

PURPOSES OF TRANSPERSONAL MOVEMENT THERAPY

The major purposes of transpersonal movement therapy, as briefly discussed next, are to expand beyond conditioning, recover the self, create authentic movement, and achieve transcendence through movement.

Expanding Beyond Conditioning

Why focus on movement as a process in therapy? Does it have some intrinsic validity, or is it a therapeutic luxury? Many movement experiences have taught me crucial lessons about my own life process and have served my evolution as a therapist. Perhaps my deepest ongoing exploration has been to complete my relationship to fear, especially the fear of expressing myself. A recent movement experience illustrates this cycle of encountering tension, allowing sensation, acknowledging feelings, and moving through to a new experience of self.

At a free-form dance with African drummers one evening, I allowed myself to go into free fall, to really explore that sensation in movement. Letting go into gravity was the culmination of my experiences in relation to fear. An equivalent to my sensations that evening would be skydiving. I discovered that when I became totally soft against gravity instead of *holding* myself to keep from failing, holding myself in any particular attitude about the way I should be, or in any kind of a position, no matter how pretty or daring, I became a kind of movement gyroscope. For about three hours I moved continually, over and over letting go of the position in space or the pattern of moving. As a result, I felt balanced in any position I tried. I didn't fall no matter what I did or how much I turned and leaped. I didn't find any limits in my ability to be grounded and to be simultaneously in motion. It felt as if I had expanded my awareness out into my fingertips (in fact, I had small hematomas on my fingers the next morning). I had totally expanded to my experience of fear so nothing was left in my body to be solid and dense, nothing left to contract. It was all free fall.

Recovering the Self

Movement therapy is essentially a recognition process, a knowing again or remembering who we are. One of its major purposes is to affirm the experience of being fully alive. The transpersonal approach assumes that one is in the continual act of becoming. As we become aware of how we actually move and relearn that we have arms and toes and genitals, we begin to remember the freedom we originally had to keep discovering ourselves in the world. We remember old feelings and sensations, some pleasant, some most unpleasant, each gradually acknowledged and integrated. Each knowing enriches the mover and the mover's kinetic sense.

The major key to open this process seems to be the recognition of inner signals, the streamings, pressures, tinglings, surges that lie below the surface tension. Most of us avoid that recognition and the confrontation with self that follows, not only by tensing ourselves but also by talking to ourselves continually so that nothing else can be attended to. Maslow called the inner signals "the impulse voices" and observed that in most neuroses the inner signals are weak or have disappeared (to be replaced by the internal dialogue, or with psychotics, whole worlds of voices). "Recovering the self *must*, as a *sine qua non*, include recovery of the ability to have and to cognize these signals, to know what and whom one likes and dislikes, what is enjoyable and what is not."[2]

Tense people are often experientially empty people, for whom others' opinions, a list or schedule, internalized Mom and Dad, make their choices for them. Recognizing the inner impulses, however, can seem dangerous and frightening after long repression. For example, what might one want to do with one's hands if one weren't sitting on them or holding them stiffly at one's sides? And besides, moving around like that is silly, isn't it?

Transpersonal movement therapy challenges the system that maturity is exclusively a process of taking on the appropriate role and doing it well. That sense of maturity looks like rigidification.

Transpersonal movement therapy supports the pulsation of energy within the human form and assists in the risk of becoming *more*. Recognition, and allowing inner impulse, is the fundamental vocabulary of life with which a person forms his or her relationship to self and to the world.

Authentic Movement

The bridge between inner impulse and form is a way of moving that we can call authentic movement. Authentic movement is more than involvement and spontaneity. It also involves a shift in the use of attention, and that ability to shift and focus free attention gives movement consciousness. The combination of attending while moving carries it beyond habitual repetition and distinguishes it from our functional movement. The quality of attention is based on a special kind of awareness.

> This *awareness* of life working within us is something fundamentally different from observing, fixing and comprehending from the outside. In such observing and comprehending he who comprehends stands apart from the comprehended and observed. But in becoming aware, the experience remains one with the experiencer and transforms him by taking hold of him. Whenever an experience changes a person, it happens unnoticed in the greater awareness of what has been experienced. To become aware means to regain the oneness with the original reality of life.[3]

Allowing, an integral aspect of attention, has two dimensions: giving permission to oneself (even if it's silly or scary or confusing) and allowing whatever emerges to be visible. From a point of relaxed, active waiting, we can "mobilize our attention so that the energy can express itself. This attitude would be the *act of attention;* we follow what happens, concentrating on it. The movement leads and the mover follows."[4]

Attentive movement can open the channel for inner experience to find form in space and time. Such movement is always surprising, especially to the mover, who has brought up the unknown from within.

My experience of people who participate in a profound movement therapy process is that they go through repeated, identifiable cycles with many instances of discrete awareness, "little learnings." Individuals learn, for example, that they have been holding their whole body in a burdened way. Then they begin to understand that the burden has something to do with their relationship to gravity and needing to "keep on top of it." They begin to explore their fear of falling and its source. Those little learnings seem to be cumulative, so that at a certain point the movement process itself takes over, if you allow it, with its own quite visible, magnetic laws. If someone in the room engages in authentic movement, it will draw the attention of everyone in the room. It is unmistakable, like an explosion. All those little experiences of awareness come together in a new form.

One client had been involved with little learnings for several sessions at the time of this particular breakthrough. While moving within the structure of following a sensation in his stomach, he found himself catapulted directly into the reexperience of his five-year-old feelings of pain and abandonment about a serious, crippling illness. His cognitive mind had already adjusted quite well to his limitations, his atrophied leg, not being able to run, and so on. His unconscious mind, however, had given previous signals in dreams, moods, recurring daily patterns, that some material was unfinished. In this movement process he let go into the full intensity of the fear, pain, and helplessness that his five-year-old body had been unable to complete. This experience effortlessly generated several others (some on his own) over the next few weeks, in which he acknowledged, felt, and expressed, in both movement and drawing, his deep feelings from that time. Tremendous energy was released in this process, which he used to move out of a longstanding impasse both personally and professionally.

In the movement process, resistance/stuckness is material to be sensed and moved. I often have people "become" their stuckness to taste its particular quality for them at that time. Any movement in which the mover is awake can transcend "going through the motions." It can enrich even the trained dancer's "response-ability," because it has the capacity for renewal and freshness that come from one's inexhaustible inner life.

Dichotomies and polarities are the stuck places that most often arise from clients in the conflicts they experience in their life situations. Some people are stuck in one polarity (retreating, for example) and have no experience of initiating or wanting. Others swing from one extreme to the other (e.g., good girl, bad girl) with no sense of the middle ground. When one follows the movement instead of controlling it, contrasts tend to synthesize, to become something else, a new possibility, new movement, new life choices.

Transcendence Through Movement

Letting go into the process of authentic movement often leads through personality issues to experiences of transcendence, connection to the self. This transcendence is visible as being moved, effortfully directing the body's action. Authentic movement means fully trusting one's body, allowing fusion between one's brain and one's body cells. The fusion creates movement that is totally involved, unpredictable, elegantly economical.

A professional man who had been working in movement therapy for a few months clearly had access to his authentic responses and had begun to work on the essential issues of his life. He kept returning to themes related to having to *do* something, to "get my act together," on the one hand, and a tremendous inner drive toward freedom, on the other hand, which he experienced as "tearing him up inside." He brought material in to sessions, needed little prompting, and usually began moving immediately.

In one session he began by circling "it" (whatever was pushing or pulling at him, represented by a pillow in the middle of the room). Quickly I could see the almost-visible cord that held him as his movement took on the involved, whole-body focus of authenticity. He was clearly stalking, encountering an aspect of himself with full attention that had a timeless quality to it. I have learned not to interrupt this process, for clients are often so involved that the room disappears for that encounter. Any comment or interpretation that I might see a need to make is irrelevant. At that point, then, my presence was important as the anchor, witness, and permission-giver.

As the man moved in response to his ambivalence and finally became "it," his movement changed, taking on a diffuse, halting, hesitant quality. He later described "it" as vague and foggy; he couldn't see clearly through it. He spent the rest of the session exploring "its" demands and his responses, sometimes moving, sometimes talking to "it." I understand this current phase as a ripening for that client. Each time he moves consciously, he remembers more childhood experience, the image from a recent dream, the connection of his bodily sensations, and he learns to become more of who he is.

WINDOW ON A SESSION

Introduction: Seeing

Because movement is a universal language, anything that occurs from the time the client walks in is potential material. Most of my work is with individuals, and I generally do not move with them. Sessions usually begin with expanding the emergent movement material. I recognize this potential movement in several ways: I look for areas where the client's body is more dense, areas that are unmoving. Any repeated mannerism, such as hand fidgeting or facial tics, can signal a condensed movement metaphor. Areas of the body that work against each other draw my attention, such as the pelvic area moving forward while the chest and shoulders are retreating. I notice whether impulses to move are recognized and course sequentially through the body to expression or whether the person stops this process, as with a yawn that forms a stretch or is held behind tight jaws and shallow breathing.

My attention is focused on the edge of the movement that is about to happen. In the therapy process the client is encouraged to literally be *more*, to take the hesitancy in his or her hands, allowing the whole body to be hesitant, to breathe around the area that feels painful or numb or hard, and to allow that body sensation space to become a form, an expression. When clients allow the potential movement to arise, they experience directly the flow of energy and aliveness. They reclaim the truth of their actual experience and recreate feedback loops that get covered and distorted when somebody else is given authority to govern their internal experience.

Importance of the Therapist's Attitudes

My attitudes and processing of my experience seem to be critical to the flow of the session. One difference between transpersonal movement therapy and dance therapy, which evolved from the medical model, is my assumption that each client already contains everything necessary for his or her perfect evolution. I acknowledge that the door to this cognition involves a lot of work with personality, as personality constructs stand between the client and his or her connection with the life source. My attitude toward the emergence of personality is to understand that it is held in a bigger container, space. Content-free space is where I rest my body and my attention.

I agree with Durckheim that "one must understand from the core of one's being that all forms are brought forth in stillness and when they are fulfilled, taken back again."[5] My degree of willingness to be present, to go beyond boundaries and roles to touch the actual current of life in clients, to go on their journey with them, modulates the flow of the session and its relative degree of furthering the client's awareness and choice. I support the client's acknowledgment that his or her body is both whole and holy.

If I'm working from a transpersonal perspective, I don't take the personality very seriously. I look for the movement that expresses essence, supporting and reflecting it with my own body attitude and with every level of my experience. I continue to reflect essence no matter what kind of role, drama with spouse, or other element emerges. I still honor that, but I don't take it seriously. I don't act as if that is the only alternative. From more than a decade of work with people, I know that supporting the emergence of essence supports the perfect next step in the client's process.

Essence and Personality

Essence is what one sees out of the corner of the eye, the underlying rhythm and context of the actual visible movement. If one were humming along to that person's movement, it would be the melody of the tune. It can't be pushed; it can't be structured; it can't be called up on demand.

Personality looks contracted. When "seeing" a person's body, most personality is quite visible. The contraction is large. The whole body is bent by it. But the contraction also can be subtle, just the slightest withdrawal from the moment.

In most individuals, movement is circulating personality all the time, with only rare moments of essence breaking through. When essence emerges, the movement has that sense of inevitability and enormous vitality. This is a transformative experience, and the transformation can be created in movement, that space where something else takes over.

One movement experience with a twenty-six-year-old married woman provides an electrifying example of essence emerging. This overweight, unhappy woman felt profoundly stuck in her body, her marriage, her life. In this session we were actively exploring feeling "stuck." She used the floor as if it were glue and stuck parts of herself to the floor alternately while continuing to move, illustrating her life stance as if nothing were amiss. She eventually shifted to her shoulders and recognized that burdened part as the nexus of her stuck feeling. She chose to allow the inner voice in her shoulders to emerge in sound and movement, with the phrases "I'll show you, I'll sacrifice, I'll give up, I love to suffer" welling up and out, much to her surprise. Suddenly she began cackling and crouching, darting about the studio like a demon. The hair on my arms stood up as I felt the presence of almost pure hatred. After a few minutes of this frenzied, inferno movement, she seemed to wake up, looked at me, and said, "I always thought I was the 'bad seed.'"

Her early life experiences had been so ugly (incest; alcoholic parents) that she decided a long time ago that she must be evil to cause such misery. As this realization swept over her in the present, she felt the need to open the windows, to put on beautiful music, and to exorcise the palpable presence in the room. This session was the turning point in her learning to love herself.

Through the Window

The actual movement continua and experiences I draw from have simplified over the years. Most important, it seems, is to know how clients experience the ongoing pull of gravity, how much space they occupy both internally and in interactions, their relationship to the fundamental axes of possibility: rising, sinking, expanding, contracting, and so forth. The structure I generally provide in sessions is to define wide boundaries around the potential material (e.g., an unpleasant stomach sensation) and to encourage clients to begin expanding out into it in their own way.

Clients spend as much time not moving as moving, and they may be lying down, sitting, standing, or using all the available space to move through. Sessions rarely look the same, because each client's process is unique. I intend to honor that inner knowing and internal direction by being as transparent as possible myself and by repeatedly returning my attention to the edge of the becoming movement in the client.

An example of expanding a habitual movement might illustrate the interrelationship between my process and that of the client. Suppose the person were fidgeting with the hands, a common pattern. Working with this from a transpersonal approach, I would first feel that process in myself, as the initial level of intervention. My fundamental process would be to alternately observe and internally attend, seeing the movement and feeling my responses, watching the quality and allowing it to move me. I would hear the quality of the sounds, as if the movement were a symphony in my head. I would take in information as openly as possible, without labeling it in myself

At the same time, I would allow another part of myself to be open to any images that might occur to me. Most often I share these images with clients as part of the process we are engaging in together. Frequently it fits some aspect of their experience that I could not have logically predicted. The image-making capacity depends on allowing whatever is coming up to do so. If clients can learn just that, it gives them enormous freedom from the pattern of clinging desperately to their current position until they are wrenched loose and grab for the next available position.

Our bodies are a visual representation of a life stance.

I also perceive the quality of the compromise, the conflict. I'm thinking of one woman I saw, and I sensed the desperation in her from her hand movement. As it emerged, I allowed that feeling to move its way through me without my impeding its progress. If, as sometimes happens, it reaches a stuck place of mine, I attend to that. This is a process of really participating in the client's process. The willingness of both parties creates the crucible where change happens.

In that session, the woman's composite realization was a surprising sense of how angry she felt and how scared she was to express that feeling directly. It literally leaked out through her fingertips.

Embodying the Concepts

In this culture, unlike others across the world and throughout time, we are not well-acquainted with the healing nature of movement itself. We need to know what it is good for, the end product. How can movement, being nonverbal, carry over into verbal communication? How can something you learn about the way you stand change the way you communicate with your spouse?

We must remember that the way one stands is not the issue, but, rather, that the quality of moving when standing in that particular way, *experiencing* oneself in the moment, is what enables fuller communication to take place. Verbal communication is the end product of the person's willingness to express.

One woman discovered that she had been habitually standing on her toes for years, but she really hadn't *experienced* standing on her toes. When she actually began standing on her whole foot, both feet, and explored her expression from that root, she realized during the next week a parallel in her relationship with her husband. Before, she had always been anticipating him, his wants, his feelings. She had kept on her toes in relation to him. When she stood solidly on her own feet, it totally changed her communication style with him.

Transformation occurs at a deep level in this style of movement therapy, and it is allowed to reverberate through the whole system. The therapy is based on the assumption that any contracted area (a hyperextended knee, for example) has life stored inside the defense system. Because the knee usually has no sensation, awareness is lacking. The knee is a part of the person that has become mechanical. But if that suspension begins to come alive again, the life that was stored starts flowing again, bringing with it any leftover, unfinished, old movement experiences, contractions that haven't expanded. All of the life of the cell that had been suspended while the knee contracted is going to start flowing through the system again. The end product of that flow may be what in our society is the basic form of communication, speech.

Core Concepts

The embodiment of three core concepts from transpersonal psychology—willingness, space, and unity—can be well-illustrated in movement process.

Willingness

Because willingness truly seems to be the key, trying to recognize and describe what a willing attitude would look like has been an intriguing study for me. If the client is willing, anything is possible, so it seems valuable to be able to uncover and encourage that attitude in the concrete arena for learning to love yourself—movement therapy. Willing clients have some commonalities. Their bodies are more toned; their skin lies smoothly connected to their muscles. Their natural movement preferences more closely match their internal experiences, seem truer. That congruence doesn't mean their internal life is necessarily in harmony or satisfying, however. In one case the client's internal life was psychotic. Her face grimaced, her body twisted, but she knew it. The germ of consistency was already present.

The movement of willing clients is generally more fluid, though rarely throughout their bodies, which contain the usual hunches, burdens, and numb areas. The quality of the movement itself deals better with transitions than more resistant clients. Unwillingness tends to look more static in time and space, as if the person were rooted to the spot. The fluidity of the more willing mover isn't chaotic or without purpose, though. It rather seems to follow an inner thread. The form of the movement looks more reedlike than steely. Possibly, part of willingness is the repeated choice to let go, even of the comfortable places. With these clients, the suspicion that no one else is going to rescue them seems to allow the risk of letting go of life stances and movement styles that no longer fit their sense of responsibility for who they are. Willingness seems to short-circuit the need to understand, the need to figure it out before they can risk change.

The man's body looked as if he had a surgical-strength rubber band attached to his chin and his genitals, so whenever he stood to his full height, he vaguely experienced a sexual threat and excitation.

This forty-year-old man's back was a reservoir of old burdens and resentments, and his shoulders were especially hunched and thick, painful. All this conflict was upheld quite tentatively on tense thighs, locked knees, and curled-under toes, making walking itself fatiguing.

Most of the movement work with this client began by acknowledging the most prominent body sensation, which he then amplified, exploring throughout his body (chasing it around), breathing around, and following. He used movement as a form of meditation; when the analyst part of his mind became active, he gently turned his attention back to the actual sensations, especially the vague, fleeting ones. The words that were apt to emerge some time in the sequence were, "I don't know," followed by a larger exhalation of relief and the formation of a definite movement expression of that vague body sensation. For example, one energetic, flinging-off movement came out of his stomach uneasiness.

His willingness seemed contingent on his acknowledging that his body is a whole system with its own intrinsic relationships and laws, not necessarily dominated by his cognitive brain. Each experiencing and expressing cycle enlarged his aliveness, his choices in his everyday life, his capacity for renewal. He began to stride more easily, throw off the burdens, and see more clearly into himself and others.

Space

Individuals' relationship to space is critical to their sense of belonging in the world and represents their method of grounding or security. How much space people use in their movement and how much internal space they are aware of parallels their cycle of expansion and contraction. I often have clients move in that particular structure in the first sessions, expanding until they feel as far out as they wish to go, then contracting as far in as feels right, and again expanding. Most people use little of their potential space, and their feelings about security, protection, and guardedness emerge with this focus of exploration. Birth issues especially are triggered by the experience of expanding right to the edge of possibility, into asymmetry and fears of falling.

Use of space also indicates degree of self-esteem. One older woman who had ovarian cancer moved through space as if she were constantly testing the water. It emerged that at home in her small kitchen with her husband, who was a huge block, a retired military man, she repeatedly made herself smaller whenever they had to cross paths. Her inner experience of herself was a mix of unfinished little-girl needs to skip and frolic and turn and the acculturated constrictions her body had accumulated from years of having her desires blocked while her responsibilities to others were accented. The choice to make oneself smaller is a giving up that breeds resentment, confusion, and eventually hopelessness.

Internal space, the sense of being at home in one's body, is a primary goal of movement therapy. A woman with many self-image issues was working with falling into pillows and noticing the stiff, deadwood feelings in her arms, whereupon she remembered a childhood incident of falling off a swing set. She had expected her arms to break her fall and remembered the fear paralysis they locked into, as well as her decision to disown them for being so stupid as to allow her to badly hurt herself. From that point, she apparently had contracted severely at her shoulder joints, so her arms hung loosely and fairly ineffectively at her sides. The process of owning her arms again involved a long movement dialogue between her arms and the rest of her, reclaiming reaching, throwing, pushing, and swinging—all the movements that arms do.

Use of space in interrelationships is largely learned, as are role behaviors. A young man was exploring "sideways" movement one afternoon when he began to feel prickly along his back and seemed to need to crouch and guard himself. He looked as if he were being held, so I asked him to imagine a tether attached to him and someone or something at the other end. The someone became his father, who stood behind him and prevented him from moving forward. The young man then recalled a complex series of memories of all the ways he had felt tethered in his lack of free time—his father's constant demands in the family store, refusal to acknowledge the son's desires, and so on. From that point, the client could begin to reclaim that widening space, and his body (especially the chest) began to fill out as he presented himself in the world as more capable and free.

Unity

The illusion of separation is most visible in the body fragmentation and movement dissonance of conflict. As long as one holds someone else responsible or to blame, experiences of unity are rare. Fears of being consumed and annihilated, dissolving—all those birth-related issues— block the free flow of awareness out into space and unity. My attitude in work is that we are exploring the obstacles between the client's present life and his or her full potential. An obstacle is like a logjam in the flow, and actively loving the obstacle frees the jam. I feel the obstacle in myself and love it, move with it. I see the obstacle in the client and love it, move with it.

Most often in sessions the experience of unity is the end result of letting go of a particular pattern of moving through the world. The exhilarating freedom of dropping an old resentment lodged between the shoulder blades, or straddling more of the ground when walking, or standing and facing a fearful situation that formerly induced averted eyes and clenched stomach are the moments of free attention, the moments of full breath and oneness with life.

The experience of unity seems to always be available behind the veil of projection. In a women's movement therapy group we spent one session exploring literally moving behind veils, as is commonplace in much of the Moslem world. The women used large pieces of cloth to drape themselves and began exploring space and the rhythms of covering and uncovering. They worked a long time individually, then in pairs, and finally in a spontaneous swaying circle dance under a parachute. The video I made of the group clearly reflected the phases of taking on roles—the harem girl, the nun, the aloof matron, the invisible slave—and the tentative and then more abandoned release of those roles. The momentum of covering and uncovering built as group members began using their cloths in elaborate coverings and uncoverings of each other, learning to include one another in that universal rhythm. At an inspired moment I put "Scheherazade" on the record player, and the movement became even more circular and inclusive. As the covered form of the women swayed quietly, the presence of unity was radiantly evident.

MOVEMENT EXPERIMENTS

Each of the following activities is designed to illustrate a particular facet of transpersonal approaches in therapy. These are based on the experience that is possible when one lets go of content and focuses on process.

Experiment 1

This experiment is to be done with a partner. Ideally, choose a time when you've put aside schedules and demands; use an open space where you feel comfortable; and have nonrhythmic music in the background (Brian Eno's "Ambient" series is especially good for this purpose).

1. Have the partners (you could be one) stand facing each other, each person with one foot about a half-stride behind the front leg. They are to experiment with rocking their weight from front to back and make any adjustments that allow them to feel more fluid, as if the hip, knee, and ankle joints were on rollers.

2. Have partner A offer his or her forearm to partner B, allowing every other body part to relax. Partner B is to place his or her fingertips on partner A's forearm, with pressure somewhere between feather-light (withheld) and anchor-heavy (giving up responsibility).

3. Ask partner B to close his or her eyes, while partner A begins to move his or her arm smoothly, slowly, and in random patterns in space. The objective for partner B is to maintain the same extent of finger contact throughout, and for partner A to consciously make his or her movement wavelike. They will notice how much information is transmitted through the fingertips. Each time partner B anticipates or tenses, partner A will feel it. Exhaling completely assists in releasing tension, for both partners.

4. After several minutes, have the two switch roles, then take time to share their actual experience.

This experiment ages well. With practice, participants report experiences of unity, not only with their partner but with life energy as well. Images of rivers, floating feelings, enlivening of unnoticed body parts, and the positive experience of giving over control to another person have also transpired for participants.

Experiment 2

This experiment can be done individually or in partnership. To simplify the activity at the beginning, use a partner as observer until the observer in oneself is developed. This structure can be a tool for discovering automatic responses and enlivening them.

1. The initial framework for this experience is relatively unstructured. Simply have the mover allow and follow movement impulses as they emerge in his or her body. This movement can be done lying down, sitting, or standing, and may involve large

movement or small gestures of hands and feet. Movements cannot be *right* or *wrong*, just that which wants to be moved.

2. Let this random moving continue for some time, even if the person runs out of things to do and starts repeating previous movements. Meanwhile, the observer (either the partner or your mind's eye) is to notice the movement to which the mover keeps returning. This may be a discrete gesture that is repeated; a way of moving from place to place, such as in short, quick bursts; or a quality or style, such as circular arm movements or a tunnel-like focus of the torso. The important aspect to notice is the repetition.

3. Let the attention focus on this identified movement now, by having the person repeat it, taking some time with each of the following variations:

    a. Make the movement larger in the sense of *more* of whatever it is. Exaggerate it beyond "everyday" dimensions and really bring it into relief. Let the whole body become that quality. Initially this may feel ridiculous or silly; allow that feeling and whatever other responses arise to be part of the experience.

    b. Take the kernel of the movement, the quality, and do its opposite. For example, if the movement involves arm circles, have the arms make only angular, straight lines in space. Notice the body's response to trying this opposite.

    c. Take the movement and let another part of your body move it. For example, do the arm circles and let the hips move in the same way.

    d. Let the movement alternate between exaggerating the identified pattern, moving its opposite, exaggerating, opposing, many times. Notice the tendency of qualities to blend, to find a new kind of movement somewhere between the two.

4. Allow a few moments of reflection time for the participant to ask:

    a. How am I creating this pattern in my daily life?

    b. Is this movement familiar, like any other experience I've had?

    c. What have I discovered about the way I think I should move and be in the world, and how do I feel when I change that habitual response?

Experiment 3

Remember the little wooden, multijointed animals or dolls, about three or four inches high, on a round stand with a button on the bottom? Push the button, and the doll collapses; let go and it springs back up. This experiment is based on that principle and is an active way to learn the art of "going with" while remaining grounded. It is fun to do in a group with partners, to experience the differences in everyone's style of resistance and flow.

1. For contrast, have partner A take a position (both feet on the floor) where the person feels he or she can't be moved. Have partner B circle partner A's body until partner B can see the "loophole," the flat place, the area which, if nudged just slightly, causes a loss of balance.

   Switch roles, perhaps a few times with various positions, to have the participants really experience the body sense of "taking a position" and to experience its relative security.

2. Have partner A take a fairly wide stance, knees slightly bent, eyes closed, exhaling each breath fully. Have partner B use his or her hand to push various parts of the partner's body lightly: shoulders, head, hip, stomach, thigh, and so on. Ask partner A to imagine his or her body as a spiraling form, allowing each push to move through the body, going with it along the spiral until the energy of the push dissolves, then returning to the central position. This is to be repeated with the next push, and so on. After about five minutes, the partners' roles should be reversed.

3. Everyone seems to have a central tension reservoir, the place that responds reflexively to a push by becoming rigid. It could be one's lower back, chest, back of the neck. Have partner A nudge partner B at these various body places. Partner B will have the experience of rigidifying, losing balance, rigidifying, losing balance, perhaps many times before deciding to let go of the automatic response and explore the sensation of "going with." Reverse roles, and be sure to take time to share discoveries with the partner and the group.

NOTES

1. T. Bertherat and C. Bernstein, *The Body Has Its Reasons* (New York: Pantheon, 1977), p. 38.
2. Abraham H. Maslow, *The Farther Reaches of Human Nature* (New York: Viking Press, 1971) p. 33.
3. Karlfried Durckheim, *Hara: The Vital Centre of Man* (New York: Samuel Weiser, 1975), p. 159.
4. Mary Whitehouse, "C. G. Jung and Dance Therapy: Two Major Principles," in *Eight Theoretical Approaches in Dance-Movement Therapy*, edited by Penny Lewis Bernstein (Dubuque, IA: Kendall/Hunt, 1979), p. 62.
5. Durckheim, *Hara*, p. 161.

11

Cross-Cultural Counseling: A Transpersonal Approach

Kathlyn T. Hendricks

How can an appreciation of the cross-cultural aspects of counseling be a transpersonal experience? Every year I inquire into that question with a dozen graduate students, and each time we end the inquiry with a universal realization: Cross-cultural counseling is transpersonal psychology in action. The first day of class I ask a question: What is culture? Students give a tremendous range of responses. Some rephrase the text's definition, which is "any group of people who identify or associate with one another on the basis of some common purpose, need, or similarity of background."[1] Others include an impassioned defense of the rap culture or the single-parent subculture. After an illuminating visit to the British Museum, I suggested that any group becomes a culture when its members start making and displaying little, decorative figures. Hummel's porcelain peasants and country girls are an example of this tendency. As the class proceeds, students begin to realize that all human interaction is cultural; it takes place in the context of the person's history within a group (or groups) that has its own rich and complex history. They also begin to see that any communication is colored by a vast layering of cultural meaning. We are all affected by "the way it's done" in our family, community, church, neighborhood, class, and part of the city.

Students are assigned weekly reading in periodicals and newspapers, and each week they come in loaded with discoveries and the growing awareness that every interaction has a cultural tone. One commonality that seems to carry through histories of all countries in all times is distrust of verbal and behavioral differences. Travels through museums and history books demonstrate again and again our first human response to the Other: separate, control, annihilate if possible. We have a dismal record of being able to bridge cultural differences. Wars have been fought over accents. We usually assume that the other guy is inferior, and thus justify our own behavior. Rare are demonstrations of cultural amiability, of bridges where differences are appreciated.

A recent newspaper article described an American military woman's experience in Saudi Arabia as part of the Gulf War. She was off-duty and covered head-to-foot to signify respect for the local dress code for women. As she walked through the market, a local man approached and berated her for not wearing a veil. When he discovered she was American, he switched to English as he continued castigating her.

Our media archives are full of cultural conflicts; they make great drama. From the cavalry and Indians to rap groups and censorers, the clash of cultures makes big box office.

We have probably all had the experience of realizing we were "different" in some way from our peers. Many students date this awareness to painful or embarrassing events in school. I remember moving from Detroit, where my saddle shoes and blazer were the height of fashion, to California, where I definitely looked nerdy among the sandals and pastels. I had never heard of a taco or a surfboard, two items of supreme importance to Southern California culture. Take a moment to remember the time and place where you realized that differences exist between people and that these differences *make* a difference. What is amazing is how often, at least as children, the person you most fear and avoid becomes a friend once the dance of differences is done.

Fritz Perls said, "Contact is the appreciation of differences." To really make contact as a therapist, the vast world of cultural diversity has to be understood to even begin to work. We have some evidence that beneath the tremendous diversity on the surface, the core human experience is unity. For example, when cultural imprints and the fantastic array of culturally determined behavior dissolve in psychosis, the communication process becomes identical.[2] Research also indicates great consistency across cultures in adult-child nonverbal interaction. Positive infant vocalizations (PIVs) were performed primarily during eye contact. When adults talked, regardless of their language, infants didn't vocalize in a positive manner. Across cultures, negative infant vocalizations (NIVs) elicited more adult touch and movement. Infant PIVs elicited more adult verbal reactions.[3] This demonstrates that people emerge from the ground of being speaking the same language. After several years living in different cultures, however, people become remarkably varied. In multicultural counseling we are looking at the tools and materials that will bridge the common human experience of feeling, contact, and unity.

Understanding cultural characteristics has become more important to meet the client and match his or her world view, especially as global communication creates a smaller world. In the course of clinical experience, therapists have learned to take a broader view of what is valuable and necessary for therapy to work. Over the last ninety years, the context of therapy has been shifting to include social, environmental, and global concerns. But, as Desmond Morris notes, we still don't have a dictionary of cross-cultural gestures that would allow us to translate some of the fundamental mores that separate us.[4]

Media reports are full of racial and cultural conflict. It is almost impossible to read a news story without seeing charges of bias, racism, or culture-bashing. Racism continues to be a serious problem that "is projecting black men to the brink of extinction." According to Herbers, by the year 2000 "seventy percent of all black men in the United States will be dead, in jail, on drugs or in the throes of alcoholism."[5] A recent review of the research on multicultural counseling concluded that "ethnic minorities receive not only different but less preferred forms of treatment than do whites."[6] Although counseling theory is gradually including the legitimacy of different cultural viewpoints, it continues to remain fairly unsophisticated in treatment approaches. Studies indicate that many cherished Western psychotherapeutic techniques, such as client-centered, intrapsychic, individualistic, nondirective approaches, are perceived as ineffective or offensive to non-Western clientele.[7]

The need for therapy is highest among those who don't understand or trust traditional methods or their well-dressed practitioners. "Both the incidence and severity of psychological problems are highest among the lowest classes. These classes commonly include members of minority cultures."[8]

I grew up with several cherished American myths: If you work hard, you'll get ahead; all parents love their children; wives and husbands respect each other; everything will get better when you're grown up. For an increasing number of individuals and families in the United States, these myths are truly foreign. They don't make sense unless you're in the middle class. Too often, until recently, therapy has been conducted as if everyone is middle class.

Multicultural counseling looks at the context in which we develop our personality and interactive styles. Especially at the beginning of therapy, people from nonmainstream backgrounds look and act very differently. Acting from an appreciation of these differences can form rapport and trust, the foundation of any therapeutic relationship. But studying cultural generalities doesn't in itself prepare the therapist for the individual's unique family and acculturation mix. The best attitude may be "beginner's mind." This is a phrase from Eastern meditation practices meaning to act as a beginner, to approach each situation as if you know nothing and can assume nothing. This attitude can actually expand our ability to see and experience the cogent moment and the appropriate action. To just look, rather than looking for, opens possibilities for seeing new connections in communication that simply disappear if you already know.

GUIDELINES FOR BEGINNING CLINICIANS

1. *Always question your assumptions.* The person across from you presents himself or herself through style of dress, use of space, facial expressions, tone of voice and hundreds of other verbal and nonverbal signals. As do you. One definition of transpersonal is "beyond or through the mask." You are definitely checking out each other's masks for suitability, availability, and a host of other factors. To constantly question

your assumptions gives you the possibility of genuine rapprochement. To assume closes doors before they're fully open. For example, I assumed that the dark-skinned woman in the front row of a new class was black and had actually assigned her to a study group before she gently corrected me in a lilting Spanish accent.

2. *Be real.* This is in contrast to following a recipe. Self-disclosure and the willingness to "get down" are all important. Most ethnic or nonmainstream clients are just as acute perceivers of phoniness as middle-class consumers are. Professional demeanor is essential to initial credibility and is greatly enhanced by the attitude of authenticity. If the therapist is interested and willing to learn, exposure to different cultures enriches both participants.

3. *Know the signs of respect in different cultures, especially your client's.* The dance of meeting is a complex protocol of ritual and cultural precedent. When the therapist honors the unique perspective each culture has for establishing trust, he or she communicates willingness to enter the client's world. More than knowing the verbal language, meeting the client with nonverbal fluency or willingness to learn the cultural language creates trust quickly.

Hispanic clients tend to value honest self-disclosure by the assertive and directly questioning therapist, who acknowledges the man's dominance in the family. Family is important to traditional Hispanics, who prefer a cooperative rather than a competitive treatment style. The therapist needs to know that in this culture admitting a problem is considered a weakness. An approach that often works is one in which life skills and problem-solving skills are emphasized as a context for considering the specific presenting issue.

Rapport with Asian clients can be cultivated most easily by understanding the individual's place in the more collective orientation. In contrast to Hispanics, Asians prefer to avoid conflict, and they value highly a way of being that revolves around hierarchies of "saving face." Face is a complex blend of respect, pride, and dignity whose specific rules an outsider couldn't possibly know. Approaching the eldest member of the family for information first is an example of entering the Asian world with respect.

Black lecturers have emphasized "getting on the same wave length" as black clients, especially by attempting to understand black language and history, which often has a stronger religious base than the white culture. For example, many therapists are unfamiliar with "Juneteenth," the name given to the date of freedom for American black slaves.

Rapport with Native Americans can be approached by moving into a much slower pace, a nature-based sense of time. Rather than the assertive authority that Hispanics respect, Native Americans honor a peripheral approach to issues. Trust forms more readily with a counselor who doesn't stare or interrupt and who can wait in silence for rapport to develop. Native American sense of time, based on the cycles of nature, may be in conflict with the traditional fifty-minute therapy session. The therapist also should be aware of Native Americans' strong sense of history and often extreme patience in contrast with the mainstream tendency toward instant gratification.[9] In fact, patience and non-assertion have contributed to the Native American's current economic and educational plight, although militant strategies have increased in the last twenty years.

4. *Let go of being the authority, and be inquisitive about the client's uniqueness.* This suggestion can be tricky, because Asians, Hispanics, and blacks often prefer and respond more effectively to an authoritative therapist.[10] But, as one of our black counselors said, "People of color want understanding and a willingness to learn" in their therapist. Several cultures still consider asking for help as a sign of weakness. It is especially difficult for many men to seek help outside the family or church. To encounter what one man called those "corduroy folks with elbow patches" is intimidating. Ultimately, this suggestion is an opening to empowerment of the client. The hardest work may be creating a context of mutual initiation. With that groundwork, real progress in the quality of daily life can be approached.

Gerald Boynton has developed what he calls the "Escape model," which stands for Engagement, Sensitivity to Culture, Awareness of Potential, and Environment. He argues forcefully for a therapeutic context that utilizes the family's existing potential:

> The issue of full family participation in the discussion of the family problem can best be handled as a "fairness to all family members" rather than from a communication model. The explanation of therapy as a process can also be presented as "working together," which presents a family and therapist coming together much like neighbors to help with a barn raising.[11]

5. *When possible, have the family assess its own differences and strengths.*[12] Another aspect of client empowerment is clients' participation in the assessment and process of therapy. As Boynton explains, "Both groups [Mexican-Americans and Appalachians] would likely engage more effectively if the therapist addressed the initial problem formulation with the parents as initial informants rather than 'entering the family system from the least involved family member.'"[13] Sensitivity to the power hierarchy, which is often traditional, fairly rigidly role-defined, and patriarchal, will produce results for the client even if the therapist's values are more egalitarian.

6. *As you proceed, educate the client as to your model, intentions and techniques.* The phrases and metaphors we use as therapists may be foreign to clients from different backgrounds. Most counselors are aware of the debate swirling around the possible cultural bias in standard intelligence tests. Many nonmainstream children haven't been exposed to the same experiences as the white middle-class on whose common background the tests have been based. The therapist needs to listen with cultural awareness for the most useful images given the client's life experience. For example, rural and community images may speak more clearly than technological and urban ones. Several studies affirm the need for straightforward communication that both educates and processes.[14]

Rapport with Asian clients is best achieved in just this way. Particular attention is needed to educate the client as to the purpose of what may appear to be invasive questions, such as treatment and family history. Because Asians tend to approach authorities with respect, the clear self-disclosure of intent may more quickly build rapport.[15]

It seems most useful to set a context for discovery that allows the therapist to gain access to the important issues facing the client. The therapist's concern, empathy, and problem-solving skill then can be truly valuable to clients.

IMPORTANT CONTEXT QUESTIONS IN THE CROSS-CULTURAL SETTING

The body of multicultural research and clinical experience suggests several questions that may be useful to consider when forming a therapeutic approach:

- ❏ Who is the family?
- ❏ What is the model for health and sickness?
- ❏ What is the relationship of individual to family needs, and individual needs/desires within the larger community?
- ❏ Who makes decisions, in the family and in therapy, and how are they made?
- ❏ What is the relationship between generations?
- ❏ How is self-expression and self-determination viewed?
- ❏ What are the major nonverbal protocols?

Let's consider each of these questions and the context they provide as a bridge to communication in the counseling session.

1. *Who is the family?* A 1991 movie, *Avalon*, documented the impact of growing mobility and wealth on the traditional extended family of a group of immigrants. Television and cars replaced conversation and walks as these foreigners became acculturated. The biggest argument in the film erupted in the context of some of the brothers and their families cutting the Thanksgiving turkey before a chronically latecoming brother arrived. That argument, which was about changing the way things had been done, created a rift that widened into a chasm that split the family.

Each ethnic population brings generations of family values to its American assimilation. These ingrained mores may clash with the current fast-moving nuclear family. First-generation immigrants are especially affected, and often disoriented, by the contrast between their values and those of the larger culture.

For blacks, the family may include uncles and aunts, grandmothers and cousins, and often is run by single women—for example, a mother and her daughter. Traditional Hispanic homes place a high value on the family. Family goals supersede individual ones and often are a source of interfamilial conflict as younger members become more acculturated to the mainstream. Different values about dating and chaperoning may create conflict in families with second- or third-generation adolescents. A frequent complaint is, "The kids don't have respect for the family like they used to." The elders in Asian families are given enormous respect and deference, in contrast to the "over the hill" attitude mainstream American elders often receive.

The therapist also must recognize that the mainstream model of working father, homemaker mother, two and two-thirds children is now in the minority in the United States. It has been replaced by a growing tendency to choose (or legally be assigned) a new family structure. Family may now be single parent with children, gay parents with the children of one, blended families of all kinds, or communal families sharing common kitchen and living areas. In the first part of the therapeutic contact, it is valuable to find out how these people form and define family. One idea is to gather family background using as many senses as possible to generate involvement. As another suggestion, "Did your grandparents tell you stories?...What kind?"

2. *What is the model for health and sickness?* Research indicates some common cross-cultural ground for healing, including the importance of faith. The client's faith is increased by evidence of the therapist's training and shared attitudes about healing.[16]

Seeking help outside the immediate family still carries a stigma in several cultures. The attitudes "we take care of our own" and "you shouldn't need anyone else when you have your family" often accompany the client into the first session. Many cultures share the conviction that problems are a sign of weakness, which can create an underlying adversarial battle before the therapist even opens the door. As with any of these broad questions, the issues are complex and the answers often specific to the setting and the client. One black speaker delighted students by advising, "You don't know—ask! Don't pretend you know it already; we can smell that coming."

Chinese and other Asians often have difficulty admitting emotional and social conflict but respond well to a physical approach, so problems are more often somaticized. Blacks and Hispanics share a strong religious faith that underlies their understanding of healing.[17] Sickness and healing take place within the larger framework of their beliefs. In addition, Hispanics expect knowledge to come from the professional.[18] Offering an outline for treatment with goals and possible approaches may be an effective initial approach for the Hispanic family.

3. *What is the relationship of individual to family needs, and individual needs/desires within the larger community?* One class survey found that most students knew who their next-door neighbors were and had little, if any, contact with them. This is in contrast to my memories, shared by others, of our mothers "borrowing a cup of sugar" and having coffee with the neighbors. Sharing rides to school and receiving invitations to

community events were common a generation ago. To minority groups the increasingly fast-paced American culture must seem like a colorfully laden merry-go-round gone wildly out of control. Assessing the extent of mainstream assimilation and the fulfillment of social bonding needs is crucial in the context of providing tangible help to minorities.

Most minority cultures are community-based, whether that community is as small as the extended family (Hispanics) or as large as the nation (Japan). The message often explicitly given them is the higher value placed on achievement of the individual rather than his or her participation in the community. For example, in President Bush's 1991 State of the Union speech, he repeatedly defined and emphasized that "we are *Americans!*" by asserting the priority and primacy of the individual's rights and responsibilities. This is a world view radically different from that of many Native Americans and Asians.[19]

In the mainstream culture it is possible to be too dependent. In nonmainstream cultures it is possible to extol oneself too much. Gaining identity through interaction and contribution to the group is a strong value in these cultures. Asians, in fact, prize the anonymity of the individual within a seamless whole of community.[20] A man who educates business people traveling to Japan underlines the necessity of blending in and avoiding confrontation. For example, it is considered very rude to object to smoking, which is common in Japan. The deference to authority in Japan and other Asian communities may be trying for the therapist reared to value the importance of the one voice of the individual.[21]

4. *Who makes decision and how are they made, in the family, and in therapy?* In part, this is a power-base question. What people and systems have to be acknowledged for therapy to progress? Boynton's previous comments address this question, as does Prince:

> There is a growing awareness that psychotherapeutic practices aimed at independence and insight are not appropriate for a large and important segment of our western population, the chronically poor...the vast majority of the emotionally disturbed of the non-western world can be successfully treated (and are being successfully treated) by techniques that foster dependency and unreasoned belief.[22]

Understanding who makes decisions can facilitate the flow of the therapy process. For example, knowing that Chinese traditionally don't initiate[23] and are unlikely to present the problem directly can enable the therapist to effectively generate probing questions. Understanding that Native Americans don't make direct decisions and prefer a peripheral approach can help a therapist avoid the pitfalls of a confrontational style. Acknowledging that the patriarch of Hispanic and Asian families considers the good of the family in decisions can assist in forging a therapeutic alliance rather than a power struggle.

5. *What is the relationship between generations?* This question considers the timeline of clients' participation in American culture. Are they newly arrived "aliens" or second or later generation? Research indicates a delineation between the needs and issues of assimilation and the needs and issues of the immigrant's children and grandchildren that may be one of the most important presenting issues. For example, one Hispanic woman described her frustration at trying to fit in at school when her father demanded she obey an early curfew that none of her friends had to follow. Amy Tan's bestseller *The Joy Luck Club*[24] eloquently describes the difference in perspective between immigrant Chinese and their daughters.

6. *How is self-expression/self-determination viewed?* This question may be one of the critical determinants of therapy outcome. The degree and style of self-expression is formed by thousands of verbal and contextual cues and experiences, not the least important of which is "the way we do things." Misunderstandings about communication signals may be minimized and effective interaction facilitated by the background knowledge of traditional cultural styles. The following examples are derived from a rich body of information about preferred expressive styles.

Blacks often act out and exaggerate the drama of opposition from the viewpoint that this expression affirms community. This style is in opposition to European whites, who minimize conflict.[25] Blacks tend to externalize conflict rather than seeking help in therapy. Emotional expression is equated with unmanliness, and blacks more often deal with feelings through addiction. The French expect more authoritative, assertive behavior from authorities, such as therapists, and respond more favorably to "anger/threat displays of leaders."[26] In a comparison involving TV game shows, Anglo-Americans were found to be considerably more expressive than Canadians. American females used their hands more than Canadians, and American males smiled more than their Canadian counterparts.[27]

Hispanics may have more trouble self-disclosing than people from other cultures,[28] and they tend to have more rigid expectations about the degree of informality the therapist displays. Mexican Americans generally expect more expressiveness from clients than from professionals. They want more formal expression from a professional, although gender differences play a part. Women expect to self-disclose more and to have less disclosure from the professional.[29]

Asians as a whole tend to emphasize decorum and conformity. For example, in Thailand, children's more aggressive behaviors are met with disapproval and are discouraged. We may interpret this disapproval as an affirmation of the importance of blending into the whole, the group identity. Compared with children in the United States, problems reported more frequently were somaticizing, fear, nervous mannerisms, and worry.[30] Asian expression may be based on intuition than the voice of reason acculturated in the West.[31]

7. *What are the major nonverbal protocols?* Desmond Morris' intriguing book *Bodywatching*[32] documents the meaning we give to various body parts and their uses. Hundreds of pictures document the cross-cultural universality of many gestures. He notes that a cross-culture reference book for gestures could be a great asset to the therapist but none currently exists. The clinician facing a culturally different client sees quickly that recipes won't work. To be most effective, he or she must respond sensitively to the subtle nonverbal feedback clues that are always present.

> In a session with a native American woman, I asked a direct question about her relationship with her mother, while I leaned forward and looked directly at her. She cringed slightly and drew back, looking over my shoulder. This combination of signals let me know that even though we knew each other well by then, I had invaded emotional and spatial territory.

We have some common knowledge of appropriate and rude nonverbal communication. Several cultures, including Asians and Native Americans, consider direct eye contact disrespectful. Smiles can be deceiving, communicating for Asians everything from joy to rejection.[33]

It may be surprising to learn that the United States is a "low-touch" culture.[34] The therapist should know if the client comes from a low- or high-touch background. The general protocol is to avoid any touch beyond the handshake. In a study of brief arm touching during the initial therapy session, however, "those who were touched judged the therapist as more expert."[35] Propriety of touch, already a gender and political issue, is complicated by the prohibition of certain body parts. For example, touching the head is considered quite rude to Asians. Different rules and roles for touch apply to each gender. In the United States mothers touch more often to comfort and groom, whereas fathers touch playfully more often. And "girls receive more affectionate touches (kissing, cuddling, holding) than boys do."[36]

Understanding the use of space has cultural implications beyond the family-systems intricacy explored by Satir and others. The Laguna Pueblos have three directions in addition to those of Westerners: up, down, and center, as well as Anglos' east, west, north, and south. Navahos value open space in any project,[37] which has interesting implications for the therapy environment.

The relative degree of nonverbal exuberance that is useful to therapy may be different for genders and across cultures. For example, blacks demonstrate a greater range of movement, quicker responses, and more energy than whites do.[38] Black men, however, traditionally express more energy in dance and communication than black women are allowed.[39]

As we consider cross-cultural themes and groups, we quickly encounter new subcultures that have emerged out of common concerns and needs. When exploring a client's cultural background, counselors should not confine themselves to ethnicity or race. For example, within the field of counseling a vast subgroup has developed that is quickly identified by the phrase, "I'm in recovery." Alcoholics Anonymous, Codependents Anonymous, Overeaters Anonymous, and other Anonymous peer groups have sprung up by the thousands to meet the common challenge of addiction. Each of these groups forms a culture with specific values, rules, language, and ritual of meeting. Former students have identified other subcultures: people with handicaps, obese people, gays and lesbians, single parents, abused women, the men's movement, and now AIDS patients and their families.

Economic and social conditions, too, may transcend ethnic and traditional background to synthesize new cultural concerns and subcultures. For example, the *Gazette Telegraph*[40] confirmed that the living conditions of children in the United States worsened over the decade of the eighties. A national survey indicated that even after several factor adjustments, blacks have "significantly lower levels of well-being than whites" in the United States.[41] And people are beginning to use the framework of common concern to encompass cultural diversity. The *East West Journal*[42] reported the combined efforts of several groups of minorities to combat their disproportionate share of pollution and food contamination. Shelby Steele[43] gained prominence and notoriety by suggesting that the facts of race often obscure and contribute to conflict between blacks and whites. The school dropout rate of minorities is growing dramatically, starting now in the third grade.[44] The world is growing smaller and the problems more cross-cultural.

When we look at the enormous richness of cross-cultural history and communication, we can begin to appreciate the rituals that each culture offers. True appreciation and exploration of this richness of expression can lead us to a sense of our core unity as humans in the common future that we create.

NOTES

1. D. Atkinson, "A Meta-Review of Research on Cross-Cultural Counseling and Psychotherapy," *Journal of Multicultural Counseling and Development* (October 1985), pp. 138–153.
2. O. Billig & B. G. Burton-Bradley, *The Painted Message* (Halsted, NY: Publisher, 1977).
3. H. Keller, A. Scholerich, and I Eibl-Eibesfeldt, "Communication Patterns in Adult-Infant Interaction in Western and Non-Western Cultures," *Journal of Cross-Cultural Psychology* 19(4) (December 1988) 427-445.
4. Desmond Morris, *Bodywatching* (London: Jonathan Cape Ltd., 1985).
5. J. Herbers, quoted in J. Hooks and M. McMillan, "Insights on African Americans," *Exchange* (October 1989).
6. Atkinson.
7. See D. Sue and A. Sue, "Multicultural Counseling," *Counseling and Human Development* 22(3) (1989); and J. Casas, J. Ponterotto, and J. Gutierrez, "An Ethical Indictment of Counseling Research Training: The Cross-Cultural Perspective," *Journal of Counseling and Development* (January 1986).
8. J. L. Hanna "Anthropological Perspectives for Dance/Movement Therapy," *American Journal of Dance Therapy* 12(2) (1990): 115–126.
9. C. Hayman and L. Copeland, "Insights on American Indians," *Exchange* (October 1989).
10. See W. Darou, "Counselling and the Northern Native," *Canadian Journal of Counselling* 21(1) (1987); and W. Mau and D. Jepsen, "Attitudes Toward Counselors and Counseling Processes: A Comparison of Chinese and American Graduate Students," *Journal of Counseling and Human Development* 67(3) (1988).
11. Gerald Boynton "Cross-Cultural Family Therapy: The Escape Model," *American Journal of Family Therapy* 15(2) (1987), p. 127.

12. J. Ross and E. Phipps, "Understanding the Family in Multiple Cultural Contexts: Avoiding Therapeutic Traps," *Contemporary Family Therapy: An International Journal* 8(4) (1986).
13. Boynton, p. 128.
14. See, for example, Sue and Sue; Boynton; J. Lappin, "On Becoming a Culturally Conscious Family Therapist," in C. J. Fallicou, editor, *Cultural Perspectives in Family Therapy* (Rockville, MD: Aspen, 1983); C. May and S. B. True, "Turning Negatives into Positives in Treatment," *Social Casework* 48(2) (1967): 95–97.
15. P. Tsui and G. Schultz, "Failure of Rapport: Why Psychotherapeutic Engagement Fails in the Treatment of Asian Clients," *American Journal of Orthopsychiatry* 55(4) (1985).
16. J. Krassner "Effective Features of Therapy from the Healer's Perspective: A Study of Curanderismo." *Smith College Studies in Social Work* 56(3) (1986).
17. R. Ruiz and P. Amadeo, "Counseling Latinos," *Counseling American Minorities: A Cross-Cultural Perspective* (2nd ed.), edited by D. R. Atkinson, G. Martin, and D. W. Sue (Dubuque, IA: Wm. C. Brown, 1983).
18. E. Gomez, "Hispanic Americans: Ethnic Shared Values and Traditional Treatments, *American Journal of Social Psychiatry* 7(4)(1978):215–219.
19. Hanna, pp.116–117.
20. Hanna, pp. 120–121.
21. J. Biggar, "Meeting of the Twain, *Psychology Today* 21(11) (1987), 48–52.
22. R. Prince, "Psychotherapy and the Chronically Poor," quoted in Hanna, p. 121.
23. Hanna, p. 121.
24. Amy Tan, *The Joy Luck Club* (New York: Putnam, 1989).
25. Kochman, *Black and White: Style in Conflict* (Chicago: University of Chicago Press, 1981).
26. R. D. Masters and D. G. Sullivan, "Facial Displays and Political Leadership in France," *Behavioral Processes* 19(1989):1–30.
27. Peter H. Waxer, "Video Ethology: Television as a Data Base for Cross-Cultural Studies in Nonverbal Displays," *Journal of Nonverbal Behavior* 9(2) (1985): 111–120.
28. Gomez, pp. 215–219.
29. J. Cherbosque, "Differences Between Mexican and American Clients in Expectations About Psychological Counseling," *Journal of Multicultural Counseling and Development* 15(3) (July 1987):110–114.
30. J. R. Weisz, S. Suwaniert, W. Chaiyasit and B. Walter. "Over- and Undercontrolled Referral Problems Among Children and Adolescents from Thailand and the United States: The Wat and Wai of Cultural Differences," *Journal of Consulting and Clinical Psychology* 55(5) (1987):719–726.
31. K. Benesch and J. Ponterotto, "East and West: Transpersonal Psychology and Cross-cultural Counseling" *Counseling and Values* 33(2) (1989): 121–131.
32. Desmond Morris, *Body Watching* (London: Jonathon Cape, Ltd., 1985).
33. Hanna, p. 116.
34. S. Thayer, "Encounters," *Psychology Today*, March 1988.
35. Hubble, as reported in Thayer.
36. Thayer, p. 27.
37. Hanna, p. 118.
38. A. B. Pasteur and I. L. Toldson, *Roots of Soul: The Psychology of the Black Experience* (New York: Anchor Press/Doubleday, 1982).
39. Hanna, p. 118.

40. S. Redmond, "An Analysis of the General Well-Being of Blacks and Whites: Results of a National Study," *Journal of Sociology and Social Welfare* 15(1) (1988).
41. *Gazette Telegraph*, Colorado Springs, CO, February 2, 1991.
42. *East West Journal*, East West Partners, 17 Station, Box 1200, Brookline, MA 02147, February 1991.
43. Shelby Steele, *The Content of our Character* (New York: St. Martin's Press, 1990).
44. Personal Communication with R. Rodriguez, 1990.

BIBLIOGRAPHY

Andresen, Gail and Weinhold, Barry. 1981. *Connective Bargaining: Communicating About Sex.* Englewood Cliffs, NJ: Prentice-Hall.

Atkinson, D. October 1985. "A Meta-Review of Research on Cross-Cultural Counseling and Psychotherapy," *Journal of Multicultural Counseling and Development*, pp. 138–153.

Babcock, Dorothy and Keepers, Terry. 1976. Raising Kids OK. New York: Grove Press.

Bach, Richard. *Illusions: The Adventures of a Reluctant Messiah.* 1977. Delacorte: New York.

Bandler, Richard and Grinder, John. 1979. *Frogs into Princes: Neuro Linguistic Programming.* Moab, UT: Real People Press.

Benesch, K. and Ponterotto, J. 1989. "East and West: Transpersonal Psychology and Cross-Cultural Counseling." *Counseling and Values* 33(2):121–131.

Benoit, Hubert. 1960. *The Supreme Doctrine.* New York: Harper.

Berne, Eric. 1964. *Games People Play.* New York: Grove Press.

Bertherat, T. and Bernstein C. 1977. *The Body Has Its Reasons.* New York: Pantheon, p. 38.

Biggar, J. 1987. "Meeting of the Twain. *Psychology Today* 21(11): 48–52.

Billig, O. and Burton-Bradley, B. G. 1977. *The Painted Message.* Halsted, NY.

Bloomfield, H., Cain, M., Joffe, R., and Kory, R. 1975. *TM: Overcoming Stress and Discovering Inner Energy.* New York: Delacorte Press.

Boynton, Gerald. 1987. "Cross-Cultural Family Therapy: The Escape Model," *American Journal of Family Therapy* 15(2):127.

Byrd, Randolph C. July 1988. "Positive Therapeutic Effects of Intercessory Prayer in a Coronary Care Unit Population," *Southens Medical Journal* 81:(7):825–829.

Capra, Fritjof. 1975. *The Tao of Physics.* Berkeley, CA: Shombala.

Casas, J., Ponterotto, J., and Gutierrez, J. January 1986. "An Ethical Indictment of Counseling Research Training: The Cross-Cultural Perspective," *Journal of Counseling and Development.*

Cherbosque, J. July 1987. "Differences Between Mexican and American Clients in Expectations About Psychological Counseling." *Journal of Multicultural Counseling and Development* 15(3):110–114.

Clarke, Jean Illsley. 1978. *Self-Esteem: A Family Affair.* Minneapolis: Winston Press.

Clarke, J. and Dawson, C. 1989. *Growing Up Again: Parenting Ourselves, Parenting Our Children.* Minneapolis: Hazelden.

Darou, W. 1987. "Counselling and the Northern Native," *Canadian Journal of Counselling* 21(1).

Dossey, Larry. 1989. *Recovering the Soul.* New York: Bantam Books.

Durckheim, Karlfried. 1975. *Hara: The Vital Centre of Man.* New York: Samuel Weiser, p. 159.

February 1991. *East West Journal*, East West Partners, 17 Station, Box 1200, Brookline, MA 02147.

Edinger, E. F. 1972. *Ego and Archetype.* Baltimore: Penguin.

Erikson, Erik. 1946. *The Psychoanalytic Study of the Child.* New York: International University Press.

Evans-Wentz, W. Y. 1960. *Tibetan Book of the Dead.* New York: Oxford University Press.

Feild, Reshad. 1976. *The Last Barrier: A Journey Through the World of Sufi Teaching.* New York: Harper & Row.

Feild, Reshad. 1979. *The Invisible Way: A Love Story for the New Age.* New York: Harper and Row, pp. 93–94.

Gazette Telegraph, Colorado Springs, CO, February 2, 1991.

Golas, Thaddeus. 1974. *The Lazy Man's Guide to Enlightenment.* Palo Alto, CA: Seed Center.

Goldstein, Joseph. 1976. *The Experience of Insight.* Santa Cruz, CA: Unity Press, p.176.

Gomez, E. 1978. "Hispanic Americans: Ethnic Shared Values and Traditional Treatments." *American Journal of Social Psychiatry* 7(4): 215–219.

Goulding, Mary and Goulding, Robert. 1978. *The Power Is in the Patient: A TA Gestalt Approach to Psychotherapy.* San Francisco: TA Press.

Grof, Stansilav. 1974. *Realms of the Human Unconscious.* New York: Viking Press.

Gunther, Bernard. 1978. *Energy, Ecstasy and Your Seven Vital Chakras.* Los Angeles: Guild of Tutors Press.

Hanna, J. L. 1990. "Anthropological Perspectives for Dance/Movement Therapy," *American Journal of Dance Therapy* 12(2):115–126.

Havinghurst, Robert. 1972. *Developmental Tasks and Education.* New York: David McKay.

Hayman, C. and Copeland, L. October 1989. "Insights on American Indians," *Exchange.*

Hendricks, C. G. 1975. "Theoretical Note: Meditation as Discrimination Training," *Journal of Transpersonal Psychology,* pp. 144–146.

Hendricks, Gay. *Learning to Love Yourself.* Englewood Cliffs, NJ: Prentice Hall.

Hendricks, Gay and Leavenworth, Carol. 1978. *How to Love Every Minute of Your Life.* Englewood Cliffs, NJ: Prentice Hall.

Hoffman, Robert. 1976. *Getting Divorced from Mother and Dad.* New York: E.P. Dutton.

Hooks, J. and McMillan, M. October 1989. "Insights on African Americans," *Exchange.*

Joy, W. B. *Joy's Way: A Map for the Transformational Journey.* Los Angeles: J.P. Tarcher, p. 129.

Kaplan, Louise. 1978. *Oneness and Separateness: From Infant to Individual.* New York: Simon and Schuster.

Keller, H., Scholerich, A., and Eibl-Eibesfeldt, I. December 1988. "Communication Patterns in Adult-Infant Interaction in Western and Non-Western Cultures," *Journal of Cross-Cultural Psychology* 19(4): 427-445.

Klaus, Marshall and Kennell, John. 1976. *Maternal-Infant Bonding.* St. Louis: C. V. Mosby Co.

Kochman. 1981. *Black and White: Style in Conflict.* Chicago: University of Chicago Press.

Kopp, Sheldon. 1981. An End to Innocence: *Facing Life Without Illusions.* New York: Bantam Books.

Krassner, J. 1986. "Effective Features of Therapy from the Healer's Perspective: A Study of Curanderismo." *Smith College Studies in Social Work* 56(3).

Krishnamurti, J. 1974. *The Awakening of Intelligence.* New York: Harper & Row.

LeBoyer, Frederick. 1975. *Birth Without Violence.* New York: Knopf.

Levin, Pamela. 1988. *Becoming the Way We Are*. Deerfield Beach, FL: Health Communications, Inc.

Levin, Pamela. 1988. *Cycles of Power*. Deerfield Beach, FL: Health Communications, Inc.

Loevinger, Jane. 1976. *Ego Development*. San Francisco: Jossey-Bass.

Mahler, Margaret. 1968. *On Human Symbiosis and the Vicissitudes of Individuation*. New York: International University Press.

Mahler, Margaret. 1975. *The Pyschological Birth of the Human Infant*. New York: Basic Books.

Maslow, Abraham H. 1971. *The Farther Reaches of Human Nature*. New York: Viking Press, p. 33.

Masters, R. D. and Sullivan, D. G. 1989. "Facial Displays and Political Leadership in France." *Behavioral Processes* 19:1–30.

Mau, W and Jepsen, D., 1988. "Attitudes Toward Counselors and Counseling Processes: A Comparison of Chinese and American Graduate Students," *Journal of Counseling and Human Development* 67(3).

May, C. and True, S. B. 1967. "Turning Negatives into Positives in Treatment." *Social Casework* 48(2):95–97.

Miller, Alice. 1981. *Prisoners of Childhood*. New York: Basic Books.

Miller, Alice. 1983, *For Your Own Good*. New York: Farrar, Straus & Giroux.

Mindell, Arnold. 1985. *Rivers Way*. Boston: Routledge & Kegan Paul.

Morris, Desmond. 1985. *Body Watching*. London: Jonathan Cape Ltd.

Moss, Thelma. 1974. *The Probability of the Impossible*. Los Angeles: J. P. Tarcher.

Naranjo, Claudio and Ornstein, Robert. 1971. *On The Psychology of Meditation*. New York: Viking Press.

Ornstein, Robert. 1975. *The Psychology of Consciousness*. New York: Penguin.

Orr, Leonard and Ray, Sandra. 1977. *Rebirthing in the New Age*. Millbrae, CA: Celestial Arts.

Pasteur, A. B. and Toldson, I. L. 1982. *Roots of Soul: The Psychology of the Black Experience*. New York: Anchor Press/Doubleday.

Pearce, Joseph C. 1977. *The Magical Child: Rediscovering Nature's Plan for our Children*. New York: E.P. Dutton.

Piaget, Jean. 1951. *The Child's Conception of the World*. New York: Humanities Press.

Ray, Sandra. 1960. *Loving Relationships*. Millbrae, CA: Celestial Arts.

Read, Herbert, Fordham, Michael, and Adler, Gehard, eds. 1953. *The Collected Works of C. G. Jung: Vol. 9, Archetypes and the Collective Unconscious.* New York: Pantheon Books, pp. 1–147.

Redmond, S. 1988. "An Analysis of the General Well-Being of Blacks and Whites: Results of a National Study." *Journal of Sociology and Social Welfare* 15(1).

Ross, J. and Phipps, E. 1986. "Understanding the Family in Multiple Cultural Contexts: Avoiding Therapeutic Traps." *Contemporary Family Therapy: An International Journal* 8(4).

Ruiz, R. and Amadeo, P. 1983. "Counseling Latinos." *Counseling American Minorities: A Cross-cultural Perspective* (2nd ed.), edited by D. R. Atkinson, G. Martin, and D. W. Sue. Dubuque, IA: Wm. C. Brown.

Schiff, Jacqui. 1970. *All My Children.* New York: Pyramid Books.

Schiff, Jacqui. 1976. *The Cathexis Reader.* New York: Harper & Row.

Sontag, Lester. November 1963. "Somatophysics of Personality and Body Function." *Vita Humana*, pp. 1–10.

Steele, Shelby. 1990. *The Content of Our Character.* New York: St. Martin's Press.

Stott, Dennis. 1973. "Follow-up Study from Birth of the Effects of Prenatal Stresses." *Developmental Medicine and Child Neurology*, 15:770–787.

Sue, D. and Sue, A. 1989. "Multicultural Counseling," *Counseling and Human Development* 22(3).

Sue, D., Sue, A., Boynton, G., and Lappin, J. 1983. "On Becoming a Culturally Conscious Family Therapist," in *Cultural Perspectives in Family Therapy*, edited by C. J. Fallicou. Rockville, MD; Aspen.

Tan, Amy. 1989. *The Joy Luck Club.* New York: Putnam.

Thayer, S. March 1988. "Encounters." *Psychology Today.*

Tsui, P. and Schultz, G. 1985. "Failure of Rapport: Why Psychotherapeutic Engagement Fails in the Treatment of Asian Clients." *American Journal of Orthopsychiatry* 55(4).

Verny, Thomas. 1981. *The Secret Life of the Unborn Child.* New York: Dill Publishing Co., pp. 12, 36–39, 41.

Waxer, Peter H. 1985. "Video Ethology: Television as a Data Base for Cross-Cultural Studies in Nonverbal Displays." *Journal of Nonverbal Behavior* 9(2):111–120.

Weinhold, Barry. 1975. *Developmental Process Work.* Unpublished manuscript.

Weinhold, Barry. 1982. *A Transpersonal Approach to Counselor Education*. Colorado Springs, CO: Author.

Weinhold, Barry. 1987. *Breaking Family Patterns*. Colorado Springs, CO: Author.

Weinhold, Barry. 1988. *Playing Grown-Up Is Serious Business*. Walpole, NH: Stillpoint International.

Weinhold, Barry. 1991. *Breaking Free of Addictive Family Relationships*. Walpole, NH: Stillpoint International.

Weinhold, Barry and Andresen, Gail. 1979. *Threads: Unraveling the Mysteries of Adult Life*. New York: Richard Marek Publishers.

Weinhold, Barry and Elliott, Lynn. 1979. *Transpersonal Communication*. Englewood Cliffs, NJ: Prentice Hall.

Weinhold, Barry and Fenell, David. 1989. *Counseling Families: An Introduction to Marriage and Family Counseling*. Denver: Love Publishing.

Weinhold, Barry and Weinhold, Janae. 1989. *Breaking Free of the Co-Dependency Trap*. Walpole, NH: Stillpoint International.

Weinhold, Barry and Weinhold, Janae. 1992. *Counter-Dependency: The Flight From Intimacy*. Unpublished manuscript.

Weiss, Laurie and Weiss, Jon. 1989. *Recovery from Co-Dependency*. Deerfield Beach, FL: Health Communications, Inc.

Weisz, J. R., Suwaniert, S., Chaiyasit, W., and Walter, B. 1987. "Over- and Undercontrolled Referral Problems Among Children and Adolescents from Thailand and the United States: The Wat and Wai of Cultural Differences." *Journal of Consulting and Clinical Psychology* 55(5): 719–726.

White, John. 1972. *What Is Meditation?* New York: Anchor Books.

Whitehouse, Mary. 1979. "C. G. Jung and Dance Therapy: Two Major Principles," in *Eight Theoretical Approaches in Dance-Movement Therapy*, edited by Penny Lewis Bernstein. Dubuque, IA: Kendall/Hunt, p. 62.

Wilber, Ken. 1979. *No Boundary*. Los Angeles: Center Publications.

Wilber, Ken. 1980. *The Atman Project: A Transpersonal View of Human Development*. Wheaton, IL: Theosophical Publishing House.

INDEX

A

Alone, fear of being, 145-146
Altered states of consciousness, 6
Arthritis, 93
Asians
  expressive style of, 216
  meaning of community to, 214
  meaning of family to, 212
  meaning of sickness and healing to, 213
  methods for working with, 209-211
Atman Project, 69
The Atman Project: A Transpersonal View of Human Development (Wilber), 46
Attitudes, 31-34
Auditory doorways, 130
Authentic movement, 188-189. *See also* Movement therapy
Awareness
  level of, 25
  of life within us, 189
  superconscious levels of, 122-123

B

Babcock, Dorothy, 120
Bach, Richard, 24
Bare attention, 171-172
Behaviors, as component of personality, 15-18
Bennis, Warren, 41
Benoit, Hurbert, 48
Benson, Herbert, 173
Berne, Eric, 119
Bertherat, T., 185

Betrayal, 102
Bioenergetic exercises, 101
Birth. *See also* Psychological birth
Birth process
  changing views of, 51-53
  importance of, 46, 123
  psychological, 47
Birth trauma, 58-61
Birthing centers, 53
Blacks
  expressive style of, 215, 217
  meaning of family to, 212
  meaning of sickness and healing to, 213
  methods for working with, 209-210
Blocher, Donald, 41
Bly, Robert, 43, 123
Body
  as component of human personality, 13-14, 16
  misalignment in, 94
  movement and, 184-186
  proportions of, 94
Bonding
  case examples of, 64-66
  components of, 53-55
  effects of partial, 61-62
  importance of, 47
  therapy tools for, 62-63
Boynton, Gerald, 210, 214
Bradshaw, John, 43, 123
Brain function, 179
Breathing
  as energy-balancing tool, 101
  hypotheses gained from observation of, 94
  process of, 59-61